dia

diary *of* a
hyperdreamer

BILL NELSON

volume 2

[POMONA]

A POMONA BOOK P-026

Mad in England!

First published by Pomona 2015

Pomona Books
Telephone: 01422 846900
e-mail: admin@pomonauk.co.uk
www.pomonauk.com

Front cover photograph by Walter Nelson

Set in Linotype Granjon
Typeset by Christian Brett

Printed and bound by
Printondemand-worldwide, Peterborough

ISBN 978-1-904590-31-6

CONTENTS

⟫⟫⟫⟫⟫⟫

PREFACE

THESE DAYS MY ONLINE DIARY ENTRIES ARE FEW AND far between. Lack of time and, I have to admit, enthusiasm, seem to have relegated them, literally, to the past. I was originally encouraged to write a diary some years ago by guitarist Robert Fripp, himself an intelligent and regular diarist. I'd never really troubled myself with diaries before that, merely jotting down occasional dates and meetings but little else.

When Robert suggested creating a public diary I had certain misgivings, mainly that my life was too ordinary, that I hardly ever left my studio, that my daily routine was repetitive and dull and would hold little interest for the reader. Nevertheless, I embarked on the exercise and soon had amassed hundreds of pages. These were gathered together in the first volume of *Diary Of A Hyperdreamer*, published by Pomona. To my surprise, the book was well-received and soon sold out.

I continued to write, although there were increasingly large gaps between entries. Eventually the entries slowed almost to a standstill. However, there were more than enough pages to make *Diary Of A Hyperdreamer, Volume 2* and this, dear reader, is what you now hold in your hands.

One of the topics covered is the death of my younger brother, Ian, in 2006. The emotional impact of that event still resonates today and I can't bring myself to read that section. He is loved and missed. But there are other, less painful entries dealing with the ups and downs of being a maker of music in a world that increasingly assigns little value to it. At 66-years-old, it doesn't get any easier but, thankfully, I'm blessed with a loyal and enthusiastic fan base. It is to those fans that I dedicate *Diary Of A Hyperdreamer, Volume 2.* I hope you will enjoy it.

Bill Nelson
May, 2015

2 0 0 5

Snow these last two days. Heavy yesterday. I decided to drive Emi to work rather than let her risk the treacherous roads on her own. Today a slight thaw and now a freeze. Icy conditions tomorrow. Still working intensely on the website images with Dave Graham. Slowly but surely coming together. This is just the 'skin' for some areas of the site. Soon, the cavities beneath the skin will have to be created and filled with content from my archived 'private' sources and also from the Permanent Flame files supplied by Chuck Bird. Still a long way to go before we're fully operational but things will be added as time progresses. It will be several months before the site approaches the kind of strength and complexity I've got in mind. I'm also working on visual content for Paul Sutton-Reeves book about my career. Due to various things beyond his control, he's had to come back to me for more photos to go into the book. I've spent the last few days scanning things from my own collection and have just put out an appeal to fans to send in any photographs they may have of Red Noise. As Red Noise's career was relatively short, I don't have much visual material relating to the band. It's one area where my archives are lacking. Duncan Ahlgren and Garry Nichol have sent in some of their own personal shots of Red Noise though and we should be able to use a couple of these for the book.

Also working on the possibility of major label re-releases, the EMI box set and Universal's proposal to re-issue the 'Mercury' years. It's a complex project though, particularly the latter as much of the material has been issued as part of my Cocteau Records catalogue. Adrian at Opium is trying to get to the bottom of it. Adrian just got back from the Grammys in LA Sounds glamorous. Not sure I'd want to go though, other than to ogle those girls in almost non-existent frocks. Oh, yes, I saw them on TV and thought, 'lucky Adrian'. Yes, maybe I would go, given the chance and drool all over their chiffon, like the shameless old dog I am. Adrian shared a table with the Foo Fighters who, so Adrian told me, said very nice things about my music. Credibility time with Elle and Elliot again, then. A brownie point for me.

My acoustic guitar-based instrumental album is at a stand-still. Frozen like the weather. No time available to work on it right now. I hope I can get it finished in time for a spring release. I've got more ideas in mind for it though, more little snippets of composition that I ought to record before they melt into air. I'd like to assemble a guitar instrumental compilation album too, as I may have mentioned before in these pages. Pull together some of my favourite pieces from across the years and add in a couple of unreleased tracks for good measure. Could be an interesting combination of things. Lots of other little things nagging away in the background. Some I can't speak about here yet but some very interesting developments coming up soon. Quite exciting, I think. I'll tell more when the time is right. Enough work for today. Maybe I'll watch TV for a while until bedtime. Unwind. A short diary entry but to be expected considering my tiredness.

·

The snows have melted and the view across the field from my studio window is green again. Quite cold, nevertheless. Became frustrated by the constant visual scanning and Photoshop work I've been so busy with and decided to put it all to one side and spend a day or two recording some new pieces for my electro-acoustic guitar album. This thing seems to take a different turn each time I return to it after a lay-off. Two new tracks completed and more ideas bubbling under. For an acoustic album, it seems to have developed a jazzy turn of phrase. Jazz has always been a subliminal force in my music, even from the pre-Be Bop Deluxe days. (I didn't choose the words 'Be Bop' just for the sound they made.) As the years advance, however, I seem to be mutating into some kind of 'jazz' guitarist, though not in the sense that other musicians would generally recognise within the academic implications of the term. As a man who neither reads music nor has ever had a guitar or music theory lesson in his life, I'm ill-equipped to deal with jazz in its orthodox, commonly accepted sense.

Perhaps I shouldn't really use the word in this context at all. It's just that, for some time now, I've found myself feeling increasingly more inspired by (and empathetic with) the lives of jazz musicians. For all the glittering (if dumb) excess of rock music's iconic figures, it seems to me that jazz music's icons lived their musical lives more completely, intelligently and profoundly. Equally as self-destructive as some rock musicians (sometimes perhaps) but even so, as a species, it's obvious that there's something a bit more evolved going on. My real bottom line is that it's all just music and that categories are as much a restriction as a help. We're all victims of the kind of conceptual packaging that sorts music into conveniently labelled boxes, boxes that not only divide the music up but also restrict our free movement within music's ocean of sound. Perhaps it is naive of me to believe that it is possible for anyone to respond positively to the whole range of musical expression available to us as 21st Century consumers but I like to think that an ability to appreciate a broad range of music is everyone's birthright, even the girls who work with Emiko in the flower shop who seem blissfully unaware of any music outside of the radio and disco 'norm'.

I've said it before but we need a higher standard of musical education in our schools. The subject needs taking much more seriously than at present, particularly with reference to music's wider implications. By this, I mean abstract thought, pure aesthetics and philosophical development. For me, naturally, it's the one true religion and always has been. All else is heresy. Which brings me to a very special event: I've now been given permission to write about a concert that I'm to be involved in on the 21st of May this year. It is (for want of a better term), a tribute concert to my long-time and very dear friend, Harold Budd. Harold announced his retirement from performance and recording last year, his latest album, *Avalon Sutra* purporting to be his last. He played a farewell concert in Los Angeles towards the end of 2004 but there is now going to be a similar event here in the UK as part of this year's Brighton Arts Festival. A number of artists are to take part in this and a band is being put together around Harold for the final segment of the concert. The artists involved in this are myself, Michael Nyman, Jah Wobble, John Foxx (of Ultravox), Steve Cobby (of Fila Brasilia),

Robin Guthrie (of Cocteau Twins), Steve Jansen (of Japan), The Balanescu Quartet and others still to be confirmed.

Channel Light Vessel was once given the title 'ambient supergroup' by the music media but this event promises to take that term somewhere else entirely. Harold has been dropping me letters and e-mails over the last couple of months or so about the project and I'm pleased to see that it is finally coming to fruition. Harold naturally had some personal reservations about the project, unsure of what stresses and strains might be involved but I think these have been overcome. Everyone taking part in this event has a personal respect and love for Harold and his work and it will be a privilege and sheer thrill for me to take part and honour Harold alongside everyone else. And, of course, I will be absolutely terrified too. Neverthless, when all's said and done, it will be a unique event that anyone who gives a damn about the possibility of art within music should not miss.

I should spend time with Emiko today. I've been working late in the studio every night for some weeks and Emi has to sit downstairs watching TV when she comes home from work. Saturdays and Sundays are usually the only time we get to do anything together socially. I'll switch off the music and visuals and take her out somewhere. Re-charge my own batteries too.

·

A quick diary entry today. Lots going on. Have now finished 16 pieces of music for my latest guitar instrumental album and I'm trying to settle on the correct running order. As I mentioned here before, 12 tracks is my goal but it's good to have more to choose from. I'm hoping that, by my next diary entry, I'll have a final list to announce. (And an idea of when it will be available.) This task is occupying me almost full time but I think it will be well worth all the effort.

Now, I have a special message to convey: Regular users of the Rooms With Brittle Views website will have noticed that it was no longer in existence today, due to webmaster Alan Myer's switching it off for good. Unfortunately, it seems that Alan no longer felt that he could spare the time and energy to operate the site and, sadly, has decided to close it down. Like many others, I want to express my thanks to Alan for his input over the last five years and for doing his best to maintain the site under sometimes difficult circumstances. I'd hoped that Alan might have felt like continuing his site alongside the forthcoming 'Dreamsville' one but it was not to be. Alan's day-to-day business has increasingly taken up more of his time of late and maintaining RWBV has become an obstacle. As I have said in earlier diary entries, I have no desire to add further pressures to Alan's situation and I wish him well and hope that he will find life somewhat easier without the time-consuming responsibility of running a BN fan site.

Which brings me to the future. We are reasonably close to opening up the new Dreamsville website, which it now seems will have to function in a slightly different capacity to the one

I originally planned. I'm looking at ways to develop the new site in a broader direction, providing some of the facilities to fans left by the closure of RWBV. By this, I mean more than just the production and distribution of my recordings, which was the original reason for starting Dreamsville. This will obviously be a little more time-consuming for me but, because of the help I've been generously offered by various people who have already contributed to RWBV's past existence, I think everyone will eventually be satisfied by our efforts. I'm now looking at setting up a discussion board to replace the loss of Northern Dreamer so that fans will continue to have a place to meet and talk. Eventually, this will be incorporated within the Dreamsville site. It will take the form of a 'pub' which, for the moment, is to be called 'The Dreamsville Arms'. This pub will be located within an area of the site known as 'The Pleasure Park'. The Pleasure Park will hold various buildings connected with general entertainment, including a 'box office' where live concert tickets and so on can be purchased on line. There will also be a facility to secure tickets to special fan events such as the annual fan convention which we're hoping to put in place as before, perhaps in an expanded form. More news of this as it develops. The Pleasure Park will also contain 'The Guitar Arcade', an essential building to visit for anyone with an interest in guitars and guitar playing. Dreamsville is a fictional town and its various buildings will have different functions. There will be a 'Villa Nelsonia' where my diary entries will be found. Villa Nelsonia will also contain other odd musings. Then, there will be 'Dreamsville Town Hall' which will act as a central office for the site. Here is where the 'Mayor of Dreamsville' will reside. The Mayor will act as a public interface for fans and will work closely with myself on the development of Dreamsville itself. My good friend Jon Wallinger has kindly volunteered to fulfil this role and will become the official 'Mayor Of Dreamsville' the moment that the site goes on line. The Town Hall will also contain a guide to the site and regular messages from The Mayor and The Architect's Department about the ongoing development plans. In the Architect's Department, a team will work on the site's structure. Obviously, I will be overseeing this with the help of my long-time design collaborator David Graham and also with technical assistance from Paul Gilby and others. News will be handled by the newspaper office of 'The Dreamsville Rocket'.

This will be a fairly regular news bulletin with the visual look of a newspaper. People will be able to subscribe to this for free and will be sent e-mails linking them to each new edition. It will contain visual treats as well as text. Copies of 'The Dreamsville Rocket' will be archived at the newspaper office in the town. Another building will be 'The Museum Of Memory'. This will hold my personal memorabilia and photographs from my private life. Much of the material contained here will not have been seen by the public before 'The Academy Of Art' will contain examples of my visual work, 'The Music Salon' will document my musical career and 'The Dreamsville Department Store' will provide a facility for people to obtain my recordings, both old and new, plus other merchandise. 'The Post Office' will contain a guest book for visitors to Dreamsville to sign. 'The Transit Lounge' will be where links to other interesting sites can be found and 'Dreamsville University' will provide an unusual educational facility where all kinds of odd ideas will be gathered together. 'Sunny Bungalow', a sweet looking 1930s style building, will contain photo's of my toy collection and other kitsch collectables. And so on and so forth. More things will be added to the town as time goes on, including a radio station and a cinema if the technical side of things works out. A LOT of work to get it up to full strength but all websites have to start somewhere and, with determination and patience (and some encouragement from the outside world), we should eventually end up with something quite special and unique. Until the first stage of the site goes on line, these diary pages will act as a news bulletin as well as a regular diary. As soon as facilities are in place for people to subscribe to the Dreamsville mailing list, I will let everyone know and we can start to populate Dreamsville with real citizens. Keep checking billnelson.com and this diary to stay in touch. More news as it happens. Now it's back to working on the new album. Its title, by the way is: *Rosewood... Ornaments And Graces For Acoustic Guitar*. It will be released on my own 'SONOLUXE' record label. A rough draft of the artwork is already underway. Patience, dear reader and stay tuned!

·

FRIDAY 18TH MARCH 2005

Rosewood now has a front cover. Dave Graham and I finally arrived at the best solution. It's appropriate, colourful and fun. It has fish on it! And electrical circuits! And a guitar! Now I have to make and choose images for the rest of the package. Went out and took more photographs of an old Hoyer archtop guitar of mine for this purpose but need to work with these in my computer before passing on to Dave for him to work his layout magic. I've now recorded 24 pieces of music to choose from for the album but haven't begun the final selection process. It's going to be difficult to boil them down to my intended 12 track running order. The tracks that don't fit will be made available on this year's Nelsonica convention album, so nothing will be wasted.

The basic form of my Dreamsville website is at the technical assembly stage and should be up and running in a week or two. It will be in a rudimentary form at first but I'll fill it with content over the next year or two. It will look great once it's properly 'stocked.' Whilst on the subject of websites, Jon Wallinger pointed me in the direction of a temporary Bill Nelson discussion board that someone has set up. He said I should check out a posting by Alan Myers on there, so I did. When I read them, Alan's comments came as a real disappointment to me as I've always been appreciative of Alan's website (and Mark and Chuck's too, for that matter), and have tried to offer what input and help I could over the years as well as be supportive of events Alan asked me to endorse. I know that Alan has had some difficult personal times of late and can only think that these have contributed to the underlying bitterness suggested by his posting. What a shame. I won't comment further other than to say that the only reason I've had to look at ways of putting a website of my own together was a direct result of Alan telling people, last year, that he was shutting down his site. And yes, as I once pointed out to some people who were getting far too unhealthily wrapped up in things, it is only a website and, in fairness to Permanent Flame, RWBV was neither the first nor only Bill Nelson website on the planet, just the one that I was once persuaded to contribute most towards. I had hoped that Alan might, once he'd come to terms with his personal life, seen fit to continue the site alongside Dreamsville, as a purely fan-oriented site, which is what it was supposed to be when it began, but it seems that was simply naive of me. After all the previous co-operation between us, I'm extremely sorry that Alan has seen fit to make such negative comments in public. What's the point in that, other than to cause damage and distress to myself and my friends? But, needless to say, there's probably much more to this sad story than meets the eye.

I'm personally upset but, from past experience, not at all surprised. So perhaps it really was for the best, after all, despite my initial doubts. Life is too short for these kind of intrigues, especially at my advanced age (and with the amount of work I've got to accomplish before I'm too old to accomplish it). In any case, people are intelligent enough to judge the real situation for themselves without me getting involved. But at least I know where I stand now. Move on, move away. Life's stressful enough.

An e-mail from Harold this morning. He's sending me a brochure from an exhibition of English watercolours that he attended. Harold's May time Brighton concert coming up soon. I'm trying not to get too nervous about it at this stage. Hal is his usual laid back, 'when it happens, it happens' self. For all his protestations to the contrary, he's one of the most Buddha natured people I've ever met. Absolutely artistically ruthless but sweet as a nut with it. I envy him his balance. And his aesthetic gifts. Finished reading *What Did I Do?* by Larry Rivers. I enjoyed it tremendously and ended up admiring the guy for his totally self-absorbed, passionate mission to squeeze as much out of life and art as possible and fuck himself senseless at every available opportunity. An irredeemable rogue who led a scandalous life driven by a fiery, burning intelligence. It really inspires one to cut the crap out of one's own life and make art with all the energy available. Ed Ruscha's book, (which I'm still reading), on the other hand, is cooler, more collected and, at times, as dull as dishwater. More greats gone to Valhalla: Phillip Lamantia, Arthur Miller, Hunter S. Thompson and Jimmy Smith (the latter the best organ grinder in the business).

One of my planned but unannounced live performances in May now cancelled due to venue unsuitability. So I won't announce it. Still one more up my sleeve though, besides the Harold spectacular. Now it's dinner time and then a mixing session. Next week the *Rosewood* assembly begins in earnest.

·

WEDNESDAY 23RD MARCH 2005

Signs of spring on the increase and some sunshine, though yesterday was wet and grey. I ended up stuck in the house anyway as I suddenly found myself unable to send any e-mails. I usually deal with the first e-mails of the day immediately after breakfast and before taking my bath. Yesterday, however, I was still stuck in front of the computer at 4pm and still in my dressing gown.

The e-mail service provider I use had changed the way their system worked, now insisting on SMTP authorisation. I followed the provider's website instructions to reset my e-mail settings but to no avail. My computer still wouldn't send any e-mails at all, various error messages flashing up on screen. It took me a long while and several phone calls to tech support teams to discover that the problem was with my e-mail browser software. It basically didn't support SMTP authorisation, being somewhat antiquated. Antiquated? Hell, it was only five years old! Software ages rapidly in Computerland, it seems.

I then had to find and download some new e-mail browser software and install it. This was accompanied by panics about whether I would lose my many thousands of stored e-mails from my older system. I eventually figured out how to make backup copies of these and installed the new software. It took only seconds to install, despite having taken almost one hour to download. Thank goodness everything worked once more and nothing was lost from my e-mail archives. I was surprised by how panicked I was by this escapade. A few years ago, before I had a computer, I poured scorn on those people who seemed unable to function out of arms reach of their PC's and Macs. I couldn't see the need for e-mails and the internet and even avoided the telephone unless it was absolutely necessary. Now, I realise just how pathologically dependent I've become on the computer to communicate with the outside world. In some ways it's quite amazing, in other's it's sad. The truth is I now have to give up a great deal of time to answering e-mails and dealing with computer-related activities, time that was once spent making music.

My intention, yesterday, was to work on the final selection of tracks for the *Rosewood* album. Unfortunately, this task was postponed whilst I dealt with the technical problems posed by my Mac. I'll try again today, after dealing with this diary entry.

Rosewood has now accumulated 27 possible tracks. As I've mentioned in these pages previously, I need to select around a dozen of these to go on the album proper, the rest being reserved for the Nelsonica Convention album. Choosing the 12 that will best work together will be difficult. The trick will be to only use tracks that work together towards a particular goal. There's some variety amongst the pieces but I think I need to make this album head off in one fixed direction, rather than become too diverse. It has elements of the *Dreamland To Starboard* album in that it is quite 'interiorised' for want of a better word … 'Mellow' might suit it better, I don't really know. Until I start to get to grips with choosing and sequencing the running order, it's difficult to say exactly what the final effect will be. At this point in time, I'm feeling a bit clueless about it all.

I recently remarked to Harold (Budd) that I approach music like a blind man with a stick. I should have qualified this further by saying, 'like a blind man with a stick approaching a dangerous highway'. I changed the titles of two or three pieces to better suit their mood. The list of possible track choices for *Rosewood* is now made up of the following pieces … [list of tracks]:

Somehow, I have to boil these down to twelve cohesive tracks for the album today. In my last diary entry, I mentioned that one of my proposed May live performances had been cancelled due to venue unsuitability. I also mentioned that I had one more live concert up my sleeve. Well, as bad luck would have it, this also didn't work out. I had been asked to play at the Coventry Jazz Festival but the organisers seem to have changed their plan and I'm left clutching empty air. So, the only scheduled appearance for me at this point in time is at the tribute concert for Harold Budd being held as part of the Brighton Festival on the 21st of May. From three shows to one.

Received a nice letter from Harold yesterday. Briefly discussing some concert performance plans but mainly talk of other things. Also got an e-mail from the Carlsbro Amplifier Company. Seems that my custom, self-designed Carlsbro amp and speaker cabinet has generated a fair bit of interest and the company are proposing that they manufacture a limited edition run of the design, with my approval. Each amp would carry a metal plaque with my signature and a number to indicate its limited edition status. Apparently, quite a few people have asked if they could buy an identical amp to mine. I'm pleased it has captured some players' imaginations.

Dave Graham has come up with *Rosewood*'s CD 'on-body' label and it perfectly suits our front cover image. I still have to create the images for Dave to fit into the rest of the package and will try to make a start on this today. I could do it whilst listening to and assembling the draft running order. I'll need to book Fairview studios soon to master the album prior to manufacturing it. I'm praying that *Rosewood* will be appreciated. Certainly, those who enjoyed my *Dreamland To Starboard* album shouldn't find it too much of a challenge.

After getting sore fingers and thumbs with the acoustic guitar at the heart of *Rosewood*, I'm itching to record some new electric guitar pieces, using a plectrum. I also ought to think about getting to grips with a new song-based vocal album. Right now, though, I'm not in a lyric-oriented mood. I'm sure that something will come to me sooner or later, it usually does.

I'm told that the launch of 'Dreamsville' is not too far away now. I'm in the hands of Adam, the technician who is building the mechanical side of the new site. I'm told he's on with the job and I'll have something to look at very soon. But, there are months and months of work ahead to get all the actual content I have in place on the site. Still, fans can watch it grow bit by bit. The idea is to get the essential stuff in place first, including the town's 'pub' (The Dreamsville Inn), where fans will be able to communicate and discuss to their heart's content over a 'virtual pint' of Dreamsville's best ale. I may even make a real bottle of 'Dreamsville Ale' available in the future, a limited brewing to be sold exclusively at Nelsonica. I'll need to liaise with a nice, small, local brewery to see how this could be manufactured and what the costs would be. Absolutely inessential, of course, but sort of fun in a surrealist way. There's no shortage of ideas for Dreamsville, just a limited amount of time available to put them into action. Ultimately, the music has to take pride of place. I've had a nice response from fans to my request for Red Noise era photos. I now have a few good ones to send off to Paul Sutton-Reeves for his *Music In Dreamland* book. Music to be selected now, so back to work.

·

TUESDAY 29TH MARCH 2005

Almost April. That time thing again. Life passing me by whilst I work myself into a state of stress. And for what? For what I hope will be a beautiful body of music. I complain, I endure, no matter what the turn of events. In an apparently meaningless world, music is the one illusion of meaningfulness that I cling to. My personal, proud folly. I've been struggling and struggling with the running order for my *Rosewood* album. I'd hoped to keep the track-count down to 12 but couldn't slim it down beyond 19. (The total recorded now stands at 29 pieces of music.) Listening back to my choice of 19 tracks in the correct sequence, I was struck by how rich the listening experience was. Perhaps too rich for some people. I worried that it might overwhelm the listener and be difficult to take in at one sitting, thereby diluting its impact. So, I eventually decided to split *Rosewood* into two separate albums. Not a double album set, but two individual volumes: *Rosewood Volume One* and *Rosewood Volume Two*. That way, I won't be frustrated by losing some of the music to lesser projects and the album's audience can access the music in two, much more easily digested, chunks. Having said that, the track-count on *Rosewood Volume One* is still more than my original 12 track target. But at least it is 15 tracks now and not 19. And, more importantly, it works a treat. I listened through to a draft CDR assembly of it last night and I think it constitutes some of my finest work. It's intense, emotional, thoughtful and spontaneous and very musical, avoiding the fashionably glamorous lure of 'avant-gardism'. I guess you could say it's a mature work. Or as mature as my Peter Panic nature will allow. I think that the final track listing for *Rosewood Volume One* will be as follows ... [list of tracks].

I e-mailed Dave Graham the sleeve notes, credits and track listing last night so that he can lay them into our design package. The album artwork is virtually complete for volume one. It looks really strong and features a lot of my photography, a package as rich as the music it contains. The next task is to assemble a running order for volume two. Dave is already making draft layouts and I need to sort out which remaining tracks fit where. I suspect though, that I'll record at least a couple more pieces of music for this to balance out volume two's 'feel'. *Rosewood*, for all its acoustic implications, is a dense and complex piece of work. It has taken a real bite out of my being, one way or another. I've worked on *Rosewood* all through the Easter weekend (and for the last couple of months as well). Emi is off work for a week as the flower shop is closed whilst its owner goes on holiday to Egypt. Our lot is far less exotic. Emi gave the kitchen a spring clean yesterday whilst I stayed hunched over my mixing desk in my workroom. We've not been anywhere. Can't really afford to, anyway. My output certainly overshadows what comes in. It's been a horrendously expensive few months, so many bills and unforeseen domestic expenses. Poor Emi. I'm so lucky that she understands and tolerates my almost non-stop work ethic. I'll try to take her out somewhere today.

Hundreds of Caravans lined up in the field opposite our house. At night, each one flickers with the cathode glow of its internal television set. These folks like to get away from it all but not too far from their soaps and game shows. Or from other people. I don't really understand the attraction of spending a weekend cheek by jowl with hundreds of other campers all boxed up together in a field. Maybe it's a social thing, rather than an escape. I'd prefer to be somewhere miles away from the herd. Of course, I'm an absolutely unrepentant social misfit anyway, so that's to be expected. More and more, these days, I look at the world outside my window with a mounting sense of semi-amused horror. I'm amazed by the shabby attitudes that seem to have become the norm in our society. What happened to the idealism, optimism and enlightened ideals of our 'swinging sixties?' Where did our liberated and liberal attitudes go? I suppose these once sweet dreams became nothing more than cheap, easily manipulated signifiers of an impossible utopia, fodder for advertising copywriters, unimaginative designers and middle-aged, one-time mods, now sofa-landlocked on an endlessly nostalgic faraway domestic atoll. Poor sods. Maybe I'm one of 'em.

Saw a rough draft of the Dreamsville site last week. Some things need a bit of a tweak. The trick is balancing graphic visual quality with practical download times. Something of a trade-off. The site is still in the hands of the technical chap and being knocked into digital shape, though the main visual components have been completed. I'm hoping we can launch the site fairly soon. But I've said that before. The consolation in all of this is that I don't want to just 'knock something up' for the sake of getting the site in place. It needs to be right. It will be (as I've also said before) an open-ended, ongoing project, something that will be developed slowly and carefully with attention to aesthetic detail. An extension of my musical and personal life, rather than a peripheral thing. I really need to escape from my room today. Health suffering again, various aches and pains, twinges, numbnesses, a general feeling of being drained, exhausted even. I really ought to limit how much of myself I allow to be damaged by all this stuff. My own fault entirely, of course. I can't even begin to address the problem. I'm hardly likely to change the habit of a lifetime at this stage of the game. If I really wanted to, if I genuinely felt more than just a romantic revulsion for this arty-farty lifestyle, I would.

Throw it all away. It's obviously a tender trap I'm caught in and my wriggling is nothing more than a token defiance. Well, there you go. In the end, I submit to the painful deliciousness of it all. What a loser, what a lucky guy.

.

FRIDAY 8TH APRIL 2005

Finally, *Rosewood* is complete. Last night, I put the finishing touches to the final track of Volume Two, a newly recorded piece to nicely round off the album and bring the listener back to the starting position of Volume One. It's hard to say which of these two albums I like most. Perhaps Volume One at this point in time but this could easily change according to my mood. They belong together, basically. One complements the other. I made an unmastered copy of Volume One for my friend Paul Gilby who, after listening to it said: "Beautiful, emotional and mature ... a masterpiece!" Well, there's one good review! Jon Wallinger, upcoming Mayor Of Dreamsville, has a CDR copy of it at the moment also and has promised to write a review of *Rosewood Volume One* to upload to my new official website, once it goes public.

More tweaks being done at the moment to compensate for varying screen resolutions amongst the computer-using public. A bit of a design compromise but nothing too drastic. A new discussion board has been arranged in the form of 'The Dreamsville Inn' so that visitors to the site can communicate with each other and discuss whatever. 'The Dreamsville Inn' will go live when Dreamsville itself officially launches. Not too long now, I think. Dave Graham has completed the layout work on the packaging for *Rosewood Volume Two* now and, once again, it's hard to choose a favourite between them. Each follows the same visual concept/layout/plan but has different colours and uses different photographs from Volume One. But, as on Volume One, these are photographs that I took of my old Hoyer acoustic guitar in various locations around Yorkshire. Together, the two albums will look quite stunning. The track listing/running order for Rosewood Volume Two will be as follows ... [list of tracks].

It has been an exhausting project, this one. I can't recall any of my previous albums having quite this intensity of effort, other than perhaps the gargantuan *Noise Candy* project. (Which reminds me, it's time to remind Lenin Imports about accounting again, I think). I feel quite drained by the *Rosewood* process but, of course it doesn't end here. The next step is to book myself into Fairview Studios to master both albums, all 30 tracks of them. Then it's time to get them physically manufactured. I'll release Volume One as soon as it's ready and hold Volume Two back a while, perhaps until the autumn.

Autumn looks like it will be an interesting time, for various reasons that I'll keep under my hat for now, but I do have a lot of work to prepare for that part of the year. A slightly new venture which I'm looking forward to. Once my Dreamsville site is on-line, subscribers to the town's newspaper, 'The Dreamsville Rocket', will be able to keep up with the latest developments as they happen. I've also spent a lot of time and energy this last couple of weeks on the 'Museum Of Memory' section of the Dreamsville site. I've been piecing together a visual history of my early life, including my great grandparents and my parents. I've found and scanned well over 50 photographs so far and I'm writing text explanations for all of them. It amounts to a sort of 'potted autobiography', not as detailed and complete as my 'proper' one, *Painted From Memory*, but reasonably interesting, nevertheless. The text accompanying each photograph tells the story behind them and puts things into a chronological context. ' The Museum Of Memory', of course, is just one area of the Dreamsville site and there are many other areas to develop. All the foundations are laid but, as I keep stressing, it will be an ongoing task to build the entire town, a task which will occupy me for a long time. Bearing in mind that my priority is music making, a little patience will be required from Dreamsville's visitors. They can rest assured though that quality is of the utmost importance and nothing will be done just for the sake of it or simply to cobble something together. In time, this will build into a fantastic resource for fans of my work and become an extension of that work for myself.

Harold's concert getting nearer, more emails from him this week. The tension mounts and all that. It will be upon us before we know it.

•

THURSDAY 21ST APRIL 2005

Today is our wedding anniversary. Emiko and I have now been married 10 years. Hard to believe as it genuinely feels like yesterday that we tied the proverbial knot. We had planned a small and quiet affair but were pleasantly surprised when a number of good friends, many from 'down south', (and one from even further 'up north'), travelled to Yorkshire for the occasion: Richard Chadwick, Roger Eno and Family, Kate St. John, Emi's friend Kyoko, my eldest daughter Julia and several others, plus local friends such as John Spence and my brother Ian. It was a lovely sunny day and we all got fruits of the vine happy after the ceremony at the Gateforth Hall Hotel, just behind the tiny apartment Emi and I were renting at that time. Besides being the culmination of a lengthy, (and beautifully on-going), love-affair, it was a treasured day spent amongst our best pals. Anyway, 10 years ago today! That old time-warp thing, yet again. Emi's anniversary present to me this morning was a little tin steam train containing chocolate hearts, (tin is the symbol of ten years of marriage) and a marvellous bottle of Pecksniff's 'Oriental Wood' Cologne. This company is the last traditional, English-originated and owned perfumiers in the country. They create some wonderful perfumes and colognes. Fragrances are one of my many passions and I'm a sucker for trying out different ones in shops whilst on my travels. I often emerge from Harvey Nichols' store in Leeds smelling like a million dollars without spending a single penny. (They have a great selection of testers). I usually try out the 'Creed' range and a few other specialist perfumier's products, mainly the one's that cost the earth and smell like paradise. I stay well clear of those obvious famous footballer colognes, the Versaces, Hugo Bosses, etc, in favour of more unusual and exotic scents. I prefer such things as Czech and Speake's No 88, I and E Atkinson's 'I Coloniali' range, a couple of Penhaligon's classics and the eternally elegant and clean 'Acqua Di Parma'. I'm more of a sensual aesthete than a macho athlete anyway, a bit of a waxed moustache twiddler, had I got the moustache to twiddle. Maybe I could adopt a decadent lothario persona, perhaps a cross between Leslie Phillips and Charles Rennie Mackintosh? Or Aubrey Beardsley and Harrison Marks? Hmm ... maybe not. But given the opportunity of a foppish ribbon bow tie, a crushed velvet suit and a boudoir filled with gilded mirrors and brocade, I'd be handing out those Phillipsian oily "Hellos" to every pretty dolly within earshot. And me married for 10 years too. Mucky bugger, says Emi, (though she says it in Japanese, which makes it sound like an exotic attribute, rather than a summing up of my senile lusts). For a wedding anniversary gift, I bought Emi a tin clockwork rabbit that plays a pair of little drums when wound up, and a beautiful antique, 1920s, costume jewellery necklace. She is going to wear it tonight when we go out for a celebratory dinner at a rather up-market and old-fashioned restaurant sited in a beautiful nearby manor house. We haven't been before but, as this is a special day, we decided to push the boat out and indulge ourselves, just the two of us and to hell with the expense. I must try not to get a hangover though, as I'm booked into Fairview studios tomorrow morning to begin the work of mastering the two volumes of *Rosewood* with my engineer pal John Spence. Then the albums go off to the manufacturers and finally to the Dreamsville Department store where the music can at last be accessed by its audience. Well worth the wait, I think. It's a complex and richly detailed work. I'm unusually proud of it.

All being well, this particular diary entry will be the first to appear on the new Dreamsville website. We're really close to launching it as I write. Hopefully, it should be live and on-line sometime early next week. It's only at the first stage of its existence but I'm soon to lay plans to launch stage two. As soon as possible, really. Obviously, there are financial costs involved in all of this but by taking things a step at a time, I hope to be able to afford the site's development. As much as cash, time is at a premium too. My year is already planned out ahead of me and I have a full schedule of projects to work on. Adrian at the office emailed me a year planner with the next seven months or so mapped out on it. I was impressed. Will I really achieve all that? Fingers crossed. It seems as if the website will need to fit around the more pressing tasks on the cards. We'll get there in the end, fear not. No holiday again this year, though, that's for sure. I grumble to myself but it's all pretend. I love what I do.

A solo tour is planned for the autumn and I intend to pursue a new direction with this. Although I've toured as a soloist in the past, it has always been based around my instrumental performances. This time, I hope to include some vocal items too. I've made a tentative start towards writing some brand new songs that I might be able to sing without the aid of a band. These would use 'foundation tracks' in a similar fashion to my instrumental performances but would be tailored to support my vocals as well as my guitar playing. At this point in time, it's difficult to say exactly what the ultimate concept or mood of these songs will be, but current working titles for the project are 'The Lovely And Mysterious Tour' or 'The Dreamy And Mysterious Tour'. At least, that's the mood I'm aiming for. A few dream-like, beautiful songs, melodic and swoony but with strong, lyrical guitar playing. I'll also include some new and some old instrumentals in the concerts. I need to create fresh video backdrops too although this will be dependent upon how much time I can spare to work on these. The videos take an eternity to make. There will certainly be some new visual material though. The plan, at the moment, is to attempt 15 to 20 concerts around the UK Also to travel further south than last year's tour. Now that Dreamsville and The Dreamsville Rocket Newspaper are in place, I'll be able to keep fans informed as this project progresses.

It will be good to have The Dreamsville Inn in place for fans to communicate, too. I have to admit to missing their input. Looking forward to a bit of good natured banter. Next year (2006), I'll be looking at the possibility of putting a new band together for another tour and creating some new songs for that project. Unfortunately, a band-based tour, as I was reminded last autumn, takes much more time and money to mount than a solo tour, even with the extremely generous sponsorship that Sound-On-Sound magazine contributed last year. Without its help, that event would simply not have been possible. Because of this year's workload, (the unforeseen need to design and build a new website, plus the intensely involved two-volume *Rosewood* project and various other 'in-the-pipeline' issues), a band project, with all its complexities and costs, is impractical. I need to be able to set everything else to one side to give such a venture my full attention. So next year will be the best time to assemble a band, particularly if all goes well on this year's forthcoming autumn solo tour. I'd like to approach the band thing from a different angle anyway, sharpen up the act as it were. It's important to me to keep pushing the envelope. In fact, this autumn's outing is intended to break new ground for me, both in terms of music and territory. It will offer an opportunity to explore a different approach to songs in a live presentation.

I'm very excited about it, although it will be quite nerve-wracking (singing alone on a stage, I mean) but it's a tremendous challenge that I'm looking forward to meeting.

I intend to release an album of these new songs to coincide with the tour plus some surprises that I'll keep under my hat for now. Talking of nervousness, Harold Budd's tribute concert is looming ever larger. We have yet to settle on a little duet piece. I've posted a couple of suggestions to Harold, just to see if there's something there that we could pursue together. Harold is also working on a piece for us at his end. I recently posted him a copy of my published *Diary Of A Hyperdreamer* book. He wrote generously about it last night, said he was very impressed by it. For me, praise from Harold is praise indeed. I'm extremely grateful and flattered. I'm also extremely nervous about the Brighton show.

Now, Emiko and I have got tickets to Rufus Wainright next month. He's bound to make me insanely jealous as he's nauseatingly gifted. I enjoy his baroque pop songs very much although they can sometimes veer from the stunningly gorgeous to the oppressively over-sauced. Sometimes, I wish a little more restraint had been applied, but he's young and I guess you could level the same criticism at my work too (and I'm not young).

General election stuff pouring through my letterbox daily. The Tory party promotional bumph seems to be never ending. 'Are You Thinking What We're Thinking?' is their chosen slogan this time. Well the answer is, "NO, I'm not, so please bugger off and take your slimy nationalistic fear-mongering with you ... " Michael Howard and his cronies give me the heebie-jeebies. What an arrogant, manipulative, condescending bunch of hypocrites they are. Mind you, politicians, eh? Fertile soil for the seeds of corruption, the lot of 'em. Steer well clear and don't let them kiss your kids. I'm tempted to go back to the kind of creative anarchism I advocated during my art-school years. But we were just kids, what did we know? Actually, come to think of it, what do I know now? Only how to make music and not much else. Ambivalent and proud of it. A bad boy. Talking of elections, seems the Catholics have got themselves a new boss. Tougher than the old boss. What's his name, Pope Rottweiller or something? Apparently he was a member of the Hitler Youth Movement as a kid. Seriously. Well, he seems to have the old hard-line attitude to contraception and homosexuality. Religion: always happy to do the devil's work. Oh, dear.

Still haven't got around to listening to the new Vic Chestnutt album that I bought the other week. Bill Frisell's on it. So I bought it. I'm still a big Bill Frisell fan. Somehow though, I've been far too caught up in my own music to have much of an ear left for anyone else's. Despite this, I have heard Emi constantly playing Rufus Wainright's latest two albums downstairs. I bought both of them after hearing the first one last year on a visit to Opium's offices in London. Richard and Adrian turned me on to him. Nevertheless, I've always liked to gild the dear old lily, so what can I say? It's back to that perfume thing again, that extravagant, lush, fertile fecundity. Music as cornucopia, fountain of plenty, sheer ecstatic sensuality. Sound you can swoon in and swim in. Naked if possible.

Better change the subject, getting a bit sticky. From the sublime to the ridiculous: Found a DVD of *Torchy The Battery Boy* the other day. A charming puppet TV series from the early

1960s, one of Gerry Anderson's first productions. Torchy has a big magic light bulb in his hat that can find things that have been lost, (my long lost youth perhaps?) He also has a spiffing rocket ship that I wish they'd manufacture as a commercially available model. But I'm probably the only saddo who'd buy it. All together now: "Torchy, Torchy, the battery boy... He's a walkie-talkie toy..." Yup, those were the days.

Reading several books at bedtime, as usual. At my bedside at the moment are: *Peter Blake* by Natalie Rudd; *The Rise Of The Sixties* by Thomas Crow; *Audio Culture* edited by Cristoph Cox and Daniel Warner; *The Making Of Modern Britain* by Jeremy Black; *Jazz Modernism* by Alfred Apel Junior; *Satori In Paris* by Jack Kerouac; and the *Lion* annual, 1957. At least a dozen more books sit in a pile on top of some bedroom shelves, awaiting their turn at my bedside. Hope they're patient. Wish we could move to a bigger house where I might have one room set aside as a dedicated library to house my treasured tomes. I used to have a library when I lived at Haddlesey House in the late 1970s and through the 1980s. It was oak panelled, had a stone 'Minster' fireplace that crackled with logs in the winter, a huge desk with a captain's chair and my Hornby train set spread out on the deep green carpet. I used to love going up there and closing myself off from the outside world. Between that and my Echo Observatory studio, I had all the cultural, creative isolation I needed. Now I'm crammed into a small box room surrounded by junk and broken keyboards. And lots of lovely guitars. Shouldn't grumble.

.

Floating in my warm and comforting bath this morning, watching rain clouds gather in the grey air above the bathroom skylight, I heard, for a few magic seconds, the first cuckoo of spring. Its call echoed on the wind from the nearby fields, summoning archetypal English Albion country images, Powell and Pressburger 'Cantebury Tale' landscapes, the music of Elgar, (although Delius immortalised the bird), Post Office film unit documentaries from the 1930s and 1940s, children's stories from post-war annuals and a host of other sweet and sentimental nostalgias. A pity that the glorious sunshine and clear blue skies of the last few days were nowhere to be seen.

Not that I've been able to enjoy the outdoor life of late. I have been and still am, feeling 'proper poorly', to use an Albert Fitzwilliam Digby style phrase. (I wonder what American readers of my diary make of such hermetically sealed British terms and references?) It all started last Saturday, whilst visiting my Mother in Wakefield. I suddenly felt that inner chill that warns of an impending cold. Within an hour I was feeling dizzy and sick and had to return home where I took straight to my bed, shivering and feeling absolutely bloody awful. My temperature shot up, my stomach sick and uncomfortable. I didn't want to move. During the night, I was throwing up acidic bile. By Sunday my temperature had dropped but I felt like a man trapped between two worlds, neither of them desirable holiday locations. I've remained in this aching, fuzzy limbo ever since, only yesterday applying a razor to my face and shaving off the four day growth I'd accumulated. It's some years since I've sported a beard and I was horrified to see that, these days, it's predominantly grey, despite the fact that the hair on my head, though thinning dramatically, has hardly any grey in it at all.

I also, yesterday, took the chance that some fresh air might revive me and ventured out of the house to accompany Emi on her trip to Leeds. This was a mistake. After 20 minutes of shopping I felt terrible: wobbly, weak and dizzy. We quickly returned home where, after a rest, I began to feel a little better. Today, there's no great improvement, although I'm certainly better than I was at the weekend. Friends inform me that there is a particularly nasty virus doing the rounds, laying people low for a couple of weeks. Well, surprise, surprise, it appears I've caught it. Emiko has been suffering ill health too. She's managed to hold off from catching my virus so far, but has been complaining of a pain under her armpit. On Tuesday evening, she suddenly announced a disturbing tightness across her chest and back. Both of us immediately thought of heart problems. The tightness got worse and Julia, a good friend and neighbour, generously offered to drive Emi to the 24 hour walk-in clinic in town. I was too ill to take her myself. Three hours later (three hours that saw me pacing the floor, worrying myself silly), Emi returned looking much relieved. The doctor had said that her heart was fine and that the problem was most likely caused by a trapped nerve. In fact, she'd lifted a heavy pot of plants at the flower shop some days earlier and this may have lead to the trapped nerve. The three hour wait at the walk-in clinic was simply because of the number of patients queuing to be seen by a doctor. These sort of incidents really make you think. I don't know how I'd cope if anything should ever happen to Emiko, (God forbid) She's the rock that I cling to in my troubled sea.

The prediction I made in my previous diary entry, (21st April), that my Dreamsville site would be up and operating by then, turned out to be overly optimistic. At this precise point in time, the launch date is still somewhere in the future. The delay has been caused by the complication of transferring the .com address over from Permanent Flame's server to the new UK Dreamsville one. It's taking longer than anticipated. I also suspect that Chuck, (Bird) is away on one of his regular business trips and hasn't been available to deal with things at the US end. We're now hoping to have it all sorted out in time to launch the site next week. This could, of course, end up not being the case. However, if you are reading these words, then Dreamsville will have finally opened its gates as this diary entry and the previous one have been posted exclusively on the Dreamsville site, and not on Permanent Flame. Permanent Flame, as I may have mentioned before, has now been enshrined as an exhibit in 'The Permanent Flame Museum' within the 'Pleasure Park' area of Dreamsville. This means that the 10-year-old website has been preserved, frozen in time, for future reference and as a tribute to Mark Rushton and Chuck Bird who began and ran the first ever Bill Nelson website, long before I even had a computer to look at it.

Last Friday, I travelled over to Fairview studios to transfer the *Rosewood* recordings and master them with John Spence. John cheered me by saying that he thought they sounded fabulous and needed hardly any equalisation changes. The masters and the packaging artwork have now gone off to the manufacturers and finished copies of Volume One will be available soon. I'm looking forward to seeing the finished result, the first release on Sonoluxe.

I had to borrow Emi's car to get over to Fairview as my vehicle has a rapidly deteriorating exhaust problem. In fact, the car needs a lot of work on it at the moment, particularly body work. There are some increasingly alarming areas of rust that need treatment. As the house is also in need of several structural repairs, both internal and external, it's a matter of deciding on priorities and letting the rest rot. Truth is, the economics of the situation make it difficult to keep up with it all. In some ways, I wish we could afford to move house, find somewhere a little bigger and more private. I really need a dedicated, larger space for my recording and musical equipment. Considering the fact that recording work is right at the centre of my creativity and career, finding myself and my gear crammed into such a small box room is both ironic and uncomfortable. Meanwhile, developers in and around the city continue to exploit every bit of land they can get their hands on. We've recently been trying to stop attempts to turn the fields next to us into an industrial storage unit. Boundary queries have temporarily slowed down their plans but you can bet that it hasn't halted them. It's all going to the dogs. (In fact, a dog track was one developer's proposal for the same field!) The area that Emi and I chose to live in eight years or so ago has changed quite a lot since we came here, particularly in terms of our own privacy and outlook. Had we known how much our immediate environment would suffer, we probably would have looked elsewhere to make our home. We're saddled with it now, of course. Things could always be worse, but still.

Sometimes, I long for the seclusion of a home bounded by its own space, immune from the claws of development. Haddlesey House, where I was fortunate enough to live in the

1980s, was such a place. I really cherished that old house and its surrounding, protective walls. Plenty of room to set up a drum kit, marimbas, amplifiers and no need to worry about noise. And a river bank at the bottom of the garden where I could sit at twilight, listening to ripples and blackbirds whilst waiting for lyrics to materialise like ghosts. Even that lovely old place, as regular readers of this diary know, was eventually raped and pillaged by the amoral greed of property developers. It's like a cheesy, up-market housing estate for accountants and insurance salesmen now. What I really need is to land a lucrative Hollywood film score commission. Then again, could I put up with all that bullshit just to earn enough money to build myself a proper studio space? Probably not ... but I could try. The truth is, my nature doesn't really lend itself to such careerist manipulations. You really need to hang out, network, put yourself about, etc, etc. Oh, I've got ambitions enough but they're not of much practical use. It's all dreams and dreaming, techniques designed to encourage the flow of (gulp) beauty and magic through my life, not to hold onto the bland material signifiers that seem to become the alpha and omega of contemporary achievers. Still, I'm no purist. I'd happily drive an Aston Martin or a Bristol or some equally beautiful, exclusive and snotty assembly of steel and leather, should I ever be able to afford such a luxury. As the old Buddhist saying has it: 'It's fine to drive an expensive car, as long as the expensive car isn't driving you'. It all comes back to the notion of attachment/non-attachment. More than ever these days, people find it hard to let go.

Watched a lovely documentary film on DVD last night. It's called *Dharma River, Journey Of A Thousand Buddhas* and was made by John Bush. It is a filmic record of river journeys through Laos, Burma and Thailand, visiting ancient Buddhist temples and communities along the way. It's visually stunning and brings home the tremendous beauty of Buddhist art and architecture. Some of the larger temples, over 2,000 years old, are breathtaking. I commented to Emi that, of all the religious options available to us, Buddhism, for me, remains the sanest, the clearest, the gentlest, most rational, simple, direct, humane and downright beautiful.

The word 'religion' however, at least in my opinion, is a limitation and an encumbrance. Buddhism's direct pointing at reality goes way beyond such limitations, right to the heart of things. But what do I know? I'm not a very good Buddhist, (as I've said before in these pages). In fact, by some people's definition of the term, I'm not really a Buddhist at all. My 'organised spiritual group' days are behind me. I prefer to walk my own path at my own pace, nor am I in search of a guru or an avatar. Perhaps I'm just trying to enjoy each moment without hurting anyone, and offering my art as thanks for that.

Insight and inspiration are all around us, always. This too, is Buddha nature. There's a key here that, once grasped and turned, opens a door onto infinite possibilities. It's so impossibly direct and simple that it is usually overlooked, misunderstood or considered invisible. That it can't be communicated by words does not necessarily make it an impenetrable secret. Letting go, is part of the process of discovering this marvellous and subtle thing. It's a jewel beyond price.

And now I'm tired again and my shoulders ache from sitting in front of my Mac. My computer screen's background image, for those who may be interested, is a lovely, vibrantly coloured painting of the Tibetan White Tara Buddha. Sometimes, I exchange her for an image of a vintage green and cream Blackpool tram. The two things, ultimately, are the same. Theories as to why this should be are welcome down at 'The Dreamsville Arms' which can be found in 'The Pleasure Park.'

More communication from Harold. Good words from him about *Rosewood*. He says: 'That's the album you've always wanted to make ...' He also has two titles/pieces settled for us to work on for his concert at Brighton next month. Nearer and nearer now. As soon as my health returns, I need to prepare a couple of guitars or more in readiness. Some set-up work needed with intonation and action. I'm planning to take several variations of equipment so as to be prepared for whatever the music demands. I have no idea, at this stage, how it will turn out, or what the music will be. I'm sure it will be fine in the end, despite my trepidation. All for today. I need to take a break.

·

THURSDAY 12TH MAY 2005

A huge sigh of relief. My 'Dreamsville' site is finally up and working and has received a very generous outpouring of appreciation from its visitors. The response has been even more positive than I could have hoped for and there are vibrant, lively conversations continually buzzing in the virtual saloons of 'Dreamsville Inn Forum '. A genuine community spirit permeates the place. Excellent!

The next task is for me to install visuals and text into the other areas of the site. First priority is 'The Museum Of Memory'. I've already gathered a large number of exhibits together for this location, as I've mentioned in earlier diary entries. These items now need to be loaded into the 'Museum' itself. Next in line, after this, is 'The Academy Of Art' and 'The Guitar Arcade'. Other duties have forced this to be put on hold though. Next week will be taken up with preparations for Harold Budd's concert on the 21st. Before that, I have equipment to repair, prepare, pack away and so on. Then a lengthy trip from Yorkshire down to Brighton for rehearsals and the concert itself.

At this point in time I still don't have an inkling about the pieces I'm to perform on. Harold is playing it very close to his chest although he has recently told me the titles of the pieces that he's prepared for us to play together. Other than that, though, no clues. Nevertheless, such a last minute approach may add an edge to things as I'll have to invent something on the spot. I have to admit that I'm flattered that Harold has confidence in me to pull whatever rabbits are required out of my hat. But at the same time (and predictably, for readers familiar with the self-doubts that regularly fuel this diary), I have very little confidence in myself at all. But fear not, the muse will find a way. Said he, setting down his glass of Merlot and adopting an inane grin.

Perhaps I really shouldn't get myself quite so worked up about it. After all, I dive in the deep end as a matter of course with my own compositions on a fairly regular basis. (Or am I just foolishly trying to reassure myself with that last comment?) Anyway, it will be what it will be. A long time ago, when Harold and I played in Portugal together, Harold said, "Don't worry, Bill, it doesn't have to be the greatest thing that came down God's pipe". But on this special occasion, particularly as it is Harold's public finale, I really want it to be wonderful, not for me, but for Harold who deserves the absolute best I can muster.

A shift of shadows, a different and far more mundane topic. Woes of all kinds on the domestic front. So, what's new? Well, here's something: back in January, I bought a new bathroom suite from MFI. Yes, I know, if only I could afford not to shop there. Anyway, I obtained what I'd thought was a bargain in MFI's January sales. Lots of convincing chat from their sales-man who assured me this was the chance of a lifetime, free taps, waste traps and fittings, a Hollywood film starlet of my choice thrown in to scrub my back, complimentary bubble bath, and so on and so forth. 'Lovely', I thought, imagining Sharon Stone's nipples giving me the Soapland treatment. I placed my order and gained brownie points with Emiko. (though not for the Sharon Stone fantasies). Eventually, I arranged for them to fit the damn thing too, not just supply it. "We have qualified fitters, Mr. Nelson, they can do any extra work you might require, such as tiling, Mr. Nelson ... whatever your heart might desire, very good quality, Mr. Nelson ... a comprehensive service tailored to your needs, etc, etc, blah, blah, blah ... ". Out came my credit card and my hard-earned cash electronically whizzed into MFI's bank account. I left the store, trying to ignore the horror stories that several people had told me about their own, or friend's, experiences with the company. "MFI? Oooh ... (big intake of breath and shaking of head), "you don't want to go there!" Time passed as we waited for their fitter to set a date. More time passed, weeks, months, an eternity it seemed. I went into MFI's store and raised a quiet storm of complaint. My face turned black, red horns popped from my skull, lightning flashed in my immediate vicinity, my voice dropped a couple of octaves, the sky went dark and I noticed that they had to switch the store's lights on. The MFI assistant appeared indifferent to any of these ominous pyrotechnics, acting as if my frustration was something so commonplace as to be not worthy of anything more energetic than sneering disdain. Actually, I'm trying to paint a picture of myself as a strong and indignant customer here. The truth is I was really quite reasonable, calm and polite. Of course, I should have been much heavier with them. Nevertheless, the assistant eventually wandered off to contact the fitter. "Wait here Mr. Nelson, just a moment, Sir." Twenty minutes or so later, the assistant returned to say that they'd spoken to their fitter who had apparently said: "Fitting on May 5th … definitely". The assistant confidently wrote on my MFI paperwork: 'Delivery: 5th of May, fitting: 5th of May'. At long last, I thought. So, on the 4th of May, Emiko and I spent the entire day clearing the bathroom of all furniture, of piles of magazines, of dozens of bottles of cosmetics, colognes, fragile mirrors, framed pictures, vintage radio, etc, etc. We also cleared an area of access from the front door, up the stairs, through the bedroom to the en-suite bathroom. Then we scrubbed the bathroom from top to bottom. Everything ship-shape and ready to go. I put my various work projects on hold so as to be available for the following day's delivery and fitting of the bathroom suite. I'd also bought boxes of tiles for the fitter to fit around the bathroom walls. All of this work agreed with him several weeks previously. AND paid in advance, as is MFI's rule. (Note: always read the small print, preferably with an electron microscope). Meanwhile, Emiko dreamed of a new bath that didn't leave rust marks on her skin. I dreamed of getting lathered up in the welcoming vicinity of Sharon Stone's thighs.

On the morning of the 5th, Emi and I are up really early, eager and ready for the arrival of both fitter and our new bathroom suite. A few hours later, Emi has gone to work and I'm still waiting. After a while, I start to worry so I call the fitter's number, as given to me by MFI. An answer machine answers. I leave a message. Three-quarters of an hour later, the fitter calls to say that MFI hadn't told him he was supposed to be fitting our bathroom that day. In fact he's doing another job. (I find this unbelievable as MFI had actually spoken with the fitter on the phone in my presence some weeks before. And it was he who gave MFI the date of the 5th). I ask him when he can come to do the job and he says, "Call me when the bathroom suite arrives". I say: "It's arriving today, so are you coming over later to fit it?" He says, "Can't do it until next Monday at the earliest, I've taken on other work". (This is Thursday). In a state of shocked stupor, I put the phone down. I eventually recover my composure and call MFI who begin to make outrageous excuses. I demolish these firmly and methodically and ask them what they propose to do to remedy the problem. They eventually say, "Well, why don't you just take delivery of the suite and we'll arrange another fitting date". I then explain to them (as I've already explained on several occasions since ordering the damned thing) that we have absolutely nowhere to store a boxed bathroom suite with all its fittings, other than in the garden and there's no way I'm leaving it there. I suggest they postpone the delivery until they organise a new fitting date, perhaps Monday or Tuesday at the latest, as now suggested by their fitter. MFI say they'll call me back. Once again I sit by the phone, trying to grasp the banality of the situation.

When they eventually do call back, they say that they can't stop the delivery as the truck driver doesn't have a phone and therefore isn't contactable. They suggest I wait for him to arrive with the suite, then tell him to go away, and take it back to the depot with him. By now, steam is coming out of my ears. I sit in the house all day, fuming and hoping the delivery truck will arrive soon. It doesn't arrive. At four thirty, I decide to go out into town as I have better things to do. When I get back, Emiko has returned home from her day working at the flower shop. She says that the delivery man actually telephoned her at the shop, saying he had a bathroom suite to deliver to our house, but no-one was in. (And this after MFI had told me that the guy didn't have a phone in his truck). Emiko explained the situation and the delivery man laughed: "It happens all the time with MFI" he said. He then took the suite back to his depot. I then await MFI to inform me of a new fitting date. I'm hoping it will be either Monday or Tuesday, as was suggested by their fitter. I hear nothing, not a sausage. On Monday, I call MFI to see if they've sorted things out. They say, "No, but why don't you call the fitter directly?" I do so, wondering why I'm doing their job for them. All I get is the fitter's answering machine. I leave a message, explaining the urgency. No one calls me back. I call again, leave another message. This goes on for a while.

By Wednesday, I've abandoned hope and call MFI to tell them that the fitter hasn't answered my calls and ask them to get it sorted out or I'll consider cancelling my order. They say they'll try to contact the fitter. Ten minutes later, they call back to say they've spoken with him and that he can't fit it for at least another three weeks as he's taken on other work. In a daze, I tell them I'll speak with my wife about it. Emi and I then talk through the problems we've had and decide that, although it makes life more difficult for us, we really don't want to give our custom to this company any more. It's simply not good enough. I call MFI back and once again explain that they've had my money since January, it is now almost the end of May, and I still don't have my bathroom suite and that enough is enough, I want a refund. The girl on the phone sniggers and says "Fine, come into the store and we'll arrange it". So today, I locate all my paperwork, receipts, etc and go into the garden to get into my car to drive to MFI to ask for a refund. And here comes domestic screw up number two: as I swing behind the wheel, I look up to see that my windscreen is sporting a large hole with cracks radiating out from it, right across the entire screen. I get out of the car in disbelief and look at the damage. A real mess. Not at all safe to drive. The cause? Our next door neighbour has been erecting a workshop the size of a small house at the bottom of our garden and the builders have, it seems, lobbed a brick or something extremely hard through my car's windscreen. Their last day today, too, apparently. A parting shot? How they did this, I have no idea. It couldn't have been something dropped from the building as my car wasn't underneath it, or the surrounding scaffolding. There was no sign of a brick or a missile either (they must have removed it). Whatever it was, it would need hurling away from the structure to hit my car's windscreen. My blood pressure went up along with my hackles but the builders had gone home. On tip-toe, I presume.

I urgently had to get into town so I grabbed my things and set off to walk into the village where there is a bus stop. I then waited almost 30 minutes for a bus. By this time, I'd tried to apply my Buddha head to the situation. Stay calm, let go, be cool. The problem with this, of course, is that people often take advantage, thinking that placidity equals pushover. I really should show them the other side of the coin once in a while, but they wouldn't like it and neither would I. Just like many other good-natured folk who try to let go of their anger and frustration and put themselves in other's shoes, when the pressure eventually builds up to bursting, I really blow my top. All those pent-up feelings of exploitation and injustice erupt in a very forceful way. And then those same people who had me sussed as a wuss and who were happy to take advantage of that presumption, suddenly whine and complain that I'm a nasty and vindictive old so and so. Well, tough titty. Sometimes bad behaviour begets the same. Oh, the horror!

There's even more bullshit going on around me right now but I'm damned if I'm going to get into it here in this diary. Okay, calm down, William. Don't over-dramatise it for the sake of your audience. Just call your insurance company and see if you can get them to send out a windscreen repairman. Or whatever it is you're supposed to do in these situations. Sometimes, although I'm the first to say money can't buy happiness, I think that if I could afford it, I'd put a certain distance, physically and spiritually, between me and these kind of things. The older I get, the less attractive they become. Man, I'd live on a little island in the middle of some warm stream, away from the herd, counting the buttercups in the meadows and listening to the skylarks sing. The rest of the world could get on with its manipulations and acquisitions without inflicting its shit on me. I'm a fuckin' misfit and shameless with it.

·

Early afternoon. Last night, the man in charge of the builders was summoned to look at my shattered windscreen. He says he already knew about it. (Well, there's a surprise). He casually apologised and suggested I get it fixed on my car insurance. I said I'd need to see what the insurance policy covered in respect to that. He said he reckoned the replacement screen would be free but, if there was an excess charge to pay, he'd pay it. I called the insurance company this morning who put me on to Autoglass who told me there would be an excess charge of sixty pounds to pay. I had to pay for it there and then, on my credit card over the phone. Unfortunately, they say that they can't get to the house to repair it until late Monday afternoon, which means I can't use my car until Tuesday. (The car can't be moved until the new windscreen 'sets').

Someone else just told me that I was stupid to do it via my insurance company at all as it will affect my no-claims bonus. I should simply have made arrangements to get the screen replaced directly and given the entire bill to the builder as it was his responsibility. Too late now, of course, as I've messed about on the phone all morning, trying to sort it out. Typical.

Now I have to catch up with the chores I intended to do yesterday, pick up some dry cleaning, go to MFI and get a refund, pay some household bills, etc. I've had to borrow

Emiko's car as a result of mine being out of action, which means I've had to take her to work and will need to pick her up later on when she finishes. Time consuming.

On the MFI front, I heard this morning that my brother Ian had also recently bought a new bathroom suite from them and it seems he's had very similar fitter problems, even though he lives in a different part of Yorkshire to me. I won't relate Ian's story here as it is just as complex and frustrating as mine. I'll just say that he too had heard similar stories from other people about poor quality service. It's nice to know we're not alone in this.

An entirely different subject: the latest issue of *Word* magazine carries a feature about important albums that have been underrated or overlooked. In amongst them is Be Bop Deluxe's *Axe Victim* album. Nice to see it being acknowledged in this way. The writer makes some interesting points though I have to say that the concept for the album was not quite as naive or innocent as he seems to think. The 'glam/Bowie' thing was done quite deliberately but in a knowing, ironic, almost parodist fashion. Particularly as, at the time of the band's formation, we had no master plan to land a record contract or to become professional musicians. It was, in many ways, just a bit of fun, the concept emerging from my art student background and incorporating the Pop Art and Warholism that had informed my art-school years. Plus, the glam look turned the girls on, as I hoped it might! Oh, yes, David Bowie and Roxy Music were touchstones but they also were seen as a source of pastiche. Remove the whole thing one step further from the point they might have removed it from. Shine a different light into the hollow centre of pop music. At least from a more personal angle. In any case, by the time EMI Records had become interested in signing the band, I was already steering things away from the glam style, but it was EMI who persuaded me to hang on to the look, (and that specific batch of material), a little longer as they felt that the band's original fan-base would expect that image and style on our first album. Actually, when *Axe Victim* was released, I'd already written most of the material that would later emerge on *Futurama*. But, perhaps I'm being overly fussy here, maybe I protest too much. Everyone has to start somewhere and, whilst I'm now somewhat squeamish about the early Be Bop material, I have to admit that it was bright and fun to play and the dressing up thing was a bit of a lark, a foppish in-joke on one hand and a crowd pleaser on the other. It helped get us noticed so served its purpose. And I met some really sweet girls. It was of its time and its time was ripe.

Time changes things and the music must change too. Sometimes on a daily basis, according to mood. This is the hardest thing for some people to deal with. Artists who move on and regularly challenge themselves inevitably have a tougher time of it than those who establish a popular product and simply stick with it. People like to be able to label or identify things, whether it be the easy familiarity of an Elton John or (and I admit I'm on controversial ground here) the equally predictable signifiers of the so-called 'avant-garde'. It seems to me that things at either end of the spectrum have much more in common than they'd be prepared to admit. (These days, the avant-garde is just as marketed and targeted a product as pop). A bit of a hobby-horse of mine this subject, I know, but just stand back from it a student bed-sit's metre or two and you'll see what I mean. At the end of the day it's all disposable, ephemeral, fickle, fashion-shackled and tribally oriented. Music, for all its grand pretensions and aspirations, is ultimately a commodity. (Unless it never escapes from one's bedroom). The minute it emerges into the world, it surrenders to the possibility of profit, either financially or in terms of perceived 'artistic' status. It gains weight (like me) and begins to live a life of its own, out of control. Perhaps Harold, with his current vow to quit and to move on into a new phase of his life, has the guts to do what I fear the most — to leave it all behind, drop the weight and walk upright again. But despite my carping, cynical protestations, I'm hooked like a junky on the stuff. Sometimes, I resent this fact so much. Too pathetic and insecure to live without my regular sound fix. A weakness or a strength? Who knows, I can't tell any more. My next album will be called *Brickie Victim* and will feature songs about breeze-blocks and blocked views. It could only happen to William.

·

SUNDAY 29TH MAY 2005

An entire week has passed since Harold's concert in Brighton and only now have I found time to sit down and write an entry for my increasingly late diary. When I returned home, at midnight on the Sunday after the Brighton event, I found my inbox full of emails, mostly accumulated whilst I was away. I seem to have spent all of last week trying to catch up, plus dealing with other pressing problems, all requiring my slightly-out-of-focus attention, many of them of a domestic nature but most of them musical or creative.

Music is a lovely thing to dedicate one's life to but, in my neck of the woods, it's a 24 hour, seven days a week job. There's always something waiting for me to work on. Not that I'm complaining, you understand. I'm just moaning a little. I like to glamorise my passion, gild it with a little self-inflicted angst. Oh, how we artists suffer!

So, here we go, my extremely nebulous and probably unreliable reflections regarding the Brighton concert: a long train journey from Yorkshire to get there on Wednesday, 18th of May. Emi and I have to drag our suitcases from King's Cross Station, dodging traffic and pedestrians along busy London streets, until we reach the Thameslink Station. Then we struggle to carry our cases down flights of stairs to the platform to catch the Brighton train. (No escalator, no lift. Only in England). As usual, we've taken far more clothes than required but, as the weather seems so changeable, we've packed items for any eventuality. How I regret it whilst struggling to get those heavy cases down the stairs. We're both getting far too old for this kind of thing.

The Thameslink train to Brighton is packed solid with commuters, all looking absolutely pissed off with their lot, overloaded with stress and thwarted ambition. The train is uncomfortable, hot, and stops at virtually every station en route. It feels like an eternity in hell before we finally arrive in Brighton, a genuine relief to get there after the tiring day's travel. We're met on the platform by a bright and breezy young lady called Amanda, who is acting as artist-coordinator for Harold's concert. Amanda's cheerful demeanour instils confidence as she whisks us off to our hotel. I've been feeling nervous about the event for days but Amanda's calm personality soothes things a little. Our hotel turns out to be 'The Old Ship', situated right on the sea front, halfway between Brighton's main pier and the old Victorian one that was destroyed by fire and water not so long ago. This latter pier's rusting hulk, stark, ghostly and forlorn, is plainly visible to the right of 'The Old Ship's' main entrance. Sad that it has apparently deteriorated way beyond repair now. The surviving Brighton pier, to the left of the hotel, has a funfair at its furthest end, complete with a traditional, inverted 'ice-cream cone' helter-skelter. Later, I will take some photographs of this, hoping for a possible album cover image for the future. Or at least one that I can use on the Dreamsville website.

The sea-front promenade itself has traditional seaside cast-iron railings, painted in what I like to call 'corporation green and cream'. Very similar to those found in Blackpool, but a little less art-deco, though from a similar period. A few scattered old public shelters along the prom too. Architectural whimsy, my kind of thing. I wonder if Brighton ever had trams, like Blackpool? Within minutes of checking in, Harold Budd calls my room and invites us down to the hotel's bar for a reunion drink. I haven't seen Harold since our ill-fated jaunt to Mexico, maybe over two years ago now. (Our scheduled concert in Mexico City was cancelled after we'd arrived there). Whilst we didn't get to play in Mexico, Harold and Emiko and I spent a week hanging out in Mexico City's museums and galleries and cantinas, enjoying a pleasant time, despite the fact that 'Gulf War Round Two' had just erupted and was dominating the TV news to depressing effect. (Check out my *Diary of a Hyper-dreamer* book to read more about this period). Since that time, we've each been back in our respective habitats, Harold in LA and the desert around Joshua Tree, Emi and I in our heavily insulated nest in Yorkshire, but we have stayed in regular contact via letters and emails, as always.

Harold looks well, dapper and not a single day older than the last time I'd seen him. (How does he do that?) He remains one of my dearest friends and time spent with him is full of laughter and companionship, even if I fall speechless some-times. The fact that he happens to be a musical and artistic treasure is simply an extra bonus. It's only when I hear him play that I feel absolutely awestruck. One minute, we're laughing at some stupid, inane reference to peas and carrots being served up to us in a pub in Selby over 12 years ago, the next I'm being elevated, uplifted and, yes, educated by the way that Harold touches the piano's keys and brings forth a chord of such exquisite shape and resonance that I could weep with envy. I hear it but don't understand it, nor would I want to. This is a mystery worth preserving. I never ask Harold how or why, I just let it sink in and settle. Somewhere down the line, the lesson that I've learned by this method makes itself known. This is part of the generosity in his art.

Harold and Emi and I then decide to have dinner at the hotel, rather than go out and brave the unreliable weather, which is by now looking windy and damp. The hotel restaurant isn't the best choice. It serves up a fairly dry and mediocre meal, but our happy conversation enlivens the table and the less than sparkling food becomes secondary to the enjoyment of each other's company. Much wine is consumed. Outside the hotel dining room window, a pedestrian crossing's light is silhouetted against a background of dark sea and grey sky, first a little red electric man lights up, then a green one. The sea and sky broods as the green and red lights alternate. I make a mental note to take a photograph of this before we leave Brighton. Later, as Emi and I retire to our room for the night, we discover that it is crippled with noise: rattling sash windows that sound like distant cannon fire, a taxi-rank beneath the window that echoes to the mad shouts and incomprehensible songs of a seemingly endless chain of drunks (this unholy racket continues well into the early hours). Then, the noise of a heavy street cleaning vehicle, followed by a garbage truck, followed by screaming, vicious seagulls as dawn breaks. After that, the regular early morning traffic, motorbikes, delivery trucks, police sirens. By 8 am, I've managed no more than three hour's intermittent sleep.

I get up to attend the first day of rehearsals, feeling terrible. I'm well past the age when I can rise above such things. I need a full eight hours to feel human. One of the problems is that I'm used to a quiet, country environment, backgrounded by gentle early morning birdsong and little else, save the occasional distant cuckoo or skylark. No chance of that here. I stagger about the hotel room, wondering how I'll cope with the rigours of rehearsals. I've not heard anything of the music Harold requires me to play. It's all unknown.

The morning weather is windy and wet and so the ever efficient and cheerful Amanda whisks Harold, Emi and I off to the Brighton Dome in a taxi. Us old folks need a wee bit of molly-coddling. The first day of rehearsals is being held here in the Dome, an entirely acoustic rehearsal too, without either monitors or pa system. The Dome is a lovely venue, right next door to Brighton's famous Pavilion It's a long time since I've visited Brighton, way back in the 1970s actually, when Be Bop Deluxe played there a couple of times. The first of those

Brighton Be Bop Deluxe concerts was a happy but poignant one for me. A girl, who I had once fallen hopelessly in love with some time previously and who had, in both presence and absence, provided me with a muse-like inspiration, had moved from East Yorkshire to Brighton to attend university there. This girl was Lisa Rosenberg who, as long-time aficionados of my music will probably be aware, I'd fallen for in a big way during Be Bop Deluxe's earliest days, when the band first played at The Duke of Cumberland pub in North Ferriby near Hull, around 1973. It was one of those transcendental affairs that change one's entire outlook. Lisa and I shared a sweet, but all too brief, romantic relationship that survived just 12 months or so. I was married to my first wife, (Shirley), at that time, though the marriage was not a happy one. All my fault, really. Too young to handle it, too wrapped up in music to pack it in and toe the line, too ambitious to be the nine-to-five husband that Shirley wanted. I'm neither ashamed nor proud of that time, it happened and I did my best, which wasn't particularly good enough. Anyway, The Duke of Cumberland gigs provided Lisa and I with an opportunity to be together, albeit fleetingly. (She lived near North Ferriby in the somewhat upper-class village of Kirkella). In between Be Bop's three sets per gig we would moon and spoon and pour out our hearts to each other in the Duke's rear garden, or on a bench in Coronation Gardens by the village crossroads, or down by the side of the river Humber in North Ferriby, watching the boats drift by on the rising tide, listening to the brass bell on the sand bank warning buoy gently toll, this accompanied by the more distant bells of North Ferriby's church.

The band usually had to come looking for me to drag me

back on stage for the next set. I could have remained by her side, looking into her eyes, all night, music forgotten. In between these monthly gigs at 'The Duke' we would write letters of longing to each other. Lisa sent hers to me at my place of work as our relationship might have been discovered if she'd sent them to my home. At that time I still had a day job with the West Riding County Council's supply department. For my sins, which were many but generally minor, I was a Local Government Officer. I hated the job, but how easily we are diverted from our dreams. It seemed that this was all that was available to me. And, in truth, it was. I doodled guitars and song lyrics on scrap paper whilst sitting at my desk in the office, much as I had when I was at school. The idea of making a living from music seemed way beyond my reach. But I lived for those few gigs the band could get back then. During that time, I wrote floods of songs about Lisa and our melancholy, ecstatic romance — *Teenage Archangel*, *Axe Victim* and *Love Is Swift Arrows* being the earliest. I was totally transformed by the depth of my feelings for her. Eventually, Lisa moved away from Hull to take up her law studies in Brighton and I wasn't to see her again until my first concert there, quite some time later. I can still recall the surprise and tender nervousness I felt when she came backstage to say hello to me once more, at the Brighton gig in the 1970s. Be Bop's professional career had started to gain momentum and I had changed the line up from the original one that had played at 'The Duke.' I was thrilled, pleased, flattered, devastated and shaking like a leaf to see Lisa again. And proud of her too. I remember introducing her to Simon and Andy and Charlie, who, unlike the original band, hadn't been witness to our earlier, aching love affair. I was like:

'This is the girl who inspired me to write those songs. Now you know why!' The impression she'd made on my life had been profound.

A year later, Be Bop Deluxe played in Brighton again and another member of the band's road crew told me that Lisa was in the audience again and that she had asked him if she could come backstage to say hello to me. But this time my second wife, Janice Monks, was with me and Jan, who knew all about my old flame, said 'No way!' I can't really blame her for that as she knew exactly how besotted I was with Lisa. So I reluctantly asked the roadie to make an excuse, and not allow Lisa backstage, even though I desperately wanted to see her. I fretted about the situation for months afterwards, nay, years. I guess I've always been (as must be obvious to those who have gone beneath the surface of my songs) an incurable romantic. Still am, by the way, and damn the consequences. The heart has its reasons.

So, Brighton revisited, but now it's the 21st Century, 30 years later and Lisa's faint ghost glows soft in the ever darkening rooms of my memory. But still there, still there, never completely vanquished. First day of rehearsals with Harold — now I finally get to hear the two pieces he's prepared for us to play together. I was expecting awkward keys for the guitar but the first piece apparently starts in E minor. A moment's relief. Then it shifts to something less comfortable, a key that denies me the safe harbour of open strings. Not beyond my reach though, with a little thought and telepathy. The second piece is in a slightly trickier key, C-sharp or B-flat, can't recall which now. I jotted it down in a notebook, then forgot about it.

Harold skims through each composition with me, he on

piano, me on acoustic guitar. All quite naked and vulnerable. He steers me away from going over the pieces too many times. In fact we hardly go into them in any fine detail at all. And this is the first time I've heard them. I do, however, presume to understand his approach. Perhaps this is just Harold's strategy to keep an edge to my performance, to stop it from becoming too slick, too busy. The less I know, the more careful, sparingly and thoughtfully I'll play. Scary for me but, obviously, Harold must feel confident that I can provide a spontaneous response to the music. I feel a tiny bit more confident than I did on the train journey down from Yorkshire, but only just.

A pleasant meal at a Thai restaurant that evening, with Harold, Guy Morley (the show's organiser), Amanda, visual artist Russell Mills, (who has designed the stage sets and lighting scheme for the concert), Steve Jansen, (gong and drums for the second half of the concert) and Theo Travis (flute). I immediately feel comfortable around Theo who is unassuming and straightforward but gifted. Russell too. He's a lovely chap whose humour belies his tremendous talent as a visual artist. I love being around people of this calibre, even if I do generally feel as inferior as hell.

Next day, after more sleeplessness, we rehearse again, this time with monitors and Pa system. Robin Guthrie arrives from his base in France and sets up a lap-top processed guitar. Robin is a lovely guy, too. Everyone's lovely. Harold decides I should play on the number he's performing with John Foxx as well as the two pieces Harold and I are doing together. He then adds one more, extra piece for John and I to play with him. So now I'm to take part in four numbers during the first half. Wow! I'm not complaining at all, in fact I'm thrilled and flattered but

I'm also terrified. Another meal with everyone that evening at a restaurant close by the Dome, right next door to a theatre that advertises, on a banner hung outside the theatre's foyer, a production called 'Julia Pastrana, The Ugliest Woman In The World'. The banner next to this one carries the qualifying message: 'Performed In Total Darkness ...' I'd told Hal about these banners earlier in the day. I thought their message was hilarious. The idea that the central character was so physically awful to contemplate, so dangerously ugly that the show had to be performed in total darkness, seemed absurdly and surreally funny. More wine back at the hotel. I'm flagging, finding it hard to concentrate.

Another night of hotel room noise with only three hours sleep and then it's sound-check and band rehearsal time. A busy day, as we have to work on the long group improvisation that will fill most of the second half of the concert. John Foxx, Harold and I run through the trio vignettes that we are to perform, but not my own duos with Harold. He says we don't need to do these, that we have them down fine. I, on the other hand, can't even remember what keys they're in. John sings some very lovely, semi-operatic, sort of Gregorian chant style vocals, processed through various vocoder/harmoniser effects. I play some half-reversed guitar chimes under Harold's piano arpeggios, trying to stay out of the way of the top line as much as possible. It seems to work. John is a really nice guy too and I'm pleased to be part of his performance, minimal as my contribution to it is.

Jah Wobble arrives from his gig in Paris. I've previously only met Jah once, in Leeds, when he'd involved Harold in his 'Solaris' band project. (This was a few years ago and Harold had invited me along to see the concert). I didn't really have time to get the measure of him then. Now, I spot him in the 'rest lounge' area of the Brighton Dome where some of us are taking a refreshment break. He's just arrived in time to run through our band improvisation piece. I go up and say hello and shake his hand. Within seconds I've decided I like him a lot. He has a good sense of humour and seems warm, genuine and down to earth. My kind of person.

Harold, earlier in the day, has been rehearsing the string quartet pieces with The Balanescu Quartet who sound magnificent. The quartet's leader, Alex Balanescu, is to join us in our group improvisation. Another musician taking part in the improv section is an old friend of mine from 'up north', Steve Cobby, who will provide lap-top sounds. Steve, who arrives not long before Jah, is his usual, absolutely cheerful self, a valuable and positive force. It's good to see him again. We finally get to run through the group improvisation. Rough and not really ready but Harold seems fine with it all. Some technical problems — noisy buzzes due to earth loops and lighting interference, but the tech guys seem to sort it out. I've got Pete Harwood and Dave Standeven with me, not just to look after my gear, but to help out with the other players' equipment too, which they willingly do. Robin has been suffering some strange noises, clicks and pops through his own system. Perhaps part of the overall electrical oddness that envelopes us and our equipment. Everyone lends a hand where needed. A supportive atmosphere.

I ask Harold if we should run through our duo pieces one more time. He says we don't need to as we're cool. I swallow hard and hope that I'll be cool enough to come up with the right

notes. The concert itself is a bit of a blur: I'm feeling the negative results of my lack of sleep and my nervousness has really
kicked in. We all sit in the wings to watch the Balanescu
Quartet perform Harold's string quartets. Absolutely beautiful.
A crowning achievement, I think. Then Theo takes the stage
with Harold and they play together, a lovely, poignant performance. Theo negotiating his parts with skill and insight. I reflect
on the fact that it will be good to hear Harold's music in all
these different contexts, with such a variety of textures, strings,
wind instruments, guitars, voice, piano, keyboards, laptop,
percussion, bass. The audience really seem to be appreciating
it too. Their concentration is tangible.

Then it's my turn. I walk onto the stage. Pete hands me my
acoustic guitar and I perch on a stool next to Harold's piano,
trying to remember how the pieces fit together. Harold glances
across at me, we nod to each other and off we go. Like a dream,
my hands moving of their own accord, the audience fading
away, the music spinning its spell around us, binding us
together. Just like at the first day's rehearsal, I feel exposed,
naked to some degree, with just acoustic guitar and grand
piano, and so much space in the music itself. Nowhere to hide.
But things seems to gel, the guitar and piano blend sounds good
from where I'm sitting. There's a tenderness to some sections
of the two pieces that feels sweet and fine. I'm enjoying it
tremendously, despite my nerves. Harold looks like he's enjoying it too. I hope that he is. Then a switch to electric guitar, (my
Gus 'Orphee' custom), as John Foxx joins us to sing beautifully,
his voice transformed by harmonisers and vocoders. I take no
chances, laying right back and allowing John space to do his
thing. It all seems to work wonderfully. Then I'm off stage,

relieved about the way that things have gone so far. Glad that I didn't keel over from lack of sleep. I go back to the seats in the wings to observe Harold's solo section, he alone at the piano. What a wonderful touch he has. I wrote to him earlier this week and said: '… your solo piano pieces, so perfectly judged and executed. That business about you having no pianistic technique is utter tosh. You have fabulous technique … I have only to hear you play a single note to realise that. Your touch doesn't so much 'make' the note as 'unveil' it. Your fingers point to the invisible and it appears, singing.

After Harold's solo performance, the interval, a quick glass of wine to steady my nerves, then Part Two. This begins with Steve Jansen performing a five minute version of Harold's solo gong piece, *Lirio*. Steve brings forth different tones and textures from the gong using mallets, varying the amount of attack and playing different areas of the gong's surface. It's a deceptively tricky piece to make work and Steve executes it brilliantly. Then Robin Guthrie takes over from Steve with an ambient, delayed, looped wash of chorused guitar chords, building the atmosphere for several minutes. He's then joined by Steve Cobby, who adds lap-top digital swoops, bleeps and phase shifts, gently distressing and punctuating the piece. Then Harold joins in on piano, then Theo on flute, then Alex on violin, then me on electric e-bow guitar, then Jah on bass guitar and Steve J. on drums, setting a rolling groove in 5/4 time, solid as a rock for everyone else to dance around. Various sound problems on stage though, it becomes increasingly difficult for me to pick out the other soloists. My eye proves more reliable than my ear for this task. I can see Alex energetically bowing his violin so I lay right back, stopping completely in some places, resisting the urge to push harder, doing my best to not impose my personal will on this thing. Let it roll Jah and Steve's groove is relentless, urgent, appropriate. An anchor for us all. Then, a high pitched microphonic squeal emerges from somewhere, feedback but not of the guitar variety. Definitely caused by a microphone. Someone will kill it soon, I think. They don't and it goes on, and on, squealing like a stuck pig, a youth club pa system run amok. Why hasn't someone located the cause and muted or adjusted the microphone? Harold seems to be indifferent to it. He sits, not playing, just digging the groove and enjoying the accumulating chaos. By now, I'm absolutely detached from it all, can't find a way into the music or think of anything worthwhile to add, so I do very little, other than just be there, adrift in the sonic ether. Then, suddenly, it's all over, the big machine grinds to a hesitant halt, the microphone feedback continuing for a few seconds before being finally silenced. We all move forward to bow before the audience. A good feeling but also a sad one for most of us — it's Harold's final farewell to live performance. But what a fabulous way to end a beautiful career. Harold's contribution to contemporary music remains unique and irreplaceable. I'm humbled and honoured to have contributed a tiny something to this.

After the show, lots of socialising, wine, hugs and exchanges of email addressess. General happy drunkenness. I'm feeling dizzy with it all. Richard and Adrian from Opium are there, as is Permanent Flame webmaster Chuck Bird and long time fan, Eric Tilley, who have flown over from America just to see the concert. I'm given gifts by the pair of them: toy rockets and an autographed photo of a US astronaut who shares my name. Whatever fog I've inhabited these last few days becomes even foggier, but with sparks and flashes of electric colour, warm smiles and feelings of empathy. And all I've consumed is wine and music!

Emi and I get to bed sometime after 4 am. Up early on Sunday morning to catch the train to London. Before leaving, we grab breakfast and I grab some photographs of Brighton's seafront. That pedestrian crossing. Then a taxi to the station and a coffee on the platform before departing for London. Upon arrival in the big city, Emi goes down to Surrey to attend one of her Buddhist meetings, whilst I stagger on alone, like some hung-over, sleepless zombie, along the South Bank, weaving my weary way to the Thames Modern gallery where I treat myself to lunch and a video of Lotte Reiniger's *The Adventures of Prince Achmed*, an exquisite, 1926 animated feature film that I recall seeing on TV when I was a very young boy. Then an afternoon of obscure bookshops and window shopping before I meet Emi for dinner at Trader Vic's bar/restaurant in Park Lane, prior to catching the late train back to Yorkshire.

We arrive home just before midnight, exhausted but happy. Since then, it's been a game of catch up. Tons of emails to deal with, some tweaks to the design of the Carlsbro Nelsonic Deluxe amp that is soon to go into production, website postings to attend to, this that and the other, including this diary entry. Busy as ever. None of it means much. All of it means everything. This is what I do, for what it's worth. *Rosewood* out now. Finished copies sounding and looking good. Not pop music but not beyond understanding. It's a heartfelt album, all the way. Well, that's one way of rationalising it. But does it need to be rationalised at all? Of course not. It's what it is. Nothing more to say about it than that. Other than an outpouring of joy.

Now: new technical breaks and breakdowns in my studio. My stand-alone CD burner hardware has developed a fault and needs repairing. As a result, I'm currently unable to burn CDs of my home mixes until it's fixed. When will this be? Knowing my form, some way down the line from here. Also, my Line 6 Vetta 2 combo amplifier returned from Brighton damaged. The master volume control broken off, a snapped spindle. (Probably happened in the van). The amp will need to go back to Line 6 for a new volume pot, spindle and control knob fitting. These are distractions I could do without. I really need to be working on the new songs for my autumn tour, recording a new album to release at that time too. Plus I need to shoot new video footage to create a stage backdrop video. And design a tour programme, t-shirt etc. There's also several Dreamsville website things to deal with, more design work to complete for Carlsbro, the Nelsonica fan convention to try and pull together. No time to rest, as usual. Re Nelsonica: The venue I'd hoped to hire for this year's convention turned out to be horrendously expensive. I would have been looking at well over £8,000 plus to use the rooms I had in mind. It would have been a very nice venue, with comfortable facilities, but, it was way outside the budget. I'm now looking at an alternative venue and awaiting prices but it may be that I have to rely on the old Duke of Cumberland again this year. We'll see. If that proves the case, I'll research a better venue for next year's convention instead. That way I'll have more time to check out different options. With the workload I've had so far this year, plus the two *Rosewood* albums, the urgent need to build a new website, etc, etc, my convention plans have become somewhat last-minute.

Hopefully, I can pull something together, even at this late

stage. I'm still aiming at the end of October. Fingers crossed. Had an email from Matt Howarth, enquiring about the music for our Neon Cynic project. I've not sent him a CDR of the music I've created so far. I meant to and should have done this ages ago. I'll try to get something off to him this coming week. He's apparently finished all the visuals and has coloured the entire comic book novel. The only thing that's needed now is my accompanying music. Here at home, (on the 'domestic' front) these last three days, we've had two of Emi's friends from Japan visiting us. I've been driving them around the Yorkshire tourist spots. Howarth yesterday (adventures in Bronte land), and today we're off to Whitby. The intention is to introduce them to 'The White Horse and Griffin' and its seafood delights, if I can drag myself away from this diary and actually get dressed, that is. Must hurry. It's a Bank Holiday weekend and the roads will be a nightmare. Caravans, pensioners, 'recreational' vehicles, 'people carriers' full of screaming kids, whimpering dogs and snarling husbands. The usual highway of life. Luckily, I know some back roads and scenic routes.

·

THURSDAY 16TH JUNE 2005

Damaged my left hand last week, mainly middle finger, by accidentally hitting the banister on the stairs whilst rolling up my shirt sleeves. Yes, I know, a dumb thing to do but, as pathetic as it sounds, it hurt like hell. The blow pushed the finger inwards, against the joints and tendon. It's been painful, swollen and red and I couldn't play guitar for a few days.

Difficult to grip things and to drive without discomfort, too. Finally on the mend but still a little tender. I seem to be either much more clumsy in my late middle-age or simply more accident prone than of yore.

Two envelopes arrived in the post from Harold last week, one containing photographs of the desert house within which he composed the *Bride in the Tree* pieces that we duetted at the Brighton concert. The other envelope contained a letter with Harold's thoughts on his 'retirement', his reflections on the concert itself, and more general chit-chat. Harold's letters are always a joy to read and I consider myself fortunate to receive them. Whilst on the subject of communications, I received a long and generous email from artist Russell Mills recently. Good to hear from him. I'm going to try to contribute a few 'off cuts' of music to a sound assembly project he's working on. Lots of interesting people involved in it. Hopefully, I can donate some prima material to the communal sonic soup.

Also received an email from Kate (St. John) and spoke with her on the phone. As I've mentioned before in this diary, I'm very fond of Kate, she's one of those rare people who I can relax around and talk openly about anything. I hope to ask her and Theo Travis to join me for parts of my London concert this coming November, if I can come up with some music worthy of the two of them. Actually, the writing of new music is not going too well right now and not just because of my hand injury. After I returned from Brighton the other week, I listened back to the unfinished tracks I'd been working on prior to Harold's concert and suddenly decided to abandon them. They just didn't tweak my nipples. Not a writer's block, just a barking up of the wrong tree. You'd think that, after completing the *Rosewood* project, I'd be full of confidence and optimism but I'm not. All I can hear is its flaws. Perhaps I need to lose my current 'weight of the world' worries, rid myself of the various doubts and fears that have been bothering me, just let things flow more. I've often given this same advice to friends who have hit a similar sort of creative obstacle but, typically, I find it hard, if not impossible, to deal with myself. I just seem to be overburdened with self-doubt and existential angst at the moment. Or is that my regular condition? Anyway, I've consigned the unfinished pieces to the 're-consider several months hence' bin.

I've now started on an entirely new piece, a vocal one, for both the tour and the tour album. I've completed a couple of mixes of it but not sure if it's right yet. So, still more tweaking to be done and then a backing track mix of the song to be made for the shows. The song is called *And Then The Rain*, yet another melancholic rain song, the sort that seem to have become a regular part of my musical vocabulary. This particular one could be said (by some) to be a 'classic' Bill Nelson romantic rock/pop tune. (Is there such a thing?) There's nothing stylistically new about it but it certainly fits into a certain melodic niche that a lot of people tell me they like. Not that I composed it with that specific result in mind. Like everything else that happens to me, it just happened. More worryingly, I'm pretty much ambivalent about it right now. I'll see how it stands up after I've forgotten about it. Let it settle.

Because my digital recording system allows me extra control, further options, I tend to spend far more time recording each piece than I did with the old analogue tape system I used for so many years. An inclination to fiddle about presents itself. And then, because I spend longer working on each piece, I become bored, indifferent or immune to it. There's a lot to be said for working quickly with limited means. It certainly speeds the process and stops the rot setting in. Not that I'd really go back to the old technology, even though I do, ultimately, prefer the warmth of tape.

The major creative problem I'm having at the moment is caused by the pressure to come up with lyrics. Perhaps it's because I'm not in a vocal-oriented state of mind right now. My passions are pulling me more towards the instrumental end of the spectrum. In fact, not just the instrumental end of the spectrum but the very abstract end of it. The bit that verges almost on silence. Nevertheless, I've been persuaded to present some vocal songs (as well as instrumentals) at the autumn concerts, so I have to come up with something worthwhile. Maybe I'm panicking unduly, but panicking I definitely am. What I really need is a holiday or at least a healthy break away from all of this. (How often have I said that?) I don't seem to have stopped for the last few years now, a constant chasing of my own tail. Is it so surprising that I'm feeling exhausted? My own fault, of course, no-one to blame but me. But because of the amount of work I've produced over the years, people often think it comes easy, that it's stress free and constantly on tap. If only that were the case. The reason I've produced so much stuff isn't because it's easy, it's because I work very hard at it and with a passion, to the point where I regularly endanger my physical health and mental well-being. Sounds dramatic, I know, but it often feels like I'm emptying my life and soul into these things. I love doing this work but it's much more of a struggle than people might realise.

Adrian at Opium asked if I could suggest four tracks from my catalogue that could be given to the agent to play to promoters to give them some idea of what my solo concerts are like. I certainly can do this, if it helps, but I'm pretty amazed that, after the extremely well attended *Romance of Sustain* solo tour I presented in 2003 and last year's sell out solo+band tour, that it's necessary for me to 'audition' for promoters in this way. Or am I presuming too much? I'm not exactly expecting two weeks at the Albert Hall, after all. Maybe these people are too worried about losing money to really make any, too concerned with certainty to take chances. It's almost boringly predictable, safe bets all round. As my father used to say, 'jobs for the boys.' How unexciting, how banal. Unfortunately, such attitudes don't sit comfortably with my own. It's way too sleepy slow for me. Still, mustn't grumble. I'm just as effective and happy in my little studio as out on the stage, probably more so. If the tour happens, it happens, if it doesn't, I've certainly got plenty of other things to get on with.

My CD burner is still not fixed. My fault for not unwiring it from the studio set up and hauling it over to Leeds to get it repaired. Must do this soon. Must also do same with my Line 6 Vetta combo which is still sporting a broken volume control. Domestic repairs needed all over the house, not just my studio equipment. Serious repairs. Trouble is, I get terribly distracted by the ongoing creative stuff. It grabs me by the throat and won't let me think about anything else until it's had its wicked way with me. And not just that but administrative stuff too, little niggly things that take up time and make the things I really want to do more pressurised than they need be. Life at this end of 'the business' is far tougher than when I used to play the commercial game. God knows if it's art or not but, whatever it is, it's bloody hard going sometimes.

One area of progress. A new keyboard is on order, a Yamaha Motif es88. To replace my busted Emulator e4k workstation. I should try to sell the latter, even though some of the keys need replacing. I've used it for the last 10 years or so, some great sounds in it, plus it operates as a sampler. It would be a fine instrument for someone who was prepared to get the keys fixed. Nevertheless, I'm looking forward to getting the new keyboard in the hope that some unfamiliar sounds will spark fresh creative ideas.

Car troubles this week. Both Emi's car and mine have been in the repair shop for work to get the vehicles through their MOT's. An expensive business. Cars are generally a nightmare, especially old, high-mileage ones like ours. Four-wheeled money vampires.

A nice series started on TV last Sunday, about the English landscape and how it has influenced artists throughout history. Beautifully photographed and uplifting. Of course, Yorkshire figured highly in the first episode. God's own county, as they say. I never tire of having that glorious landscape on my doorstep. I consider myself blessed to live amongst it.

It's not all glorious landscapes though. Royal Ascot horse races are being held in York this week. A Royal pain in the arse, I call it. (Arsecot?) It disrupts the roads around here dramatically. An entire week of being stuck in traffic on some routes. (And when I say 'traffic' I mean mostly those flashy, 'look how much cash I've got' sort of cars, the type I gave up for lost 20 years or more ago.) Still, I've been able to giggle at all the drunken, flimsily clad women tottering around town on their high heels with their spotty boobs hanging out. Bolly dollys a-go-go. Cheap as chips and twice as greasy. Pink and purple and yellow and green and that's just their faces. You can tell I love 'em though. Flirty tarts dancing to dated disco music around their tacky pink handbags at after-race parties all over town. Pissed as arseholes. Absolutely! Desperate! The men are as just bad too, puffed up like red faced baboons in grey morning suits and top hats. Makes the place look untidy. It's hilarious to see the fuss being made about the event locally. Shove the Queen (and the few other Royals that bothered to show up) into the equation and everyone starts strutting around as if they're suddenly in on something of earth shattering importance. 'It's The Queen, you know … Yes, my dear, here in our town, on our doorstep.' (Actually, she's staying in our village, just a short walk from our house, so shove that down your majestic pipe and flush it. Of course, me and ol' Charlie were down the local boozer the other night, riffing about Abba. We're the same age, don't cha know). What this event has proved is that most people are so transparently desperate for celebrity that any slight brush or association with it will be gobbled up greedily. Endless lines of local traders clambering over each other to genuflect in front of the old boiler. Sad really, if it wasn't such a comedy. Still, keeps 'em in idle chit-chat if nothing else. Maybe I'm cynical and jaded, the 'been there, done that' attitude. I shouldn't begrudge them their little stab at self-aggrandisement. God knows life is dull enough for most folks around these parts. Let 'em enjoy their brush with 'royalty' whilst it lasts. Mind you, the weather has been less than cheerful for the event most of the week. Certainly dampened the silly hats down a bit. Then again, it's made those exquisitely flimsy dresses even more amusing. Wish I'd have had my camera handy to show you what I mean. What's the word you're looking for to describe me? Incorrigible? Rude? Disrespectful? Scandalous? Anarchic? Jealous? (Gimmie a break!) Probably something much stronger if you're a saddo royal limo chaser.

If nothing else, this event has provided me with a useful stage on which to act out my grumpy old man scenario. Royalty and advocates of blood sports. Ripe for scorn in my book. Still, the betting shops and bookies will be happy. Plenty of pseudo-posh dosh being squandered, despite the current local opinion that the event has been something of a failure. Not enough people bothered to show up apparently. A case of Southern snobbishness and indifference meets Northern greed and shiftiness. Hotels and other local businesses were hoping to be run off their feet, dreaming of train-loads of cash flowing in from the migrating Southerners. Local prices went up with local expectations. Trouble is, the buggers stayed home in droves, (thankfully). Well, it's crowded enough around here at this time of year without mock-toffs and posh totty adding to it.

Obviously, I've never been one for frequenting the old betting shop. Can't afford it, of course, being a tortured artist and all that. And probably wouldn't if I could. My Dad used to like the 'gee-gees', though. But personally, those high voices and beards never appealed to me. Actually, Dad used to occasionally win some money on the horses. Even though he was far from being a wealthy man and couldn't place large stakes. But he had a certain way with 'accumulators', the winnings from one race being immediately placed as a bet on the next, and so on. A sort of a 'system', he claimed. He was pretty good at it. Won enough to pay for our family's entire holiday in

Blackpool once. The bookie behind the Pleasure Beach banned him from placing bets there ever again, told him not to come back. Dad cleaned him out, it seemed. Oh, how we laughed. It was extra sticks of Blackpool rock all round. My Dad liked soccer too but that never appealed to me, either. I do know the name of one football player though — Stanley Matthews. Little guy with big shorts and Brylcreemed hair from what I recall. A 1950s schoolboy hero for some. Actually (and obviously) I'm playing the fool a bit here. I did actually go to a soccer match once. My Dad took me to a game in Blackpool, when we were on holiday there (but not the time when he got banned from the bookies). He hoped I'd be enthused by a real live soccer match but I was bored rigid. Much preferred going to the Tower Circus or listening to Reginald Dixon play the mighty Wurlitzer in The Tower Ballroom. Or go for a spin on a promenade children's ride called 'Fairyland'. My mother says I really liked that one. Sounds about right. I was, so I'm told, a sensitive kid and according to my school chums something of an odd-bod. And there's me thinking that it was everyone else that was strange. Times change but maybe not so much.

Watched Fellini's delightful and shouty *Amacord* on DVD the other night. Music by Nino Rota. Great name that, 'Nino Rota'. I really like Fellini's colour sense and the way that his camera moves against the wonderfully choreographed crowd scenes. *Juliet Of The Spirits* is one of my Fellini faves. And *Eight And A Half* of course. Great opening scene in that one. Let's go fly a kite but dreamy-weird. I'm reading *In The Half Light* by Anthony Lawrence. The author is a poet and this is his first novel and it's a cracking one. The entire book is imbued with the quality of poetry, a flowing, beautiful, compulsive read.

I highly recommend this to anyone who enjoys intelligent, unusual, imaginative and elegantly written prose. This is a book that doesn't treat its reader like an idiot. I was initially attracted to it by the cover image which is subtly haunting. These days, in my opinion, book graphic design has overtaken album sleeve design for inventiveness.

Recently bought a 'moleskin' blank notebook and a graphite pencil from Salt's Mill. Had a late Sunday lunch there again last weekend. Emi and I love visiting the place. The combination of Hockney's work and the historic 'utopian model village' setting creates a very civilised atmosphere. The excellent book shop in the gallery previously had several copies of *Diary of a Hyperdreamer* on the shelves, but they've sold out now. (I know because some Japanese friends whom we took there recently wanted to buy copies but the assistant at Salt's Mill said they'd all gone.) Anyway, I intend to carry the moleskin notebook with me in my shoulder bag at all times, to use as a sketchbook. Always to hand should inspiration strike. Of course, I'll either forget I'm carrying it or I'll be too busy trying to create music for the autumn tour to get any sketching done, more's the pity.

Must write to John Foxx soon. Harold and John and I should try to get together to record something. Despite Harold's retirement. I meant to contact John a week or two ago but seem to be constantly distracted by one thing or another. I really should make more of an effort to stay in touch with people. By 'people', I mean those whose sensibilities would encourage me towards a less pessimistic outlook. Those who would inspire me to take a few more sunlit chances. Positive creatives who understand all this stuff. But, left to my own devices, I retreat into shadow, spitting and hissing to no effect at all, other than to alienate those who might otherwise share their time with me. Darkness and light, and not much of the latter. Something's up, but what? Depression again? Maybe, but as I said, it doesn't get any easier. Come on, William, you're raving. Buck up. Just get on with it! Sound of helicopters passing overhead, ferrying the wealthy to and from their royal race meeting. There must have been 30 or more helicopters parked in a field near the race course at the start of the week, just opposite the allotments. Less now though. Some local farmer will probably be making a few extra bob by allowing them to land there. I've seen the pound signs in so many people's eyes these last few weeks, the sudden lust for personal glory. Can't say it's a surprise. Police everywhere too. What this nonsense is costing us locals is anyone's guess. Outrageous, probably. Never mind. Back to normality next week. The right wing nouveau-rich will be back in their kitsch little boxes where they clearly belong. What a relief! All that frilly, fluffy pink bad taste makes the place look untidy. Pip pip! Cheerio chums!

·

SUNDAY 24TH JULY 2005

A long gap between the previous diary entry and this. Far too long. Work demands have been overwhelmingly intense and I've had little time or energy for anything else. Perhaps this is not so unusual considering how many projects I seem to regularly juggle these days but I do seem to have bitten off more than I can chew this time. I've been constantly struggling against physical exhaustion and a kind of mental/spiritual malaise, every day being tinted and tainted with a combination of dread, self-loathing and panic. Just too many things dragging my concentration this way and that, a sense of hopelessness gradually overwhelming whatever optimism I've attempted to muster. I've felt as if my work has suffered as a result too, though this may be entirely subjective. Whatever, it still feels like too little energy spread too thin.

The task taking up most of my time is the continuous writing and recording of my forthcoming album. For reasons not quite clear, many of the pieces of music have turned out to be long and complex. They are mostly heavily layered, orchestral textured songs with intricate, fussy arrangements. Each song has taken several days to complete, not just in terms of the writing but also in terms of the actual performance and recording. Mixing the finished recordings has proved problematic too, as there is so much going on just beneath the surface of the music. Getting the correct balance between the myriad interwoven components is not exactly a quick and easy job, so many details to consider. I'm still toying with the idea of remixing a couple of songs, though I'll hardly have time for such a luxury if the finished package is to be ready for the autumn release schedule. There's all the artwork/packaging to consider too.

If these songs were ever to be performed in a completely live context, (i.e.: no use of backing tracks) they would require a large group of very broad-minded and eclectic musicians in tandem with a small symphony orchestra to duplicate the recorded effect. As I originally intended to write intimate pieces that would only require three or four musicians to perform the songs live, it's a shock that what eventually came down my cantankerous muse's pipe ended up being so densely layered and epic sounding. I haven't a clue as to why this should be, it's just as mysterious to me as to anyone else. I'm subject to the surreal dictates of my own unconscious and am often as much a victim of its unpredictability, as well as a beneficiary. The songs' lyrical content has been problematic too, reflecting, perhaps, my troubled state of mind. They're not overtly angst-ridden, heart-on-sleeve, chest beaters but they do seem to suggest a certain world-weariness and resignation. These are confusing, dualistic, personal songs whose shiny veneer maybe hides something deeper and darker. As I so often say these days, maybe it's just a result of my age and the weird times we live in. But, regardless of these thoughts, I still want to push on, to see where the current thematic or conceptual thread leads me. Luckily, the idea of making it a 'mini-album' provides a much needed safety net. At least I now know that I can 'switch off' the project and deal with the rest of my workload when the time comes to do so. A little bit less pressure, though there's still plenty more to deal with. As an explanation for my sense of urgency and panic I'll list the current workload in this diary entry, in a moment or two, BUT before I do, here is the latest information about this 'album in progress' of mine:–

The songs I've decided will be on the 'possible inclusions' list are as follows … [list of tracks]. All these are vocal pieces. There are also two as yet unfinished and untitled instrumentals. The list does not include everything that I've recently recorded, i.e.: abandoned tracks or tracks that have been completed but set aside for other possible projects (as they proved unsuitable for this one). The album is very much a work in progress at this stage, although it now has a reasonably fixed title. What is the title? Well, unless I radically re-think the album, it will be called *The Alchemical Adventures of Sailor Bill*. There are deeply personal reasons for this apparently surreal and light-hearted title, which I may explain at some point in the future. Needless to say, it springs from my usual internal pre-occupation with the absurdity and seriousness, beauty and ugliness of our human condition, and mine in particular. So the cut-off point with this album will be entirely dictated by the deadlines and demands of my other work. Whether 'mini' or otherwise, there WILL be a new album, despite the pressures.

And here, by way of example, is the list of the work I'm attempting, as promised above:–

1. Prepare autumn tour set, including the making, choosing, mastering and assembly of performance backing tracks, both old and new.
2. Design tour advertising material, flyers, t-shirts, posters, etc, for above.
3. Shoot and edit new video material to use as back projection on the autumn tour. (An extremely time consuming job, this one.)
4. Prepare various items and performance events for Nelsonica 05 (to be held in October) including design and preparation of all visual material, tickets, limited edition screen print poster, etc.
5. Create a Nelsonica 05 convention CD, including the selection and mastering of appropriate musical material, and suitable visual content, sleeve design, etc.
6. Create an exclusive music track for *Sound On Sound*'s magazine's 20th anniversary issue.
7. Give a talk to music college students in September.

8. Prepare tracks, both old and new, for the early August guitar festival performance in Lewes. (And boy, am I behind schedule with this one!)

9. Choose and assemble an appropriate selection of music onto CDR to send to Ronald Nameth with regard to a possible collaboration on the Ginsberg *Howl For Now* documentary film.

10. Contribute an article/written Q+A for a book being written about the above event.

11. Transfer to Mackie removable media hard drive and then mix the very early Be Bop Deluxe Decca audition tapes for possible release in autumn.

12. Design packaging for above.

13. Help to oversee the release of major label back catalogue. (Mercury and EMI.)

14. Select appropriate equipment for upcoming live shows, unwire from my studio and repair where required. Then pack and haul downstairs in preparation for transportation to venues.

15. Schedule a full day's rehearsal for autumn tour and ensure that everything is in place that needs to be.

16. Allocate sufficient time at home to allow a personal rehearsal schedule for the tour material so that the main rehearsal is freed up to concentrate on technical/equipment/ sound mixing matters, rather than musical ones.

17. Complete the writing and recording and mixing of the new album.

18. Decide track running order, book Fairview to master the final album and design packaging art for it.

19. Attend and possibly contribute towards the performance

of Ginsberg's *Howl* poem, anniversary reading.

20. Begin a possible collaboration with John Foxx.
21. Ditto with J.F. and Harold Budd.
22. Ditto with Cipher. (Theo Travis and Dave Sturt.)
23. Try to get back on track with my collaboration with American comic book artist Matt Howarth.
24. Open up further areas of the Dreamsville site, including the long promised 'Museum Of Memory' feature, the 'Academy Of Art' and the 'Guitar Arcade.'

But, as I've already said, the priority for me at the moment is to constantly work on the new album. (11 am to 11 pm, with a 45 minute dinner break, every day, with a couple of guilty Sundays off to give Emiko some kind of life other than sitting downstairs watching television whilst I furrow my brow in the studio.)

So, this is the kind of life I lead right now — obsessive, unhealthy, anti-social, grumpy, angst-ridden, insecure, depressive, stressful, etc. (Oh, poor, poor me, so many guitars to play!) But also, dreamlike, magical, creatively fulfilling, educational, enlightening and privileged too. Yes, it's that special. I'm just one of those common or garden, pathetic but fabulously lucky tortured artists that you read about in tacky romantic novels. AND I've got the dysfunctional lifestyle, psychological quirks and expanding waistline to prove it.

And now on to other, more serious matters. Terrorist attacks in London. What can I or anyone else say? The horror, disgust and revulsion that we all feel about these events requires no explanatory comment from me. Nevertheless, I'll say this, if only to release a little of the pressure in my own angry heart.

That people commit such acts of depravity in the name of religion (whatever religion) is a sickening measure of the ignorance, stupidity, gullibility and downright self-centred, ugly righteousness of those who think of themselves as 'agents of god'. ('God' is, increasingly it seems, a convenient concept for abdicating individual responsibility for vile criminal acts.) The indoctrinated dupes who carry out these cruel, pathetic and ultimately ineffectual attacks are deluded lost souls, terminally infatuated with the ecstasy of self-immolation, death and glory, holy-martyrdom and all the other banal, historically tested, psychologically potent appeals to the dangerous idiot within us all. These young fools bought the tired old lie of a righteous martyr's paradise. And couldn't see past the illusions woven by their hate-filled puppet masters. What a tragic world we live in. As always, the innocent suffer the most. And don't get me started on the political issues. There's ignorance on all sides. Enough disgust from me? More than you need. Let's move on.

Despite my relentless work schedule, I have conspired to take a couple of Sundays off. A visit to Castle Howard and visits to the East and North Yorkshire coast, Reighton Sands, Whitby, Spurn Point. The latter two locations allowed me a chance to paddle like a kid in the ocean, to savour the waves and breath some fresh air (though I wish I had more time to do it properly and without guilt.) I justified the time away from my studio by taking along my camera and camcorder to capture images that might prove useful for the tour's video projection, or for this very website. My trip to Reighton Sands or 'Reighton Gap' as it was known to my family in the 1950s, was only the second time I've been there since I was a child. (My earlier diary entries reference this.) On this latest visit, Emi and I ventured down the steep incline, cut into the cliffs, to the beach. It was the first time I'd walked on these sands since I was a very young boy. Nothing much had changed, apart from some coastal erosion, but the view of Flamborough Head from Reighton Sands was just as striking as I remembered, the beach just as sparsely populated.

The crumbling ruins of the concrete World War II bunkers, almost exactly as they were in the early 1950s when my family stayed at a bungalow in Reighton Gap, still stand, braving the North Sea winds and guarding the little pools in which I once, all those years ago, sailed my cream and red painted, battery powered, toy boat, 'St. Christopher.'

I wrote 'Hello, Sailor Bill' in the sand with my walking cane and Emi took a photo. Emi and I then stood, trousers rolled up, at the edge of the sea, up to our calves in the incoming tide, which was cold and sharp and clear. We'd done the same thing at Spurn Point the previous weekend (where I'd photographed the patterns made by fishermen's tractors in the sand on the Humber river side of the estuary peninsula.) I love this entire stretch of coastline, its variety, its history, and never tire of it. My late father loved it too, as I've probably mentioned before. In fact, he loved the ocean and the coast generally, wherever we roamed as a family back in those simpler times. I still vividly recall standing next to him on cliff tops on the east coast or on harbour walls in Ilfracoombe in Devon, watching the storm-tossed waves. The wilder the seas, the more my father enjoyed observing them. He could be a difficult, sometimes angry and occasionally volatile, violent man, but also generous, kind, thoughtful and soulful. Certainly contradictory. Those moments standing beside him, in awe of the waves, stay stronger in my memory than his darker moods.

One of my latest songs directly references my father's love of the sea. In fact, it starts with a simple statement: 'My father loved the sea, summertime, wintertime, anytime … My father longed to be, a sailor on the sea.' It sounds much better in the context of the whole song. (The song is called *The Ceremonial Arrival Of The Great Golden Cloud*.) It's over eight minutes long.

Weather cool verging on cold today, cloudy and no sun. The recent warm weather vanished for a time, or so it seems. But it's been frustrating to have to stay in my hot, airless studio whilst the sunshine has been transforming the surrounding landscape into an archetypal English pastoral summer scene these last few weeks. It will soon be harvest time though; fields of barley have turned from green to gold already. Leaves turning before we know it too, I suspect. The seasons change so rapidly. I continue to make music and must optimistically return to the work, pushing on regardless. Minutes, hours, days, weeks, months. Time passes and life sings.

·

MONDAY 29TH AUGUST 2005

August is about to end. 2005 seems to have moved towards autumn at a terrific pace. I've not realised just how quickly time has flown and I'm now in even more of a panic than before. This year has been an unrelenting attempt to hit deadlines and targets that I'd somewhat optimistically set myself several months ago (and which were listed in the previous diary entry to this one). Did I miscalculate just how much I could achieve in that time? Or am I simply slowing down with the weight of the years?

Somewhere along the way, summer seems to have happened to everyone else whilst I've been stuck in my little workroom, assembling one dream or another, trying to make my imagination tangible to others with the aid of smoke and mirrors. The thing which is draining me most intensely, but also, conversely, proving to be the most rewarding, is the ongoing creation of my *The Alchemical Adventures Of Sailor Bill* album. This, for me, has been the most important task of the year. It is only now, after working on the album for a long time, that I'm beginning to understand exactly what it's real meaning is. At first, there was a general fishing around for direction and some songs I initially recorded for the project seemed to go off at too much of a tangent. I was searching for a style that might lend itself to my solo live performances on the forthcoming November dates. This approach, it turns out, was a mistake. I found that particular 'angle' less than satisfying for some reason. It just didn't feel as if I was hitting the right emotional target. It was only when I totally abandoned the idea of making these songs 'practical' (in live performance terms) that the sparks began to fly. The move away from performance-oriented material to pure studio soundscapes opened the creative channels for me and I suddenly felt free of the 'keep it live' restraints I'd saddled myself with. Then, with the realisation that a 'theme' of sorts was presenting itself in a couple of the pieces, I struck out in an even more singularly defined direction. I made the decision to build the material around a symbolic nautical/coastal theme which put things into clearer perspective and, before long, the album's current title emerged from the mud. The use of ocean, shoreline, ship, lighthouse, harbour, pier and seaside fairground images seems, somehow, to manifest, or symbolise, my present emotional and metaphysical state of mind (and life's journey generally). These images also resonate with a romantic, nostalgic wistfulness which suits my current feelings of melancholy. They also demand a little more than the usual rock music vocabulary and tonal palette, something more epic, enigmatic and subtle.

The 'alchemic' notions of transformation of base matter into a higher state also seems apt, as does the reference to myself as a fictional character called 'Sailor Bill', a salty old sea-dog on one side of the coin, an elegantly dressed matinee-idol Captain on the other. Both pop culture caricatures of sea-going stereotypes but all the more interesting for their whimsical artificiality. Sometimes, the more 'unreal' an image or character is, the more alive or convincing it becomes. We live in several mental/metaphysical states at once (multi-verses as opposed to universes?). Some of these states, usually the ones we consign to the box labelled 'everyday life' are dull and mundane. They mask who we are, rather than reveal. On the other hand, the states of being that we put into the box marked 'dreams, fears, hopes, longings and imaginings' are vibrant and alive, brightly coloured and compulsive. They are somehow closer to the truth than the visible 'reality' of our public selves. Much more authentic and unique. The 'me' that exists deep within my outward physical form is far more beautiful, liberated, adventurous, unselfish and wise than the nervous, unconfident, aging melancholic who gets presented to the world these days. I'm always much more than I seem to others, and to myself too. It was with all this in mind that the 'Sailor Bill' persona took root. Can you see where this is going and why?

The next turning point came when I decided to unify as many of the songs as possible by building them around orchestral textures, rather than the more usual rock music instrumentation. Some pieces go further with this premise than others, of course, but I've had to curb the temptation to please some of my audience by adding a veneer of guitar to pieces of music where no guitar veneer is required. One piece in particular immediately sounded less than it should have sounded simply because I overdubbed a guitar solo where it wasn't appropriate. You'd think that, by now, I'd not give such a thing a second thought but, for a brief and undisciplined moment, I almost turned a perfectly beautiful piece of music into a horrendous rock anthem, worthy of Queen or one of their ilk, simply by adding a 'rock out' guitar part, merely to elicit a predictable response from what I'd mistakenly thought of as 'the average listener'. I wiped it straight away after playing it back. Too easy, too cheap. I'm more than just a guitar player, damn it (and not much of a guitar player at that, in my opinion)

This, I now realise, is not an album for the average listener. Nor is it a product for the average 'me', whatever that might imply. Just as I've had to abandon all pretext of ever performing this material live, I've had to also abandon any thought about what anyone else might make of it when it is eventually released. In fact, the ever sharper focus I'm bringing to bear on the music has made the creative process much more difficult and challenging. Despite this, it has proved to be an unusually rewarding, if somewhat time-consuming, exercise. There's now almost a hint of a concept album or opera about the project, though not in the usual linear storytelling mode of such genres. The lyrics, in fact, are fairly minimal, quite direct but visually evocative. The visual dimension is reinforced by the music which has, in places, an epic 'largeness' that I hope will paint a suitable oceanic picture in the listener's mind. There's a very odd chemical marriage of antique and modern in the sound-scapes of these pieces. I've made no attempt to rein in my sentimentality, my nostalgic yearnings and there's no deliberate stab at dissonance or commonplace minimalism. It's all richly romantic, densely textured, fantasy-fuelled writing that evokes the feel of old Hollywood or, better still, Golden Age British cinema, movies. But, at the same time, because of my lack of formal musical education, there's something else at work in the music, something that seems to exist apart from academic considerations of form, style and era. Simple but not minimal-istic? Innocent but not naive? I don't really want to speculate too much in fear of driving the spirit of it away but it's perhaps this intuitive element that gives the work an odd sort of quality. It feels, somehow, 'present'. I think this is simply because I'm writing from such a personal, idiosyncratic, untutored position. Stubbornly determined *not* to do what other's might prefer me to do or would advise me to do.

Maybe this is music that no one else would want to make. Maybe it's what's left on the table when everyone else has eaten and gone to bed. It's the residue of something already consumed but a residue transformed into an entirely unexpected confec-tion. A rich feast? Or maybe it's just warmed over scraps. For me, it is, at this moment in time, all consuming. I'm besotted with it and it refuses to let me rest. The hours I've given to it are never going to return to me. I've had moments of elation writing and recording this material, and moments of doubt and despair. It has not, by any stretch of the imagination, been an easy ride. Certainly not one of those albums that fall easily from the blue empty void onto the composer's table. I've yet to finish the project or even to listen to a possible sequence of tracks but I'll hesitantly say that it is possibly one of the best things I've ever done. Of course, I reserve the right, being the artist, to damn it to hell at a later date if the wind changes direction. But, so far, I'm feeling that this is a wee bit special.

Last week, a disastrous event. My plug-in 24 track Mackie hard disc drive decided to shunt weeks of recorded work off into another dimension. I'd almost completed the recording of a new song, over which I'd laboured for four solid days (a song that might possibly have provided the high spot of the album), when I turned off the recording equipment in the usual way. When I next turned it on, the hard drive showed no files present, basically a blank drive. I stared at the screen in utter disbelief. Where were all the songs? Weeks of work? And my brand new super-song of which I'd felt so pleased? Also on the drive had been *The Man Who Haunted Himself*, a song I'd already mixed down to DAT tape but which I'd decided needed a more considerate re-mix before it would be fit for the album. All this and more, it appears, vanished in a digital puff of smoke. I was absolutely gutted, depressed, heartbroken. Calls to my friend Paul Gilby got me connected to Mackie themselves who, after some over the phone prodding and probing, seemed to confirm that all was indeed lost.

I then noticed that the hard disc recorder's real-time readout was showing that there was only 3 minutes 44 seconds of available recording time left on the empty drive. If the drive was truly empty, surely it would show more time available for recording than this? The Mackie techs then seemed to think that this might indicate that the song files were still present on the drive but that their index page had become corrupted, thereby making it impossible for the machine to open any particular song file. So, later this week, Paul is generously going to take the hard drive to a specialist company in London to see if the music files can be recovered. If so, I may get my precious material back and finish the song I felt would be so important to the new album. (And remix the *Haunted* song). Fingers crossed. If this process doesn't recover the apparently vanished songs, then I'll have to use the earlier mix of *Haunted* and attempt a total re-recording of the new song I've lost. It won't be at all the same, however, as the original was so complex, so detailed, so full of 'happy accidents' that it would be impossible to reproduce exactly the same combination of magic and chance that created it in the first place. I can't even remember all the delicious melodies and counter-melodies that made up the orchestral sections of the piece, let alone reproduce all the minute adjustments to tone and timbre that each instrument had been subjected. The vocal performance was unique too, a product of time and place, never to be quite as convincing again Plus, the proper moment for its creation has now passed, my enthusiasm cruelly dampened and diminished by the original's loss. But we'll see. I've not completely given up hope yet.

Since then, I've been working on the machine's internal drive and not risked using the malfunctioning external plug-in one. I've almost completed another new song. Not bad going, time wise. It's called *Here Comes the Sea (The Captain's Lament)*. Another big orchestral score and a few guitar parts scattered here and there, but nothing 'guitaristic', just appropriate colour where needed. No gratuitous applause seeking. The album's opening track will be a pure instrumental though, something to set up the correct atmosphere for the songs. This piece is called *The Lighthousekeeper's Waltz* and has a sort of 'overture' effect.

But enough talk of this. The album has already turned me into even more of an anti-social semi-recluse than usual. I need to get it finished and off my chest, clear the decks (to use a nautical pun). I have stolen the odd day or two from my work to appear human (although I'm told that I always appear distracted and distant on these occasions). My daughter Julia and my grandson, Luke, came up from London and we all went to a quite spectacular air show together. Absolutely terrifying but thrilling. Took some camcorder footage for videogram use. Great to see Julia and Luke, though. He's a real bright spark and a credit to Julia's patience and love. Also, my mother's 77th birthday. Mum's such a gem and I'm a terrible son. I don't spend nearly enough time with her. Or my children. Or my wife. (Though I have spent most of this Bank Holiday weekend attempting to take Emi out and about). It's all music, bloody music. And very little else. Now, back to the mixing desk. Need to push on. I'm way behind schedule.

•

I've begun to look at the calendar with the same feeling of horror I get when looking in the mirror. It's scary and something I'd rather avoid dealing with, but have no choice. Time is of the essence and deadlines are looming in all directions. The mastering session for the two new albums is set for the 29th. This coming Thursday. No more changes to the recordings are permitted now so things have to stay as they are. Nor am I allowed to change the running order of the songs as I've given my erstwhile art and design assistant, Dave Graham, the go ahead to typeset the text for both projects. In fact, we're close to having the packaging art finished although I've just now sent Dave more images for possible inclusion; photographs I took at Whitby and Robin Hood's Bay earlier today. I made the trip specifically to gather photographic images and camcorder footage. I'm supposed to have video projection material ready for the November tour dates too but, at this moment, there's neither tour material, nor tour concept, to work with. I've simply not had enough time, what with everything else I've had to do these last twelve months.

I think one of the problems is that everything seems to become focused on a single point of time in the year (i.e. autumn). There's the fan convention with it's now obligatory album, visual work and live performance, plus the tour schedule and it's equally obligatory new album and staging. But, it's not just that. Alongside these major projects are other tasks, some associated, some completely separate. Many of these seem to occur at the back end of the year also. Naturally, it all ends up being a sort of juggling act, a crazy attempt to keep various balls in the air at once. But, I shouldn't really blame anyone but myself. I guess I'm the sort of girl who can't say no.

Hope I'm not in a terrible mess. I just feel drained and empty at the moment. Some information has been missing from this diary of late due to writing it in a rush, particularly when other things have been on my mind. In some ways, the music-making part of my life should be the easiest. Why should I complain about workloads? It's a privilege, a sort of 'calling', a natural by-product of my being. It's unavoidable, automatic, self-evident. It's essence. On the other hand, it's dangerously unhealthy, sometimes questionably unhinged and, whichever way you look at it, hard work. For anyone else to understand just how hard, they'd need to be with me throughout an entire year, spending the same time as myself (in this tiny room that I'm audacious enough to refer to as my 'studio') working constantly without reference to real time or real life, being totally immersed in the creation of something that begins with blind faith and usually ends up with what I can only describe as either self-doubt or godless despair. The former is preferable to the latter but neither is much fun. I wonder how many people would continue to put up with it, the boredom, the insecurity, the selfishness, the obsessive and remorseless attempt to elevate a meagre musical ability beyond its sorry limitations? (And why the hell do I do it?) How quickly would the fun wear off, the glamour be exposed for what it really is? A few months, or, as in my case, more than 30 years?

And yet, despite all this angst-ridden, pathetic, mock dramatic chest beating, I still can't give it up. Sometimes I'm actually disgusted by the hold this thing has over me, how weak I've become in its grasp. Too eager to swoon, that's me. Too desperately in need of love from strangers. But, oh, how wonderful to be given the chance to try, to be given the gift of creating music from such dreamy weakness. What a stunningly beautiful two-edged sword I've been handed! Praise the lord and load the water pistols. You know, sometimes dealing with words is almost as much fun as making sounds. Almost. Everything is drama and our lives vain fictions that rarely advance beyond a short run at some local theatre. But, during the brief time that the footlights burn, we play the part to the hilt, believing every red velvet moment, playing it as if our lives depended on it. Which, perhaps, they do. Gilded fictions, beautiful illusions, fables made real by our sheer desperation.

So what activities of mine have I forgotten to include in the last episode or two of this diary? Well, I omitted to mention my quite probably broken foot. A couple of weeks ago, I was reminded that, earlier in the year, I'd accepted an invitation to officially open a new recording studio at the College of West Anglia in Kings Lynn. The opening was scheduled for September 15th. At the time of accepting, I'd no idea that September would see me pushing things to the limit in terms of project completion. When I received the reminder about the opening, at the start of September, I realised that it had completely slipped my mind. However, determined not to let anyone down. I made plans to travel down to Kings Lynn to do the honours and to talk to the students.

The night before the journey, I was dashing around the house trying to prepare clothes for the trip. I hadn't got my house slippers on and clumsily hit my right foot on the edge of either a door or a bookcase nearby, my toes taking the brunt of the blow. Instant pain but I thought it would fade after a few minutes. It didn't. That night, sleeping was difficult. The slightest contact of the bed sheets with my toes brought on more pain which kept me awake. The next morning I was a wreck, limping about the place and grimacing. My toes and foot were black and blue, badly bruised and it felt as if a couple of them might have been cracked or broken. For a moment, I considered calling Jon Lawrence (the tutor who had asked me to open the new studio) to beg off the engagement but I felt that this would not be a good thing. So I decided to go ahead as planned. Getting a shoe onto the injured foot was another problem. I had to force myself through the pain barrier but, once my foot was in there, I grabbed a walking stick from my collection and set off for the station by cab. Luckily, Emiko had taken time off from work to accompany me so she was able to support my injury, spiritually if not physically.

It was a long journey from Yorkshire to Kings Lynn, involving a change of train at Peterborough and then again at Ely. It rained all day as we sat on station platforms awaiting our connections, gazing out at the grey skies. I felt like an old, old man, limping around, clinging on to my walking stick. I was also embarrassed to have to explain to the college staff why I appeared so decrepit. A stupid injury. Nevertheless, I managed to get through the event which involved an interview with local media, the opening ceremony itself and a question and answer session with the students.

The tutors and staff were all very kind to me and I was glad that I'd made the effort to get there, despite the physical difficulty. Jon kindly gave us a lift to the station where we waited 50 minutes for the train before making the long trip back home. More long waits for connections at other stations required medicinal administrations of wine from platform bars to ease the pain. By the time I got home, I was pleasantly inebriated. Now, over a week later, the foot is looking much better although still bruised in some places and my little toe continues to be uncomfortable, particularly when walking. But on the mend.

Last Friday brought me another invitation. This time to travel to Liverpool where Gretsch guitars were holding a promotional roadshow event. The show was at the Cavern Club, appropriate considering the late George Harrison's endorsement of Gretsch guitars. Fans of my own music will already be aware of my passion for Gretsch instruments and will have seen them grace the stage of my concerts over the last few years. Once again, Emi accompanied me on the train journey to Liverpool, another unusually long trip, especially considering the distance. Not a high speed intercity train though, just a sprinter type that stopped at many stations en route. We were met at Liverpool station by Fender/Gretsch artist relations whizz Hoda Armani, a lovely man who did his utmost to make us feel comfortable and welcome. After treating us to dinner, we were taken to the Cavern Club where a very tempting array of Gretsch guitars glittered from the stage, including the new 'Billy-Bo' model, an adaptation of Bo-Diddley's unique custom built Gretsch Jupiter Thunderbird guitar that Billy Gibbons of ZZ Top has helped Gretsch to adapt from Bo's original design. As I said: tempting, very tempting!

I was introduced to Gretsch's current main man, Mr. Mike Lewis, who was going to give the audience gathered at the Cavern a talk about the history of Gretsch guitars. Not only did Mike do this in an entertaining and informative manner but he 'illustrated' his talk by playing guitar instrumentals to backing tapes, in a similar fashion to the way I do at my solo concerts. Not only was Mike knowledgeable about Gretsch guitar history, he could play the hell out of them as well. He opened with a wonderfully affectionate instrumental version of The Beatles *Please, Please Me*, but finished his talk by playing one of my all-time favourite instrumentals, Santo and Johnny's *Sleepwalk*. Mike has an adult understanding of the roots of rock guitar and his playing was direct and soulful and I sat there with a big smile on my face. He even played some Duane Eddy, Chet Atkins and Eddie Cochran licks so it was worth the trip just to hear him perform, as much as to see all those juicy guitars. I wanted to stay longer, pick up some instruments to try out, talk to people more, but the trains back to Yorkshire were a somewhat inhospitable. We were left with two alternatives, catch the 9:30, change at Manchester and arrive home just after midnight, or catch the 10:30 and get home around a quarter to two in the morning. My foot was still playing me up too so we opted to catch the 9:30 train. Hoda bundled us into a cab and saw that we got to the train in time. Eventually arrived back at Rancho Nelsonia around 12:20, feeling tired but happy, not least because of Hoda and Gretsch's generosity with the occasional glass of vino!

Another recent (ish) thing of mine which I seem to have overlooked in the diary was my concert at the Lewes Guitar Festival, not far from Brighton. The event took place in what was once a small but very pretty church. There was a full house and I spent some time after the concert chatting with fans and friends, a very pleasant evening altogether. Someone asked me what guitars, if any, I might still lust after. Well, as I once said, you can never have too many guitars and there are certainly a few out there I wouldn't mind getting my hands on, from the cheap and cheerful to the seriously luxurious. Of course, Gretsch have a few models that would be nice to own, including the 'Jupiter Thunderbird' adaptation mentioned above but also a Syncromatic 400 acoustic archtop, the big one without cutaways, a real swing band of a guitar. Then there's the 6120 model that apes Eddie Cochran's guitar with the P90 style neck pickup and transparent pick guard. Then there's the White Penguin or the Duo-Jet. Of course, what would really constitute a dream come true would be to work with Gretsch towards a custom instrument. I already have strong ideas about styling and so on, but, pointless going into details, it's just a dream. Another guitar would be a re-issue 1960s Fender Stratocaster in Fiesta Red, just like the one Hank Marvin played in the Shadows heyday. But with a rosewood fretboard, rather than a maple one. (I think Hank's had both at different times.) The semi-hollow Partick Eggle Vienna is very tempting too, a kind of larger version of my Berlin model, but with 'f' holes. And of course, a full sized, big bodied D'Angelico archtop would be fabulous for my sojourns in the jazz joints of my imagination.

As far as cheap and cheerful guitars goes, well, there are things like the De Pinto Belvedere Deluxe, which is a cool retro styled guitar that doesn't cost the earth. The same company's 'Galaxie 4' guitar is fun looking too. Aother US company, Eastwood Guitars, do some great reproductions of 1960s era cheapo guitars. They have a wonderful version of a Guyatone LG200-T solid body which looks great in white and costs only $399 direct from their site. They also do a nice reproduction of two Airline guitars, the one with full set of pickups and trem is a real mad scientist of a guitar. Nice in red, this one, or white. Of course, all this is sheer greed on my part, an addiction, but one that I manage to turn into music, somewhere along the line. Enough of guitars, I'm starting to drool.

The weekend has been mostly spent dealing with artwork

tasks. I'd already spent most of last week sourcing images to use for the *Sailor Bill* album. It can take a while to find ones that are interesting and just as long to discover where the actual 'feel' of the album might lay in visual terms. There's a fair bit of trial and error to start with. Some of my earlier image selections were too much on the jolly or jaunty side. Whilst looking at the ones I'd accumulated, I played back the *Sailor Bill* album to see if they fitted. The album's moody and melancholic nature ruled out some of the more modern, zippy images and I ended up making the decision to go down the 'antique' route. A call to Dave on Saturday morning to prime him on the general direction and things got properly underway. The initial searching around now done, we're currently in the fine tuning stages (apart from the possible addition of today's coastal photos to the package). The album will be mastered this coming Thursday and the artwork should be ready to go off to the pressing plant along with the master by the start of October. Same goes for the Nelsonica album, *Orpheus In Ultraland*. Before long, these two intensely detailed projects will be set aside as 'finished'. All that will remain is the process of getting them into people's hearts and minds.

Last week, I gave an interview about the creation of the albums. The interview will appear in the forthcoming issue of 'The Dreamsville Rocket' on-line newspaper and is intended to prime the imagination for the music's arrival. The *Sailor Bill* album requires 'slow ears…' It isn't an album that reveals itself in a hurry but, with a little care and patience, should reward the diligent listener for some time to come. A quaint and old-fashioned album but not for the narrow minded. I'm hoping to have a playback/preview party for friends and members of the Dreamsville-Nelsonica team. I'm thinking of holding this at Fairview studios so that the album can be heard on some pro-standard studio monitors.

Another side project now completed (and I may have mentioned this before in the diary) is my contribution to a book that is being published by Leeds University. This is a book about the Beat Generation, written to coincide with the university's School Of Music celebration of the 50th anniversary of Allen Ginsberg's *Howl*. I've written, for the book, a piece about my own encounter with the Beats and the inspiration that they generated in terms of my work.

And, amongst even more new work (though I'm keeping real details under my hat for a short while), is a project I've undertaken for *Sound On Sound* magazine's anniversary issue. I can't say any more at this point in time (sworn to secrecy) but Dreamsville will inform you of what this involves soon. Stay tuned!

Bob Dylan documentary on TV tomorrow evening. Must make time to watch this. Essential viewing for me, being a great admirer of Dylan's work. Recently finished his *Chronicles Vol. 1* autobiography which Emiko bought me last Christmas. Only recently got around to reading it but it was an interesting book.

Not much time for reading now, though, still far too much to do. Nelsonica rushing up, as is the solo tour. I ought to start thinking about the material I'll perform. God knows how I'll get that *and* the accompanying video together in the few weeks that are left before things get underway. If I'm exhausted now, what state will I be in by the start of November? I hope things work out. Looking forward to a break in December, though Christmas will take up a fair amount of time and energy. Before

I know it, it will be New Year and a new set of projects to get to grips with. As tough going as it sometimes is, the joy is in the making of all this stuff. Well, I must enjoy it to devote so much of my life to it.

.

A sense of relief and satisfaction this morning. And a hangover. Yesterday's annual Nelsonica Convention turned out to be another grand day out for all its attendees and particularly for myself. It's always a pleasure to spend the day with such devoted fans and friends but yesterday's event was particularly heart warming for me, in so many ways.

As always, before these conventions (and indeed, before any public appearance of mine), I seem to get myself worked up into a state of nervousness approaching outright panic. I had been working flat out over the past few weeks, preparing new material for the forthcoming tour, including video pieces to project behind me on stage. In fact, I lost a lot of time when two day's worth of video footage and seven day's worth of render files were inadvertently erased from my computer's hard disc, the second such loss this year (although the first time it happened was on my multi-track hard-disc recorder, rather than my computer). The days before the convention saw me working into the early hours to try to catch up with lost time. In the end, I managed to make videograms for 10 of the pieces of music in the set. But it was tough going. My friend Paul Gilby burned my finished digital video tapes to DVD for me, literally on the night before Nelsonica opened its doors to the public. It was all very much a last minute thing.

Fortunately, Jon Wallinger and the convention team of Ian, Eddie, Ged and Dave had pre-planned the actual event to perfection and didn't suffer from the computer malfunctions that blighted both myself and Paul's efforts. Everyone attending the event commented on how extremely well organised the day was. But, what appears on the surface as relaxed and smooth running is actually the product of months of hard work, forward thinking, careful teamwork and organisational skill. The Nelsonica team coped superbly with all the logistics involved and, apart from a frustrating mistake at the pressing plant involving the manufacture of both the *Sailor Bill* album and the convention's limited edition *Orpheus in Ultraland* album, all went like clockwork.

The pressing plant problem was completely unforeseen and entirely out of our control. It seems that they hadn't printed up the albums sleeve art in time to deliver to Nelsonica and it was only after some very formal complaints from Paul that we got anything from them at all. In the end, they sent up just enough convention albums to give to ticket holders, but, unfortunately, minus cover artwork and sleeves. We now have to send each convention ticket holder the artwork through the post. Once the factory gets around to delivering them to us, that is. Annoying, frustrating, etc, etc, especially after all the hard work that went into finishing those albums in time to get them manufactured.

Nevertheless, this problem didn't seem to mar people's enjoyment. I heard nothing but praise from attendees and the event was a great success. There were many familiar faces there but also many new ones, too. People are always extremely sweet and kind to me at Nelsonica and this year's convention was no exception. I was bowled over by the warmth of sentiment shown to me by everyone I spoke to. It was also a pleasant surprise to meet up with someone I hadn't seen for many years, someone I remember fondly from the very earliest days of Be Bop Deluxe, before we were professional musicians. The band played the Leeds pub circuit in the early 1970s and the person I'm referring to used to be a regular audience member. Although she was usually accompanied by her boyfriend, she managed to slip away from him to spend a little time with me. I was very flattered by this attention, particularly as she was an attractive 17-year old at the time and I wasn't the typical, 'party animal' type of rock guitarist. I hope I was a bit more sensitive than that. I'll admit to always having a deeply romantic nature and I guess that was the way that this particular relationship took me, although I was actually married at the time. But not happily, or for long, I must stress! Of course, I was a much younger, less wise man back then, skinny, selfish and ambitious. What time does to us though, eh?

Well, the years have certainly changed my waistline for the worst, if not my ambition. But maybe the ambition is focused elsewhere now, less concerned with commercial success and glamour. But I still want to achieve so many other things. But I do hope I've developed more compassion for others and have tamed the wilder aspects of my ego. Anyway, it was lovely to see that the person mentioned above looked hardly any different from those long ago days, apart from a rather vivid change of hair colour! I, on the other hand, have less and less hair to worry about these days (probably as a result of bleaching it blonde, back in the 1980s!). The stresses and strains of a life spent battling to preserve some kind of musical freedom have left their unfortunate mark, I guess. I'm sure my appearance must have come as something of a shock to someone who hasn't met me for over 30 years. It comes as a shock to me every time I catch my reflection in a mirror! But life is strange and things go around in circles it seems. Old faces return out of the mist with warm smiles and welcoming eyes. It's beautiful, sad and poetic all at the same time.

As well as the happy opportunities to meet with friends, Nelsonica this year provided a new item on the programme. I was the subject of a 'live on stage' interview with Simon Warner who coaxed out my thoughts about the arts in general and their influence on my musical career. I really enjoyed this part of the programme and, from what I can gather, the attendees did too. There was also an opportunity to give everyone a preview of the *Sailor Bill* album, even if we had no copies available for them to take home. I included a piece from the album in my live performance, the song *The Ocean, The Night And The Big, Big Wheel*. I chose this track as it is one of the easier songs to tackle from the album, at least in a 'solo performance with backing tracks' style (which is what my forthcoming November tour will be). I had some reservations about including vocals in the set at all, but the four I've allowed myself to perform seem to work quite well. Much better than I expected

As with all the recent Nelsonicas, I end the day feeling a little bit melancholy as well as happy. It's the celebratory aspect of the event that both encourages and warms one's heart but it also helps to underline the passing of the years and how much is still to be achieved. So many possible ideas to pursue and yet nowhere near enough time to fulfill them. I could never be one of those self-conscious minimalist types who squeeze out an album once every few years as if it was some gargantuan triumph over a kind of creative constipation, or some precious god-like artefact torn from deep within the soul. Music for apartment dwellers and aging yuppies? That sort of approach feels a little too restricting for me, too tedious and slow and too obviously tweaked to fit a certain marketplace. I prefer the constant fireworks display, the snowstorm of thought, the perpetual fountain of sound. The Kerouac continuous roll.

Having said that, *Sailor Bill* just about exhausted me beyond anything I've ever done before. A lot of work and attention to detail. But it was made over a few months, not years. I'm still very pleased with the way it came out though, compromised or not. Considering I made it on a non-existent budget, without the help of other musicians, engineers or whatever, I think I can allow myself to feel a little pride and satisfaction with regard to the end result. I think that time will vindicate me on this one. Now I'm back in video making mode, creating further videograms to project behind me on next month's concert dates. More slow and painstaking work, but it is getting there, bit by bit.

Weather definitely colder now, leaves falling faster from the trees, rain and grey skies, darker earlier. I'm glad we have such seasonal changes and not the less dramatic seasonal uniformity of Mediterranean countries. Living here in Yorkshire, the landscape really allows one to see nature's cycle in a vivid and wonderful manner. I consider myself extremely lucky to have such beauty on my doorstep. And, as Nelsonica serves to remind me, to have such beautiful, warm hearted fans to share my music with. I'm hoping to dream up some new ideas to incorporate in next year's Nelsonica, to try and make it even better and more unmissable. With a fair wind and the blessing of the fates. Thanks to everyone involved in this year's event, both on the organisational side and the attendee's side. You gave me a day I'll never forget.

•

TUESDAY 20TH DECEMBER 2005

Such a long time since the last diary entry. Why? Well partly an insane Christmas preparation schedule and partly the November tour dates. Five concerts in all, not the 15 to 20 that were originally rumoured. A real disappointment that it ended up being so few after all the effort I put into preparing new material and video for the shows. (I'll draw a discreet veil over the reason for this.) Nevertheless, it was far from disastrous, despite a gremlin-infested first date.

Here's my take on the tour, for what it's worth. The concerts I enjoyed the most (and thought musically the best) were the Bilston Robin 2 concert followed by the Manchester Life Cafe event. Enthusiastic and warm audiences at both, particularly at The Robin 2. And, surprise, surprise, more females in the audience than I'd seen for a while. Thank heavens that a set comprised of mainly instrumental guitar pieces had enough of a hint of (ahem) the 'erotic' to attract at least a few attractive ladies to say "hello" afterwards. As much as I enjoy talking to male fans about guitars and so on, female input is most welcome!

Leeds and Liverpool tied for second place but London, I have to admit, was something of a struggle. It also was the first date of the tour but really should have been left until last. So many technical problems on stage that first night. A monitor system that sounded like it was infested with insects, a pa system without enough headroom, effects pedals that didn't work and a cock-up over projection screen hire. Plus a very nervous Bill Nelson, still trying to get to grips with the new set and the malfunctioning equipment. One good thing about the London show, though, was the contribution made by Theo Travis, whom I'd met for the first time at Harold Budd's concert at the Brighton Dome earlier this year. Theo played fabulously, completely unfazed by the monitoring problems. I'm glad that there was someone up there with me who actually knew what he was doing. I did end up feeling quite depressed about that particular concert though. Really wished I'd not agreed to make it the first date on the tour.

Just as the tour came to a close, I was finally starting to relax and get the measure of things, playing much better and getting to use more suitable, better quality pa systems. Given more concerts, I suspect that it would have gone from strength to strength. Unfortunately, after concert five, it was time to pack the gear away for at least another year.

Video projection duties on these shows were shared by Paul Gilby and also superfan Ian Clarke who, gallantly and efficiently, stepped in at the last minute to take over the shows that Paul wasn't able to do. When I perform these solo concerts, the video backdrops are an essential part of the presentation. Psychologically, they help me to feel that I'm not entirely alone up there. (I like to think that I'm not the only point of visual focus for the audience.) Plus, of course, the videos provide a suitable counterpoint to the music, each piece being created to reflect the content of the songs.

I do get stressed out about playing live without a band, though. The solo concerts put a lot of pressure on one person playing alone for just over a couple of hours, especially as I'm not the most natural of performers. It's always a bit of an ordeal for me. One of these days, I'll retire back to the studio environment, as I did in the mid-1980s and leave the live thing alone.

The new thing about these concerts however, was the inclusion of some vocal pieces, something that I'd previously only felt comfortable performing within a band situation. But singing and playing guitar to backing tracks wasn't quite as traumatic as I'd expected. In fact, from what members of the audience told me afterwards, it seemed to provide a surprisingly workable solution and it is certainly something I'd consider including again in future solo shows.

Already those November concerts are fading into memory. Other projects are already occupying my time and more are hovering on the horizon. I've been trying to read through the as yet unpublished *Music In Dreamland* book, written by Paul Sutton-Reeves. Just before the tour began, I received a proof of the book (in email form) for me to read through. I'm told by the author that approximately 30,000 words may have been trimmed by the publisher from the original text, so it is important that we check for continuity errors as well as factual ones. Because of the tour and other duties, time has only now become available to work through the book. Nevertheless, I'm finding that, because of Christmas, I'm not as readily available as I'd like to be. I have spotted various things that might be corrected (as has Paul) but there's a certain amount of pressure on us both to get the book corrected and out there, particularly as it has languished in the publisher's office for over a year since the author completed it.

As of writing this diary entry, I haven't had available time to deal with it for several days. In fact, I've really only scratched the surface. I'm hoping that there will be more time after Christmas to give it proper attention. I would really like to do whatever I can to check any factual errors or misunderstandings but I expect that a certain amount of compromise will be necessary. Other projects looming on the horizon:

1: I have to mix the Be Bop Deluxe 'Decca Audition' tapes for release as an album.

2: Negotiations are underway for me to produce another recording by the Russian band Nautilus Pompilius who are now known as Jupiter. This may happen in February.

3: I would like to assemble a new guitar instrumental album based on the live pieces that I've incorporated into my solo shows this last two years and which have previously not been available. This means recording my solo guitar onto the various backing tracks and properly mixing everything to create a finished album of instrumentals. The album will include tracks such as [list of tracks]. They will become part of an album with the subtitle, *Painting With Guitars, Volume 2*.

4: I intend to go through some of my 1980s and 1990s archive material and release an album of previously unheard music from those eras. There is a tremendous reserve of material from the past that would definitely be of interest to the committed listener.

5. I have already made a (very) slight in-road into what will eventually emerge as an autobiographic/poetic video about my life, told via images, dialogue and music. I hope to find enough time during this coming year to complete a larger section of it.

6: Nelsonica 06 requires planning. I'd like to take the current high standard a little higher this coming year. Research a new venue and add even more to the curriculum. I also need to create a new Nelsonica limited edition album for convention attendees. This one will most likely include the songs *Snow Is Falling* and *Ghost Show* amongst others.

7: I'm burning to begin work on a brand new album. The bar has been raised by the *Sailor Bill* project and the next step must be equally, if not more, important. This means working very carefully and abandoning anything that doesn't hit the target. A time-consuming process.

Right now, I'm favouring something a little more stripped down than the orchestral *Sailor Bill*, *but* until I get to grips with the writing, it's hard to say which way things will go. Titles and mood are already falling into place though.

8: I need to consider what form any live concerts may take in 2006. I have some ambitious ideas but, whether they are practical or not will depend on the support I get from fans and business associates alike. One possibility is that they won't be in the form of a trek around the country's arts centres. I may attempt just two shows, one North, one South, but with a much more ambitious production than this year's concerts, and covering a great deal more musical ground than of late. Something really special is what I'm aiming at. It may be that I need to schedule this for '07 rather than '06, simply to get everything properly in place. But at my time of life, I can't afford to be cautious. Cocteau said that 'A young man should not make safe investments.' Well, I might add that an older man cannot afford to make safe investments! Time is of the essence as my youth is increasingly far behind me now. Speaking of which, it was heart warming to receive so many good wishes from fans on my recent 57th birthday. Frightening to think that, in a mere three years, I will be 60. However, in my age-addled head, I'm still a 17-year-old. Okay, 23 at a push!

One really exciting bit of news is a connection that has been forged between myself and an American guitar designer by the name of Dean Campbell. I recently came across a Campbell 'Precix' guitar in Music Ground's store in Leeds and was knocked out by the instrument's sheer playability. It's a solid body guitar, handmade in New England, USA and is a very practical but high quality instrument. Dean Campbell's work-shop is staffed by luthiers who have, in the past, worked for Guild guitars. I've had a Guild x500 archtop guitar since the 1970s so I know just how skilled those people are. Dean and I have been in contact these last few weeks and he is building me a Precix model, tailored to my needs. The really exciting thing is that we are going to bat ideas back and forth about a brand new design that Dean has on the drawing board. He's asked for my input as to the ongoing development of the instrument and I'm thrilled to be able to add my thoughts to the project as it develops. The Precix model that I've been trying out (and am keeping well within inspirational playing distance, an arm's reach from me as I type these words) has an action and response that really makes me want to play. It's one of those guitars that is difficult to put down, once picked up. I'm looking forward to using this instrument on my next set of recordings as it has a precision, resonance and clarity that is very special. For readers of this diary who are also guitarists, I recommend that you check out Dean's website.

Well, there is probably much more to write but I really seem to have exhausted my reservoir of memory for this particular diary entry. Life has been a blur of late and every day rushes by without enough hours in it to fulfil my intentions. For now, this will have to suffice.

To all those who read these words, I wish you the HAPPIEST CHRISTMAS and a PEACEFUL AND HEALTHY 2006! May all your dreams come true. Thanks also to everyone who has given their time, their talent and their interest throughout 2005. Thank you so much for helping me to manifest my dreams. I'm eternally grateful and couldn't achieve any of this without you. At the start of 2005, there was a brand new website to design and construct. Then four new albums to create, plus the Nelsonica convention extravaganza and a solo concert tour. (And a few other bits and pieces.) Let's see what next year brings. Cheers!

2006

Last day of January 2006 and no diary entry since 20th December last year. Should I put this down to a Christmas/ New Year letting go of the reins? Or is it simply the usual pre-occupation with all things creative? A lot of the former and quite a bit of the latter is the answer.

The usual over-indulgences at Christmas and New Year have taken their toll, as they always do. Last year's constant pace came to a halt as soon as the shops closed on Christmas Eve and I dropped my accumulated stress at the door along with the final bags of shopping. I'd eventually posted all my Christmas cards, found gifts for everyone, bought enough food to see us through to the New Year and stocked up on wine, mulled and otherwise, to keep the cold at bay.

It wasn't a white Christmas but it snowed a little the day after Boxing Day, enough to make the landscape momentarily magical. Walking through York's Museum Gardens at twilight, snowflakes spinning in gentle orbit around the amber glow of the old street lamps, the river gleaming silver at the foot of the hill beneath an indigo and rose pink star studded sky, I felt a welcome sense of wonder. It didn't last, of course, the snow that is. Within a couple of days it was a brown muddy sludge that made everything grimy and forlorn. A sudden grey plunge into the annual January doldrums. For a few brief days though, it had been a hedonistic, friends and family-centred celebration of, not just the season, but for me, the completion of a year's constant work, a year with hardly a breathing space between one project and another.

Early in the year, I had worked hard on the design of the

Dreamsville website, gathering visual material and bouncing ideas back and forth with David Graham until we got a look that suited the site's purpose. Then 'stage one' of Dreamsville was opened up to the world, generating a very positive response from all those who accessed it. Later, there was the release of the two *Rosewood* acoustic guitar instrumental albums. Again, artwork had to be created for them, once I'd completed the composition and recording of the music. (And yet another challenge for Dave and myself.)

These two albums, particularly *Rosewood Volume One*, I found very satisfying to make. I'd wanted to create a set of acoustic flavoured instrumental compositions for several years but, somehow, had never got around to it until the *Rosewood* project.

What really took me by surprise though was the next of the year's albums: *The Alchemical Adventures Of Sailor Bill*. For some reason, I was gripped more tightly by the hand of the muse with this album than anything I'd done for a long time. It completely took over my life and I worked longer and harder on the composition, arrangement and recording of the songs than I would normally have thought wise. Nothing's ever perfect, of course, but this set of songs comes as close to being personally fulfilling than almost any other album of mine. I think the reason for this is to be found in my current state of mind, conditioned as it is by advancing age and thoughts of mortality. Not morbid thoughts, just melancholy ones. At least some of the time. *Sailor Bill* successfully captures a certain mood, something that could, I think, genuinely be called an indicator of the 'essence' of myself. It is, if I may be allowed the indulgence, a 'mature' statement. In three years I'll be 60 (and how fast three years travels in this light-speed era of ours). But 60, damn it! I can't really comprehend this, it's somehow beyond belief, staggering.

My childhood seems only a few heartbeats away, its memories still vivid, its hopes and fears hardly changed. Nevertheless, the face in the mirror reminds me that young Billy has vanished with the passing clouds of time and now only grandfather William remains, hobbled and earthbound. And do I feel my age? Well, yes, and no but increasingly yes. Aches and pains and other little annoyances, a brittle creakiness, an inevitable erosion of flexibility, physical or otherwise, a stealthy dulling of the senses, an increasing world weariness. Life as she is lived, with wear and tear an inevitable part of the living. Yet still a mystery and still a wonder.

What else occupied my energies last year? Have I forgotten? Already it seems to have become a blur. A lot achieved though, all told. Here are some of the other things that I found time for: the recording of the limited edition *Orpheus In Ultraland* fan convention album. The Nelsonica 05 fan convention project with its attendant preparations and programming of content. The 'Popular Music from Other Planets' concert tour around the UK. And yes, of course, lots of new music and video was created for that.

But even earlier last year, before the above, more live concerts: The Harold Budd tribute that I took part in that was held at Brighton's Dome. Fun with Harold and John Foxx, Jah Wobble, Theo Travis, Steve Jansen, Robin Guthrie and others. A lovely, memorable event. Then the Lewes Guitar Festival with more new material to perform. And some other bits and pieces that slip my thoughts at this moment.

Too much time spent in my room though, hidden from the world. Whichever way I look at it, the last two years have been intensely creative. Maybe I should feel a much higher sense of achievement than I currently do? Here and now, at the end of January, there's the usual weight gain to contend with, the usual promise to myself that it will be easier come spring, that the return of outdoor weather will coax the bike from the shed and encourage some sort of exercise. What usually happens is the opposite of course. I end up trapped here in the studio, hypnotised by guitars and keyboards and computer screens whilst time accelerates around my wristwatch in dizzy circles. A little vortex of used-up life.

Some progress already. A couple of days ago, I completed the task of checking through Paul Sutton-Reeves' book about my career (*Music in Dreamland*). It's taken me most of January to get through it all as I felt that I should explain to Paul in some detail my observations and reasons for suggested amendments. Due to approximately 30,000 words being edited from Paul's original text by the publishers, I felt that there were places where a little re-clarification might help. I've left it entirely up to Paul to incorporate or ignore these suggestions as he sees fit but I'm hoping that the time I've spent typing out emails to him will prove valuable to the book's integrity.

It has been a weird experience reading about my career in this way. I imagine it would be disconcerting for anyone who had been made the subject of such a book, but I found it particularly strange. Sometimes I don't recognise the person on the page and am not even sure that I want to. At other times it's like being caught with my clothes off in public. I'm too unguarded, too ready to explain the music away, this eagerness to please resulting in some invented 'on the spot' descriptions of what the songs are about when often, in truth, I don't really have a clue as to their meaning. Do songs have to mean anything? It seems that, most of the time, mine do. I can't find a suitable justification for this though and would be equally happy if they contained no meaning at all. Here's something I've learned over the years but still regularly ignore — a honest pop musician does not generate as much public 'mystique' as a dishonest one. (Or one that plays his cards close to his chest.) And in pop music, mystique is everything. This indicates two things to me. First of all, I'm not by nature a pop musician, despite once, many years ago, pretending to be so. Secondly, I'm more interested in unmasking the conceits of celebrity than perpetuating them. This, of course, is not a formula for a successful commercial career, nor is it an attitude welcomed by those who benefit from such jiggery-pokery. The cult of fame, that so captures the imagination of the 'general public', thrives on fake glamour and artfully manipulated image-mongering.

People, it seems, prefer being hoodwinked to being liberated. Certainly my own experience backs that up. Whilst the majority of my own audience appears to be reasonably intelligent and sane, there have been (and sometimes still are) worrying exceptions. I've occasionally got into quite heated arguments with zealous fans who have taken issue with the fact that the 'real' Bill Nelson doesn't quite fit the 'virtual' Bill Nelson of their dreams. In fact, one sure way to experience just how negatively the cult of celebrity affects the human mind is to enter the arena of popular music. No matter how modest the level of celebrity one attains, sooner or later comes encounters with people who will obsessively claim you as the spiritual centre of their own fragile lives. You will be unceremoniously crowned the tin-pot God of their tin-pot universe. And woe betides you, should you ever seek to unburden them of their illusion. Hell hath no fury like a fantasist brought down to earth.

How easy it must be to create a spurious religion with so many willing, potential disciples. But such unhealthy mystification is all part of the entertainment business and is accepted as its general currency. Entertainment over enlightenment? As Brian Eno said in a recent article, 'We're all entertained to death.' Or something like that.

Anyway, back to the book. All said and done (and taking the above into account), I enjoyed reading it and expect that fans will enjoy reading it even more. It's Paul Sutton-Reeves' first published book and the first published biography of my career. A cause for celebration or trepidation? Well, perhaps we're both nervous of its reception. Will I have to hide from old girl-friends and ex-wives? Will my children understand their father any more than they do now? Will my friends still talk to me or look at me as if I've escaped from some travelling freak show? (Or do they already see me in that way?). The problem with books is they exile our frail lives to cruel islands of print. They banish fleeting experience to the state of permanence. Books adopt a form that appears, on the surface, substantial. We invest the printed word with a faith that would do the Pope proud. Words on a computer screen can be made to vanish with the click of a mouse but that thick brick of a thing that sits on your bookshelf or coffee table in constant view? Well, it can't be denied so easily. It can't be switched off by the removal of its electricity. Well, let's see what this thing unlocks when it's published. Maybe I'll have to leave the country.

There was some sad news just after Christmas which I've already commented on in postings on the Dreamsville Inn forum. Derek Bailey, pioneer free-music guitarist and someone who has proved constantly inspirational to me over many years, passed away on 25th December, 2005. This came as quite a shock. I knew he had suffered some illness in recent years but didn't realise quite how serious things were. Derek died from complications arising from motor neurone disease. I learned of his death a couple of days after it happened. Ironically, I'd finally completed Ben Watson's lengthy biography of Derek and the free-music scene on Christmas Eve. On Boxing Day, when my son Elliot and daughter Elle came to the house for a seasonal dinner, the conversation got around to Derek and I played them some selections of his music. The following day, the news came that he'd gone.

Perhaps many of my fans might be puzzled as to why Derek was so important or as to why I found his work inspirational. It could be argued that, in terms of form and intent, our approach to music was quite different. Derek's playing might be seen by some fans of mine as being too abstract, too confrontational, too fractured, too something or other, but certainly not comfortable listening. But these 'too whatevers' were exactly what attracted me to his work. He appealed to the part of me that resists the herd mentality, that awkward, stubborn, 'I know best' part of me that rudely and clumsily and sometimes stupidly resists compromise. His music also worked as a purely aesthetic art form, sound and gesture for its own sake, open to appreciation without it always being dependent upon the academic theories that surround much of free music's barbed history. There were threads, I might have argued, that connected Derek's music to Cage and Partch, though I'm sure he'd have considered these slender and quite possibly totally subjective. There was humour and mischievousness, grace and fire in Derek's playing. In his hands, the guitar was elevated to gallery status, a legitimate instrument of art. He was, in my mind, astonishing, revolutionary, the one player who I hoped I might one day be given the pleasure and challenge of playing with. Too late now.

Like Cage, like Partch, like Picasso and Pollock and all of Art's far scouts and secret agents, the world required only one Derek Bailey. To attempt to play like him, (and some people did and still do) would be a travesty. What he created was his and his alone, unique, absolutely essential and unrepeatable. The world of music was made more curious, more kinetic by his contribution to it. And that's an achievement.

There's an eloquent and reasoned account of Derek Bailey's life in the latest issue of *Wire* magazine, a piece written by David Toop, (who curated the Hayward Gallery's 'Sonic Boom' exhibition that I contributed some music to a few years ago). It's worth reading, especially as David had the opportunity to talk with Derek on numerous occasions over the years. It's as fine an introduction to the man and his music as possible within the restrictions of a slim magazine. Derek's own book, *Improvisation*, is an essential read too, even for musicians who aren't naturally sympathetic to the free-music cause. Yet another positive force gone, gone, gone. But not yet forgotten.

Whilst on the subject of books. Christmas brought me new ones, as it always does. They were added to the small mountain that has accumulated throughout last year and which pressure of work has denied me access. I've made a start, although my reading is still done at the end of the day in the minutes before sleep. Here are some of the titles stacked by my bedside: *Despite The System: Orson Welles Versus The Hollywood Studios* by Clinton Heylin; *Lovesick Blues, The Life Of Hank Williams* by Paul Hemphill; *Dylan Thomas, A New Life* by Andrew Lycett; *Quicksilver* by Neal Stephenson; *The Sea* by John Banville; *The Spirit Of Place, Nine Neo-Romantic Artists And Their Times* by Malcolm Yorke; *Untold Stories* and *Writing Home* by Alan Bennett; *Audio Culture, Readings In Modern Music* by Christopher Cox and Daniel Warner; *The Rise Of The Sixties* by Thomas Crow; *The Making Of Modern Britain* by Jeremy Black; *Surrealism In Britain* by Michel Remy; *Lost Highway* by Peter Guralnick; *Ted Hughes, The Life Of A Poet* by Elaine Feinstein; *American Odyssey, The Letters and Journals Of* Wilhelm Reich edited by Mary Boyd Higgins; *Fritz Lang, The Nature Of The Beast* by Patrick McGilligan; and *Bill Brandt, A Life* by Paul Delaney.

Some of the above I made a start on earlier last year but because I was so busy I broke off reading them and need to begin again when time allows. I also was given some very welcome DVDs, the most special of which is a boxed set of a mammoth 12 and a half hour long film/series called simply, *JAZZ, A Film By Ken Burns*. I'd caught some of this when it was screened as a series on television quite a while ago now, but never got around to buying the DVD, partly due to its high price. However, Christmas presents are one of life's little luxuries and Emiko generously bought it for me as a surprise gift. Whilst some have said that Ken Burns' view of Jazz history is a particularly selective one, for me the film is beautifully put together. I could watch it over and over again. It's uplifting, inspiring and heartfelt. Watching it is a wonderful way to unwind at the end of the day, the film's music and musicians providing a poetic reminder of why some of us became so besotted with music in the first place. It's the kind of programme that makes me feel proud to be part of a tremendous chain of musicians stretching back through history, meagre though my own contribution has been. Anyway, I'd recommend this fine piece of work to all music lovers, irrespective of whether Jazz rings their bell or not. If, after watching this film, the penny still hasn't dropped, then they're beyond redemption.

In terms of listening, when I've found the time, (usually over dinner,) I've been in a retro mood, albums by Ella Fitzgerald, Artie Shaw, Duke Ellington and Count Basie, Billie Holiday, Django Reinhardt, Ben Webster, Wes Montgomery and Joe Pass. Also Bill Evans' *Conversations With Myself* album and (not exactly a 'retro' record) Bill Frisell's *East-West* live album. There's a real sense of elegance, intelligence and sophistication in these jazz albums, qualities that seem to have gone missing in action amongst our current pop/rock luminaries. To listen to these classic recordings is to enter another world, a world, I have to say, in which I feel comfortably at home.

So, what are my plans for this coming year? Well, the *Music In Dreamland* book's obligations now discharged, the next thing on the agenda is the possibility of working with Russian musicians again. My old Nautilus Pompillius friend Slava Butusov and his new band Jupiter. Still awaiting budget conformation on this, though.

The next thing I'll need to do after this is to mix the Be Bop Deluxe Decca audition tapes. I'm hoping to make these available on my own 'Sonoluxe' label before very long. Current favourite title for this cd is *Tomorrow The World*. (Which was the title of an early Be Bop Deluxe song but equally suggests the group's ambition back in those early days.) Also, I've been asked by EMI Records to mix some later Be Bop Deluxe live album tracks, different takes from those that found their way onto the *Live In The Air Age* album, but from the same tour, or so I'm presuming. These tracks will be part of EMI's proposed big Be Bop Box set which will contain just about everything the band ever recorded. This is due for release later this year.

Then I must work on a new instrumental guitar album, volume two in the *Painting With Guitars* series of which *The Romance Of Sustain* was volume one. I've yet to choose the 'main' title for this album but it will contain versions of the more recent instrumental material that I've incorporated into my solo performances these last two years, tracks such as *The Girl On The Fairground Waltzer*, *Blue Amorini*, *Blackpool Pleasure Beach And The Road To Enlightenment* and *Electric Milkcart Blues* amongst others.

Also planned is an album of unreleased sketches and demos from my 1980s archives. The main focus of my attention will be a new vocal album, the next step on from *Sailor Bill*. I want to take my time with this though and, bearing in mind the archive material already planned for release, I may not find time to complete a brand new album this year. We'll see.

This year's fan convention, Nelsonica 06, is yet another project to deal with, and very soon too if it is to be ready for a proposed autumn event date. New venues to check out first. I have had an idea about including a sort of guitar 'masterclass' as part of the convention, a non-academically inclined one that will allow me to talk about aesthetic approaches to the instrument as well as technical ones. A special, limited edition CD will be required for the convention too, as is usual, and *Snow Is Falling*, a song which I featured in last year's tour, is definitely going to be one of the tracks on it. Live dates? Well, I have some ambitious plans but I'm not sure at this stage how practical they will be. As always, it's down to funding.

And that's plenty to be getting on with, I think. Letters from Harold who is moving house. A jolly note from Roger Eno, too. Emails from Peter Coulombe and Chuck Bird with reference to a possible Nelsonica USA fan convention. They are starting to get results back from a survey to discover how many American fans would be interested in attending such a thing. I'm told it looks promising at the moment. If all goes to plan, it may be that there will be two Nelsonicas next year, one here in England and one in the States.

Three new doors being fitted to the house due to weather damage. Awaiting quotations from decorators to repair all the exterior woodwork which will need doing once the new doors are fitted. One door has been hung today (though only under-coated at the moment). The other two were not quite the right fit so have been taken away to be adjusted and will be fitted next Monday I'm told.

Elliot passed his driving test, first time! I'm pleased but now I've something extra to worry about. Part of being a parent, I suppose. My mother still worries about me when I'm out on the roads, even though I'm 57-years-old and have been driving since the 1960s. (Why does that last sentence remind me of Alan Bennett?).

Emiko has had one day a week cut from her schedule at the flower shop and is looking for a way to fill the financial gap.

She's thinking about putting in some time at an old people's home as a carer. Whilst I'm sure that she'd be able to do this quite well, it seems a shame as her talent is really with flowers. Sometimes, I wish she had more ambition and would make more of her gifts but she says she's too old to do so. I think she's too easy-going in some ways but I love her as she is. She accepts the difficulties of being married to someone whose career is always up and down and insecure so I have nothing to complain about. I'm very lucky to have her share my life with me.

Outside my window: grey, undistinguished January weather. Nothing much to uplift the spirits, just that typically flat, beginning of the year mood-dulling atmosphere. Roll on spring and the saffron song of daffodils.

·

MONDAY 10TH APRIL 2006

Once again, an extremely long gap between diary entries. Perhaps they will appear more frequently in future however, as new software has been installed on the Dreamsville site that will allow me to upload my diary direct to the server, rather than having to ask tech-support people to do it for me, as has been the case until now. I've felt quite guilty of troubling others to post my diaries, though that hasn't been the only reason for their infrequency. Distracted by music making the main cause, as usual.

So, what has been happening here in the weeks since I last wrote? More of what usually happens, I suppose. Intense work in my modest studio, as always, along with various mild domestic dramas. I'll record the musical progress first.

My proposed production job for Slava's new band, Jupiter, has, unfortunately, been cancelled. Or at least postponed for the indefinite future. Disappointing, for both them and me. The band couldn't raise sufficient funding from their record company to travel to Britain from Russia for the recordings but are hoping to seek additional funding from other sources. They hope to come here later in the year to record the entire album with me. Having experienced the music business first hand for over 30 years, I'm not holding my breath. If it happens, I'll be very pleased, but that 'if ' is a big one.

I've finally completed *Neptune's Galaxy*, the instrumental album that I've created as a companion to my *Alchemical Adventures Of Sailor Bill* album of last year. It contains just five tracks but they are long ones and the album clocks in at a total of just over 75 minutes worth of music. Some might describe the album as 'ambient' though the music commands more attention than that categorisation would normally suggest. Three of the five tracks feature electric guitar and beats, one is an electric piano improvisation and the other features electronic keyboards and some subtle orchestral textures. The nautical themes are carried over from the *Sailor Bill* project but, of course, without lyrics. The track listing is as follows [list of tracks]. The entire album is very relaxing, gentle and meditative, occupying a sonic landscape, (or should that be seascape?) somewhere between *Dreamland To Starboard*, *Crimsworth* and my Harold Budd collaborations. Listening to the *Sailor Bill* album and then immediately afterwards to *Neptune's Galaxy* is a satisfying experience, the final track of *Sailor Bill* providing a perfect bridge to the first track of *Neptune's Galaxy*.

Although David Graham and myself are currently creating packaging artwork for the album, I've yet to master the tracks in preparation for manufacturing, so a release date has yet to be fixed. I'm hoping to make this album available as soon as possible though.

I've also attempted to make a start on the mixing of the Be Bop Deluxe Decca audition tapes. I've had these transferred to a Mackie external hard-drive so that I can work on the four songs here in my home studio. Unfortunately, technical problems have thwarted this for the time being. My HDR 24/96 hard disc recorder is an early model and the transfers were made using a newer version of the software. Basically, my machine can't read the files. My friend Paul Gilby has been helping me get to the bottom of the problem which we eventually discovered hinges on the conflict of operating systems. Updating the OS has not been as straightforward as hoped though. The HDR 24/96's floppy drive appears not to be working. (Required to load the latest operating system.) I also need a new e-prom fitting to cope with the larger external drive on which the Be Bop audition tapes have been transferred, so the saga is ongoing. It's been a frustrating and time-consuming piece of detective work. Hopefully, I should be able to access the files in a week or two when time will allow me to have the machine out of commission for a couple of days whilst the technical repairs are done.

Meanwhile, I've been recording more new material, six songs for what started life as a limited edition 'mini' album. It may yet turn out to be a full-length album. The direction is jazz inspired. I've often featured jazz stylings on some of my albums but, as Paul pointed out to me, I've never actually made an album given over to that particular style. This set me thinking. Anyway, I've now completed six songs for the project and there is still enough inspiration left over to write more. At one point, I wasn't sure how long I could sustain that particular mood but, at the moment, the ideas continue to flow. The six songs completed so far provide just over 30 minutes worth of music. If I can come up with another four songs I'll have a complete album. The songs are [list of tracks]. All are vocal based compositions and I'm particularly fond of *Windswept* which has a jazz blues mood somewhere between the worlds of Billie Holiday and Chet Baker. (But still 'me' somehow. How could it be anyone else?) *Always You* has a touch of Bobby Darin on Mars about it. Or a Vegas show tune from a parallel universe. Could this be the closest thing I've done to an easy-listening lounge album? Well, not quite, but close. The overall perform-ance of these tracks is a little looser than the performances on *Sailor Bill* but that is appropriate to the style. These are 'feel' pieces with improvised solos. They are not strictly jazz, of course, but just 'jazzy' or 'jazz inspired.' (Emiko described them as 'techno-jazz' but I'm not sure about that either!) As usual, I'm too close to the music to know what the hell it is. It's probably a curious side-project rather than a major statement. Other's may feel differently when they hear it. I will confess that there's some slick guitar playing on it though, if you like that kind of thing.

Working title for the mini-album is *Return To Jazz Of Lights*. It may be a keeper.

I'm working through some visual concepts for the packaging at the moment, before sending images to David Graham for him to lay-out and add typography. The path I'm pursuing is based around some old 1960s snapshots of Emiko. I've been going through her family album. She was a stunningly beautiful teenager and I couldn't have imagined myself landing a catch like her back then if we'd ever had the good fortune to meet (which would have been impossible anyway, bearing in mind the distance between Tokyo and Wakefield and my reliance on the bus at that time in my life!). One photograph I've selected for use is very odd. It could almost be a still frame from a dramatic moment in a movie. The young Emi is standing centre frame, gazing off to the right and slightly up into the sky. She is surrounded by people, nearly all of whom have their back to the camera, looking over the edge of a railing, beyond which a white statue stands, its back also to the camera. Emi is dressed in a fashion that wouldn't look out of place on a young teenage girl of 2006, low slung skinny jeans, a tight fitting Japanese Boy Scout shirt with embroidered badges, a large white bag. She looks, to use the well worn vernacular, 'cool.' The photograph's colours have faded over the years since it was taken, so I've scanned it and subjected it to a long sequence of colour, contrast and filter manipulation, giving it a vintage cinematic quality. It's an enigmatic picture, achieved without artifice. Whoever took the photo did it quickly and unthinkingly. The camera angle isn't straight but this adds to the tension. Only one person in the crowd is looking at the camera, a plumpish Japanese lady sat at a table in the middle ground. She has an inane grin on her face. It's an intriguing photograph. Using it (and the others I've picked) is not an obvious choice for the style of music on the album, but then again, it twists the album concept in a slightly surreal, ironic way. As the songs are all love songs, using Emi as an iconic image is perfectly apt anyway.

Guitars have loomed large in recent months. I may have

mentioned on the Dreamsville site a while ago that Campbell American Guitars have been working towards a signature guitar for me. Dean Campbell has sent various drawings and ideas over for me to add my own input. I've sent drawings and suggestions back to Dean and a limited edition Bill Nelson signature model is not only on the drawing board but currently being developed in prototype form. It's all under wraps for now but all will be revealed when ready. Like all Campbell American guitars, it will be a hand-made in the USA instrument.

Meanwhile, I've been playing my green Precix model and will soon be getting delivery of a blue vibrato-arm equipped Precix. These instruments play beautifully and respond sensitively to the touch of the player. I'll also be appearing on the Campbell American stand at the London Guitar Show held at the Wembley Exhibition Centre on the 6th of May. Not to perform but just to 'meet and greet' fans and fellow guitarists. A very early version of my signature guitar may be ready to display, although we're aiming for a more developed version by June. Naturally, I'm extremely excited about having a signature model after all these years of playing. If all goes to plan, it should be something really special.

But the guitar magic hasn't stopped there. I've long been a fan of unusual 1950s and 1960s guitars. When I first became besotted by the instrument, at the end of the 1950s it was almost impossible to see, in my local music shops, any of the expensive Gibsons and Fenders that our early guitar heroes played. Import restrictions on American goods meant that they were rare and definitely out of reach of the average player's pocket. In my home town of Wakefield, the local music shop, Webster's (later to become The Wakefield Music Centre) only stocked British and European guitars. These were inexpensive instruments, often with unusual design ethics, lots of chrome and push buttons, bright colours, accordion factory plastic, retro-sci-fi creations that really looked 'electric.' Burns and Fenton Weill guitars were amongst the main British makes but there were also a variety of quirky models from continental makers such as Hagstrom, Hopf, Gallanti and Wandre. Japan was also starting to license designs to, or build for, some of the European manufacturers and some Japanese instruments were often 're-badged' for the western marketplace. Of course, these weird and wonderful guitars didn't have the finesse of the more expensive American instruments but they did have a flashy visual appeal. These originally inexpensive guitars have now become collector's items and exchange hands for high prices, particularly the Wandre models which are rare and sought after.

Generally though, these budget instruments didn't play too well and their appeal was mainly in the visual department. And even then, perhaps, only if you had a taste for the kitsch. I still harbour a fond enthusiasm for them, despite being able to play much more upmarket brands these days. But I do prefer to play my guitars, rather than just look at them. Enter Mike Robinson, a musician and collector of oddball vintage guitars, who came up with the idea of manufacturing reproductions of some of the most sought-after instruments. His plan was to make them look exactly like the original rarities, but have them play and sound better. With this in mind, he started Eastwood Guitars (based in Canada) and set up a manufacturing operation to re-issue some vintage 'thrift-store' brands using modern man-

ufacturing techniques. The results are guaranteed to attract
players such as myself who grew up with those kind of guitars
during our teens. (And some younger players who have taken
notice of the 'Airline' models favoured by The White Stripes
and Calexico.)

But, whilst nostalgia is one part of the Eastwood appeal, the
sound and playability of the re-issues is something else. They
are much more solidly made and player-friendly than their
original inspirations. I recently got myself an Eastwood reproduction of a Hopf 'Saturn 63' in black and chrome. The original
late-1960s/early 1970s European instrument was quirky, a
semi-hollow body with two cat's eye style sound-holes, both
mounted, unusually, on the bass side of the body. Chrome metal
strips were used to 'pipe' the guitar's edges and sound-holes and
the resultant effect was retro sci-fi in keeping with the model's
'Saturn' name. The modern Eastwood reproduction re-creates
the vibe wonderfully and the guitar has a very unique sonic
character as well as being an unusual looker.

So, my guitar dreams continue to inspire my imagination.
Fans who have attended my live concerts in recent years will
have noticed that all the guitars I favour are somewhat out of
the ordinary, not a Les Paul model amongst them, (as much as
I adore Les' playing.) Maybe it's my art school background but
a guitar's appearance is as important to me as its playability and
an instrument's visual style will always be a major consideration
in my choices. Nearly all the guitars I play reflect some special
design ethic, whether modern or retro. My Gretsch guitars also
sit in perfectly with that sensibility, as does my Gus 'Orphee'
which pushes that approach into a 21st Century, midi-
equipped, industrial design arena. What's truly wonderful for

me though is that, after all these years of playing the instrument, I still get a thrill out of looking at my guitars and using them to make my music. I'm as in love with the instrument as I was when I got my first guitar at the age of 11 or 12. And I still can't read a note of music or espouse any musical theory.

Despite all the recordings I've made, I've yet to understand how the music gets from 'in here' to 'out there'. I'm just thankful that it does. I've spent some time with my friend Jon Wallinger recently, tracking down a new venue for this year's Nelsonica fan convention. After exploring various alternatives, we've settled on the York Hilton Hotel. I think this will prove to be an excellent location for the event, certainly for those fans who travel from abroad to attend. York is a beautiful, historic city with lots to offer its visitors. Hopefully, some fans will bring their families and make a weekend of it. There's even a York version of the London Eye big wheel being constructed. Should be open soon, certainly in time for Nelsonica 06. Along with the historic Viking and Roman sites, York has the National Railway Museum, the Yorkshire Air Museum, two more general museums, river trips, the gothic minster, a good art gallery, plenty of interesting shops, old pubs, modern cafe-bars and restaurants, almost all within an area that can easily be accessed on foot. Convention attendees can stay in the venue itself at preferred rates which we will negotiate with the Hilton Hotel so the whole package is much more attractive than ever. And easier to get to than North Ferriby.

The next step is to create the content for the convention. There are some new ideas that I'd like to introduce, including a presentation aimed at the guitarists amongst the fans. I think that, if all goes to plan, this year's Nelsonica will be even more special than previous ones. Jon and the team are really professional in their attitude to organising the convention and put a lot of thought and effort into making it a special day. It's impossible not to respond positively to such dedication and enthusiasm.

Another project that I'm about to immerse myself in is the mixing of some old live Be Bop Deluxe tracks to be included in a box set that EMI Records are planning to issue later this year. The box will collect together everything the band recorded, every official album and some out-takes and alternative mixes, plus a few unreleased live tracks. I will be going into Fairview studios soon to take care of the mixing of the latter.

On the domestic front, the usual stresses and strains. Far too many bills piling up on the kitchen table and repairs needed for the house. Cars have been up to their tricks too, both Emiko's and mine requiring new exhausts and tyres. Mine is rapidly going rusty but a re-spray would probably cost more than the car is worth. Perhaps the weather will improve soon and I can get the pushbike out of the shed.

My son Elliot has joined the car set, having passed his driving test recently. He's got himself an old VW Golf and came to pick me up to take me into town the other week. It seems like only yesterday I was helping him to learn how to ride a little two-wheel bike. I can remember the day that I took his stabilisers off and ran behind him, holding on to his saddle. I let go and off he went, perfectly balanced. When he turned around and realised that I wasn't holding him upright, the look on his face was priceless. He was just a little kid then, that thing of time evaporating so quickly. Life is so short. Well, having said that, I'll get back to the music making.

·

Perhaps I shouldn't be writing a diary entry right now. I certainly don't feel in the proper state of mind to do so but I desperately feel the need to write something down, if only to help me to work through some of my grief. I couldn't imagine, last week, that today I would be in such a state and for such an unforeseen and unwelcome reason.

On Sunday I was taking my usual morning bath when I heard the phone ring. I hadn't brought the cordless phone into the bathroom with me as Emi was at home. I thought it might be one of her Japanese friends calling, as often happens at weekends. But then I heard her rushing up the stairs and her footsteps coming along the corridor towards the bathroom. I realised that the call must be for me. She came into the bathroom with the cordless phone in her hand, holding it out to me. She was in tears and could hardly speak. With difficulty, through the tears, she said: "It's your mum, it's bad news — Ian's died."

I felt as if the whole world had ground to a sudden, violent halt and then I began to shake and weep uncontrollably. I felt as if my guts were being wrenched from me. My mother was crying as she told me what had happened only a short time earlier that morning. She had telephoned my brother Ian sometime around 11 am to wish him a happy birthday. (Sunday was his 50th.) Ian's wife Diane had answered and told my mother that Ian was still in bed, having a lie-in, but that he really ought to be getting up as they were going out soon. She asked my mother to hold the line whilst she called up the stairs tell him that his mother was on the phone. There was no answer and when Diane went upstairs to wake him she found that Ian had died in his sleep. The shock has been terrible. Feelings of disbelief, denial, sickness and bottomless black pits of emotional despair. A violent assault on the depths of our hearts and souls. And it keeps on hitting and hurting. I'm battered and exhausted by its brutality. I feel as if a precious and essential part of my life has been suddenly ripped out of me.

And, of course, it has. Ian was my 'little' brother. I'd known him all his life and, despite those silly sibling rivalries that all brothers experience from time to time, loved him deeply and respected him far more than he probably ever realised. Far, far more than he realised. Oh, Ian, if only I could tell you.

Even though Ian had survived a stroke nine years ago when he was 41, I always expected him to outlive me, to always be there with his warm smile and dry sense of humour. Ian had become a physically big man, partly as a result of the diabetes he suffered from in recent years, but this largeness suggested solidity, a rock that would stand strong, despite the surrounding waves. He seemed indestructible. Perhaps he felt that he was, too.

I saw him last a few weeks ago on Mother's Day, in March. Emiko and I had driven over to my mother's house in Wakefield with a gift and some flowers for her. Not long after we'd arrived, Ian arrived too, to give mum his gifts. I think it was actually the first time I'd seen him since the start of the year. I'm always so intensely, stupidly busy with one project after the other that family relationships and friendships regularly suffer as a result. Ian too had been busy with his freelance career as a funding consultant for arts projects. Both of us had been feeling a lot of stress, under pressure, the usual outcome of trying to keep things together on an unpredictable financial income. But Ian seemed cheerful. He'd recently got himself a new car and proudly led me outside to show it to me where it was parked in the drive of my mother's house. We chatted and joked freely for a while, just the two of us. I asked him if he fancied coming along to this year's Nelsonica convention in October, to play his saxophone with me as part of my solo performance there. I also asked him if he would like to perform with me at a special concert being planned for next year as part of a contemporary music festival at Leeds University's school of music. He was happily enthusiastic and positive about being involved in both projects so I promised I'd keep him up to date with progress for each event. (I've always enjoyed the instrumental duos we've had in the past, feeling much more comfortable in those situations with Ian alongside me than being up there on my own.)

Eventually, Ian had to leave for a prior appointment and we waved him off from my mother's doorstep. I had no idea then that that would be the last time I'd ever see him. Remembering that day now, Emi has pointed out to me that Ian had seemed really pleased to see me, his face being lit up with one of his warm smiles when he saw that I was there. I'm so pleased to have that pointed out to me because I needed his love more than he realised. More than I realised.

Last week, Emi was sorting out clothes of mine and came across some that were like new but that I hadn't worn. She'd put them to one side to see if Ian might want them. When she told me this I thought that I should give him a call and see how he was. As so often happens, I became so wrapped up in trying to finish some recording work in time for a mastering session next week that this intention slipped from my consciousness. (And now, I've cancelled that same session. I have no appetite for music. Its joy has left me.) Time always warps when my mind is concentrated on work, as my family and friends and regular readers of this diary know. I look down towards the faders of the mixing desk and it's winter. When I look up, it's spring. Or so it seems. Months pass like minutes. Life evaporates. How I wish I'd made that call last week. I can't begin to express the anguish I feel at not being able to call Ian now, at this very moment. I can hear the sound of his voice clearly in my head, the way he sounded on the telephone.

My mother called a few minutes ago to tell me the results of the coroner's report: Ian died because of heart disease. A blood clot touched his heart and he was gone. Apparently, there would have been nothing anyone could have done to save him. It was inevitable. Had he been awake when it happened, it would have felled him in an instant. That it happened whilst he was sleeping is a comfort of sorts. What if he had been driving his car with his family on board? A mercy, that he wasn't.

The last two days have brought us a kind of hell. Ian's wife Diane and Ian's three children must have been truly in the depths of it. My mother, who is not in the best of health herself, is suffering terribly from the loss. We all are. We want him back. The next few weeks will be hard too, particularly the funeral which is to be held on the 2nd of May. I have no immunity or resistance to grief. It comes in sudden waves and drowns me every time. All composure gone. I want to say something about him at the service but know that I wouldn't have the strength, that tears and sobs would be all that would escape me, words buried beneath fathomless anguish. But we will have to get through these next days as best we can, together. I'm sure that Ian would have poured scorn on any solemnity. He wasn't a particularly religious man, in fact, almost the opposite. He often took a cynical stance regarding my own 'spiritual' foraging over the years.

I remember, one lost summer back in the early 1980s, when I lived in West Haddlesey, the two of us sitting atop a haystack in a field outside the village, discussing various philosophies as the warm harvest sun sank towards the horizon. I was heavily involved in Rosicrucianism and esoteric occultism at that time and had been enthusiastically propounding its theories and principles in the hope of firing up Ian's imagination. I could, as they say, 'talk the hind leg off a donkey' in those days, such was my passion for the subject. But Ian remained scornful and humorously cynical about the whole thing, as he was about every other 'ism' I experimented with. He couldn't see the point of all that and was far more down to earth and pragmatic than I ever was. It may be that, in this respect, as in so many other things, he had a better grasp of reality than myself. He might have been my 'little' brother in years but he was strong and stubborn and independent too. And sharp and bright and witty. There was so much in him that I admired. I was, and always will be, proud of him. He was his own man and lived his life the way he wanted to live it, and damn the torpedoes.

I have so many fond memories of Ian. I couldn't possibly recount them all now but here are a couple. Back in the late-1970s or early-1980s, I was visiting my mother in Wakefield when she was still living on Eastmoor Estate, where I grew up. Ian, I think, was living there too at this point in time but had gone into town. Suddenly the phone rang and my mother answered it. It was a local corner-shopkeeper who knew my mother. He was telephoning to say that Ian was in his shop, injured. I jumped into my car and drove the half mile to the shop and found Ian in a bad way. He had been on his way home to my mother's house and had walked through a subway en route. In the subway, a gang of youths were trying to mug an elderly lady and were shoving her around. Ian had stepped into the situation and tried to stop these thugs from continuing their actions, trying to reason with them, asking them to leave the lady alone. The gang violently turned on Ian and beat him up before running away, leaving him to stagger to the nearby shop where the lady explained to the shopkeeper what had happened. He recognised Ian and rang my mother. I rushed Ian off to the hospital to have his wounds attended. I then set off in my car to search for the bastards who had done this to him. I drove up and down every street on Ian's route but couldn't find them, which is probably just as well as they would have more than likely done damage to me too, had I challenged them. But I was so angry that they'd done this to my little brother, I just wanted to beat the shit out of them. But this incident was a measure of Ian's public spiritedness and bravery. Many people would have left the old lady to her fate and kept out of danger but Ian's compassion wouldn't allow him to walk on by. He had to try to stop what was happening. He had principles and the guts to do something about it.

I have memories of Ian and I first recording music together, in the mid-1970s with Be Bop Deluxe on the song *Ships In The Night*. It was the first public recording of mine that he was involved with and it was at Abbey Road studios in London. He was really young and must have been intimidated and overwhelmed by the experience. He'd only just begun playing saxophone at that time, though he'd played clarinet for a while previously. I knew he was talented and capable and pushed him hard, as big brother's do. I was often too demanding of him, all throughout his musical life, knowing just how good he could be, given that push. I wanted him to excel, to be great, to be the best he could possibly be. My only consolation now is, if I was too hard on him, too exacting, I at least treat myself equally as hard, was just as critical of my own attempts. I thought that, together, we could change the world with our music. But I was stupid and naive, too. I demanded too much from both of us. Ian was a great player without need of any pressure from me.

Later on, he became a member of Red Noise, playing sax, clarinet and second keyboards in the band. Red Noise was also his introduction to life on the road and to television and radio appearances. In the 1980s he contributed his gifted playing to several of my solo albums and songs. One of the most memorable was *Do You Dream In Colour?* which featured Ian's incredibly catchy harmony saxophone hook, an important, essential component for the song's commercial appeal. It was one of the most perfectly appropriate parts he ever came up with, an absolutely classic line that everyone who ever heard the song remembers. It was a great pleasure, on the 2004 'Be Bop And Beyond,' 30 year celebration tour, for me to be able to perform that song live and have Ian in the band to reproduce the saxophone part perfectly. The song would be incomplete without it. How can I ever perform that song again without Ian standing next to me?

Ian later became part of Fiat Lux, a band that I initially had produced and released on my own independent Cocteau Records label. The band showed great commercial potential and the single that Cocteau Records released earned them media attention and landed them a deal with a major label, only for them to later fall foul of incompetent and corrupt management. An old and far too familiar story. Poor Ian suffered from the financial fallout of that situation for several years afterwards. I was going through similar tribulations myself so we both experienced the corruption and callousness of the industry at first hand. Ian's experience soured his hopes of being a full-time musician and he decided to reserve his music for situations that were less likely to produce further unhappiness. He began playing with friends in local bands and occasionally taught music, teaching both privately and in college situations.

Of the two of us, Ian was the one who had a formal, academic musical education. He began playing clarinet under the tuition of our late father, Walter Nelson, and then had more formal lessons that resulted in him passing various examinations and gaining certificates of accomplishment. He eventually earned himself a place at Huddersfield College of Music where he studied the subject academically. Ian was the real deal, not a dumb 'busker' like me who, to this day, still can't read a note of music. My father was so proud of the fact that Ian had done it the proper way. The ironic thing was that, whilst my formal education was in fine art and Ian's was in music, Ian eventually worked in the field of art, and I found myself with a career in music. Not what either of us had originally intended.

Years ago, Ian took a temporary job at the Yorkshire Sculpture Park. He worked in the on-site shop, selling Sculpture

Park merchandise. The park's director was, and still is, Peter Murray, who had been my painting tutor at Wakefield School of Art when I was a student there in the 1960s. Ian was eventually employed at the Sculpture Park full time and worked his way up to become part of the park's management team. It was a job he enjoyed tremendously and I was impressed by the way he handled it whenever I visited him at the park's office. I was so proud of his achievement with this. It was a job that I would have had neither the intelligence nor the social skills to do well. He was apparently in line for a directorship until his stroke put him out of commission, nine years ago.

Eventually, he recovered from the stroke, only to discover that he had to deal with diabetes as well. Of course, all of those who loved him got sanctimonious about it and we gave him our glib advice, admonishing him if we felt that he wasn't strictly adhering to whatever health regime was appropriate to his condition. Ian, characteristically, didn't respond well to being prodded about these things. His life was his life and back seat drivers were not easily tolerated. To use a nautical metaphor, he was the captain of his own ship and he intended to sail it wherever *he* wanted. Both of us were born stubborn so-and-so's but perhaps Ian had the upper hand on me in this department too. So, stubborn, yes, but he was never unforgivable.

One of the things that people seemed to remember most about Ian was his warmth and the way he had of putting people at ease. There was something relaxed, open and easy going about him that made this possible. Again, I lack that quality, being too self-absorbed, nervous or intense (or something) and was often surprised and amazed by the positive response he elicited from total strangers. He could make people feel they'd known him for years. And he did it without any artifice. It was 100% genuine empathy.

Neither of our first marriages worked out. I also had a second one that didn't but when Ian met Diane it felt as if he'd found his soul mate. I remember Ian and Diane's wedding day and the good vibes they gave off. And when Emiko and I had our wedding day, Ian and Diane were our witnesses. Diane has stuck with Ian through good times and difficult ones and she has a deep understanding of Ian's character and life. What she has endured these last two days is powerfully moving and impossible to fathom but she has shown kindness and bravery to all those in her circle and I know that Ian would be proud of her, and of his three children.

Ian's eldest son, Julian (from his first marriage), has been a pillar of strength to Diane, to my mother and to his step-brother, Louis, and step-sister, Lucy. I've been so impressed by Julian's thoughtfulness, sanity and compassion. Ian's younger son Louis and daughter Lucy (both from Ian's marriage to Diane) have shown tremendous dignity and self control, too. They are a tribute to Ian and Diane's parenting skills. I'm proud to be an uncle to all three children though I ought to have been a much more present and regular one. I hope they realise just how much their father meant to me.

During these last two days, I've been overwhelmed. I've been overwhelmed not only by what has actually happened, what also by the changes it has thrust upon so many people, over-whelmed by emotions that were far deeper and far stronger than I'd ever expected. At night, a little cinema of memory has opened up in my mind. I close my eyes and, there on the flick-

ering screen are images of Ian and I as young children, antici-
pating Christmas. Me reading to Ian the story of Peter *And
Pam's Christmas* from a now long-lost childhood book, huddled
under an eiderdown together on a snowy Christmas Eve at our
home at number 28 Conistone Crescent, Eastmoor Estate on
the edge of Wakefield. We were electrified with excitement and
anticipation, unable to sleep, eager for the morning and our
presents from Santa.

A dissolve. School holidays now. I've built plastic model
aeroplanes from Airfix kits and hung them from the bedroom
ceiling. Ian takes pot shots at them with his popgun and deci-
mates half a squadron. We run around the back garden in
super-hero capes, Batman and Robin, Superman and Superboy,
Dan Dare and Digby. Other kids, more inclined to army games,
think that we are weird. We don't care what they think. The
scene shifts and Ian and I are at the coast, or outside a caravan,
or on the beach with a toy boat named St. Christopher, or on a
clifftop flying a home-made kite together. There are images of
us standing by our father's car, me with my arm around Ian,
protecting him, my little brother. (He had curly blonde hair
when he was small, cute as a button.) These images keep coming, flickering, changing, on through the years, our innocence
gradually being left behind and with it the wonder and sim-
plicity of childhood. Exhanged for something wilder and more
dangerous: real life itself. And real life has taken Ian from us,
as real life does. It takes us all eventually. What can we do?
What's the point? Well, to live until we can live no more. But
above all, to love and be loved in return. And I love my brother
so much. I'll miss him terribly.

Ian carried with him a part of my life, a shared childhood,

memories of distant times. I think it's not overdramatic to say that a part of me has died with him. But, conversely, a part of him lives on with me. I want to recall more of our times together, to share them with readers of this diary, to let them know what a lovely person he was, to help them understand just why I'm so sad and heartbroken about losing him. For today though, perhaps this is enough, a beginning. So many warm tributes have appeared on the Dreamsville website forum for him. He would have been amazed by how much love he'd generated, how respected he was. You left too soon, Ian, too soon.

·

Two weeks and two days have passed since my brother Ian died. Although I frequently note, in these diary entries, how quickly time flies, the last two weeks have gone by at hyper-speed. Life has been a blur, a world in a spin, glimpsed through a watery lens. I'm tempted to say 'dreamlike' but it's been more like a waking nightmare. I am still struggling to grasp the reality of it, to understand just what has happened and why. The 'why' evades me.

Ian's funeral was held on Tuesday the 2nd of May. Exactly one week ago today. Already. I should try to capture a little of that painful event here in my diary, both for posterity and my own failing memory's sake. The funeral service was held in a little church in the village of Walton on the edge of Wakefield (not far from Ian's home), followed by burial at the city cemetery in Wakefield itself. Ian's wife Diane had been a little unsure about Ian's wishes in this regard, whether he would have preferred a cremation or burial. She said that she seemed to recall Ian saying that he'd never felt comfortable with the idea of cremation. I remember that Ian and I, in our distant youth, talked about the subject sometimes. We talked about it in the casual way that young men do when life seems to stretch on infinitely ahead of them and death seems nothing more than a vague, abstract concept. Nevertheless, neither of us were favourably disposed towards cremation and thought that a burial, in pleasant surroundings, would offer more comfort to loved ones and leave some form of an indication to others that we'd existed in this world. So, with all this in mind, Diane decided that Ian would have opted for a burial. My mother and myself felt that this was more appropriate, too. It provided us with some small comfort that there would be a place where we could visit him from time to time, a kind of 'bridge' to his ethereal world, even though he would always be close inside our hearts. This need came as a surprise to me as, in recent years, I'd adopted the attitude that there would be no survival of spirit, soul or essence when life ends, just a slow dissolution of the elements, a scattering of atoms in the void. A poetic, Zen-like emptiness. But of course, religious belief isn't for the departed but for those who are left behind to grieve. Any comfort, no matter how scant, furnishes our consolation. We grasp at any passing detritus the ocean of mortality throws at us, in the hope of staying afloat.

My cousin Ian Boyle travelled all the way from Canterbury to attend the funeral. He stayed here with Emi and I from Sunday through to Wednesday. My brother Ian was actually named in honour of my cousin Ian, who is the youngest of our father's sister's two sons. (Dad and his sister passed away many years ago now.) My brother's middle name, Walter, was also chosen to honour family members. 'Walter' was both my father's name and my father's sister's eldest son's name. Sadly, cousin Walter was away in Venice so couldn't attend my brother's funeral. The passing-on of family forenames seems to extend to me too. I'm named after my father's younger brother, Bill, who was killed in a motorbike accident before I was born. The Nelson family history has many lost chapters. It is shrouded in mists and forgotten memories, as I discovered when I began work on my autobiography a few years ago. Trying to piece together a complete picture is almost impossible. My mother, though originally from the Griffith's side of the family, is the oldest living repository of our family history but, as she admits, she has limited recall of the facts. My autobiography does what it can with what little information is available but a perpetual twilight mist hovers over certain aspects. Perhaps I'll never know the full story.

My two daughters, Julia and Elle, travelled up from their homes in London to attend the funeral. It was the first time that the surviving members of the Nelson clan had all been together in the same place for quite a while, the last time being a Christmas gathering at my home some years ago when cousins Walter and Ian, my mother, my youngest daughter Elle, my son Elliot, brother Ian and Diane, joined Emi and I for a pleasant day of family talk and seasonal celebrations. I can remember my brother Ian's laughter on that day. As usual, his ability to make people feel at ease in his company was clearly evident.

Emiko created the family's funeral flower arrangements. It

was nice to have that personal touch and I think that Ian would have been pleased that Emi took care of his flowers, rather than a stranger treating it as just another job. Emi made a very large arrangement with lilies and roses from Diane, an arrangement spelling out the words 'DAD' in delicate, tiny blue blooms with cream roses from Ian's children, a posy with roses and other flowers from my mum and an alto saxophone constructed from flowers from myself and Emi. I created a short verse to go with the message on the card that accompanied the floral saxophone. The verse part of the message read:

'Go blow your Saxophones of Golden Eternity,
wild and free in The Blue Beyond ...
Go blow your Saxophones Of Golden Eternity,
safe and sound inside our hearts ...'

I felt that it had something of Kerouac and the Beats about it that Ian might have enjoyed. Jack Kerouac shared Ian's sense of the immediate moment being all that mattered.

The days leading up to the funeral were filled with grief and a kind of dread. We all knew that the day of the funeral itself was going to be a grim one, an inescapable confrontation with our loss. I travelled over to Wakefield to see my mother almost every day. Although we were all devastated, we knew that my mother was suffering in a way that only a mother does when she loses her youngest son. Mum is 77-years-old and fighting her own battle with illness. That she should have to face this kind of grief too is so very sad. But my mother is an amazing, beautiful person (and yes, I'm aware that all sons think that of their mothers.) She has borne the weight of so many problems throughout her life, as many mothers do. My father's long illnesses, his confinement to a wheelchair after suffering the amputation of both his legs, her own medical problems, the worrying wayward nature of both her sons, my two failed marriages and their unpleasant side-effects, etc, etc. Through the years she has always cared more about other people's sufferings than her own. She has never complained, never been judgemental. Mum has always been steadily supportive, a perfect example of unconditional love. Her generosity, strength, dignity and compassion are self-evident qualities, recognised by all who know her. And she thinks the world of Diane and Ian's children. And I realised, this last couple of weeks, that they think the world of her, too.

On the morning of the funeral, Elliot and Elle and Julia travelled in Elliot's car whilst my mother, Emi, cousin Ian and I travelled in one of the two funeral cars. Diane and Ian's family led in the other, directly behind the hearse bearing Ian's casket. The emotional moment of the arrival of the hearse at Ian and Diane's house that morning, prior to setting off for the church, is beyond my ability to describe. I'll never forget it. A conformation of everything I'd tried to deny.

The little church was filled to capacity with Ian's friends. As part of the family, the church's front pews were reserved for us and Ian's flower-covered coffin was displayed a couple of feet away from where we sat. Here was the hard reality of it all: my brother, the one person (other than my mother and late father) who had been a stable part of my life for so long, was now about to be laid to rest forever. Sitting there, looking at that polished, crafted, dreadful symbol of finality, I remembered so many things that we'd shared, both as children and as adults. The sadness engulfed me, drowned me, crushed me.

The vicar, whose first name, I believe, was Rupert (somehow

appropriate as Ian and I grew up with *Rupert the Bear* stories) read a few Biblical passages. I could almost hear my brother, a passionately non-religious person, groaning, 'Get *on* with it!' Ian would have favoured an Irish style wake or a New Orleans style musical blast off with Bacchanalian revels and joyous memories. He wasn't really one for morbid melancholia. That curse, it seems, has been left to me.

Then Ian's sister-in-law, Angie, read a tribute to him, after which, as part of the service, some recent recordings of Ian playing saxophone with his friend John were played to the congregation. The music unlocked the floodgates. The grief was unbearable. Everyone wept openly. So poignant and sad.

After the church service, the funeral procession slowly wound its way out of the village and headed towards Wakefield and the cemetery. We travelled in silence and tears. I kept getting glimpses of the hearse ahead of us as it turned this way and that through the blossom filled, tree-lined lanes that had been so familiar to Ian in life. In the car in front of us, Diane, Julian, Louis and Lucy followed Ian on his last ride. I can only begin to imagine how painful it must have been for them, losing a husband and a father so suddenly, and at such a relatively young age. The morning weather had started out reasonably spring-like but, when we arrived at the graveside, the sky had turned a uniform grey and a cold wind animated the priest's vestments as he stood at the head of the grave that had been dug to receive Ian's casket. Ian's family, my mother and myself were beckoned forward to stand at the edge. The coffin was lowered down to rest at the bottom. The grave was much deeper than I'd imagined but I could clearly read Ian's name and the date of his birth and passing on the polished brass plate that was fastened to the lid of his coffin. I really can't begin to describe the emotions and thoughts that flooded me at that moment. Here was my little brother, whose coming into the world had been part of my own life and whose exit from it will haunt me forever.

Ian was born at home, at my parent's ground floor flat, number 28, Conistone Crescent on Eastmoor Estate on the 23rd April 1956. When mum went into labour, the midwife had suggested that my bed would be more comfortable or suitable for Ian's birth than my parent's, so I was moved into my parents bedroom whilst mum occupied mine at the front of the house. (The move was softened by a pile of comic books that my father had bought for me.) As a result, Ian was actually born in my bed, in my bedroom. It was in this same room that we would spend so much time playing with our toys when we were kids. I remember Ian being a big fan of Gerry Anderson's 'Supercar', as was I. My dad bought the family an early domestic tape recorder, a two-tone grey plastic Phillips model with a 'magic-eye' device that flashed whilst recording to show the level of sound. Ian and I recorded little 'plays' on that machine, often re-creating 'Supercar' or 'Stingray' stories. I can still hear his high-pitched young voice saying 'Stand by for action! Anything can happen in the next half-hour!' (A phrase from the opening sequence of 'Stingray.') I wish I still had that recording. Our bedroom was filled with model cars, aeroplanes, trains, toy spaceships, books and games. We shared that room for many years, our theatre of youth, filled with the symbolic contents of our nascent imagination.

And now, here I was, gazing down at all that remained of that life, those far memories, reduced to just a name and two dates etched on a brass plaque. I could feel my mother shaking as she clung to my arm next to me. I was shaking too, an icy combination of the cold wind and the deep emotions we were suffering. It seemed unreal, surreal, film-like. Ironically, Wakefield Cemetery features briefly in one of my favourite films, *This Sporting Life* and Wakefield Trinity rugby football ground, which plays a big part in the film, is close to the cemetery. Richard Harris played the central role in the film, a hard-living, down to earth character. I'm sure Ian would have appreciated this connection and felt it appropriate.

I can remember long-ago visits to Wakefield cemetery when I was very young. Walking trips on Saturday mornings with my mother to place flowers on the grave of my great grandfather, John Henry Griffiths (who died when I was three or four, I think). My great grandmother is buried somewhere in there too and also my father's brother, Bill, mentioned previously in this diary entry. I've been unable to locate their graves in recent years and my mum can't recall exactly where they were buried. I think they had extremely small, modest headstones. Maybe just initials and a date. The area where I seem to remember my great grandfather's grave being located has several such small stones, now heavily worn away by the weather. Impossible to decipher. I'll try to locate them through the cemetery archives later this year, they must have official records of the graves, maybe a plan to help me locate them. I'd like to take flowers to my ancestors. They've been neglected for so long.

My brother Ian's grave is in a newer part of the cemetery, across the quiet road called 'Sugar Lane,' that runs off from the main, busy, Agbrigg Road. Sugar Lane divides the newer cemetery from the older part. The older section is mostly filled with

Victorian and Edwardian graves, some of them marked by grandiose monuments, obelisks and angels. The 'newer' part, opened in 1961, is simpler, without the gothic trappings. Ian rests at the end of a tree-lined walk on the right hand side of the path.

After the burial, everyone went on to the Yorkshire Sculpture Park where a reception had been organised in Ian's honour by his former colleagues, including park director Peter Murray (one of my painting tutors from Wakefield Art School days) and Ian's sister-in-law Angie who has worked there for many years. Ian's children had prepared a slide show of photographs of their dad, taken at different points in his life, which moved everyone deeply and reduced me to tears again. Ian's eldest son Julian, after giving a moving and eloquent speech which impressed everyone there, proposed a toast to his dad. Ian would have been so proud of his children.

I had the opportunity to speak with many of Ian's friends including members of Bolt From The Blue, the band that I'd enjoyed playing a few gigs with back in the late 1980s (or very early 1990s). Ian had been a member of the band, as had an old art school friend of mine from the 1960s, drummer Martin Foye. (Martin sadly passed away in the 1990s, another one gone too young.) Bolt From The Blue had been very kind to me, back then. At the time of those gigs I'd been struggling to survive. My problems with business management and the music industry were at their peak and I had virtually no income at all. My life was filled with stress and fear. It was suggested that, if I performed a handful of gigs with them in local pubs, I could make a little money to help me out of some of the financial mess I was in, or at least pay an outstanding bill or two. I hadn't played live for quite a while and was understandably nervous about performing, but I ended up having fun. The first performance I gave with them was in Wakefield at a pub called The Post Haste. I recall playing covers of Van Morrison's *Dweller On The Threshold* and Muddy Water's *Got My Mojo Working*. The local *Wakefield Express* newspaper kindly wrote a generous review of the show. We even travelled to Manchester, if I remember rightly, to do a gig in a pub there. It was an enforced return to my roots, a reminder of what it was all about. The generosity and care that Ian and the rest of the band showed me has never been forgotten, so it was good to meet up with some of the original members again at the sculpture park last week, despite the terrible circumstances.

Amongst many other people attending the reception were musicians who had been part of my Lost Satellites band: Dave Standeven, Steven Cook and my long-time friend, Jon Wallinger. They all have fond memories of Ian from the 'Be Bop Deluxe And Beyond' 30 year anniversary tour that we undertook in 2004, and from the annual Nelsonica fan conventions. As they're much valued friends of mine, it was extremely supportive for me to see them there. Two more very dear friends were also present to honour Ian: John Spence who had worked with Ian in various musical situations over the years and Paul Gilby who had worked alongside the Lost Satellites on the 2004 tour. It was so comforting to have all these familiar faces close by at such a difficult time and everyone recalled their experiences of Ian generously.

Another warm and welcome gesture was the presence of several loyal fans and regular members of the 'Dreamsville' on-line community. Everyone was extremely kind and I was touched by their considerate and compassionate concern. At the end of the afternoon people began to drift away. In a manner that Ian would have approved of, I was feeling somewhat woozy from the wine that had been served up by the park's staff. I was hoping it would act as a kind of anaesthetic but it simply heightened the unreality of it all. Paul and Elliot provided transport to get Mum, her husband George, Julia, Emi and I back to our cars which had been left at Ian and Diane's house that morning. We then collected my grandson Luke from his grandmother's house (my first wife, Shirley). Once Luke was on board, Julia, Luke, Elle ,Elliot, Emi, Mum, George, my cousin Ian and my friend Paul Gilby, drove out to Heath Common, another old village on the edge of Wakefield. We all went to The Kings Arms pub, a place that still has gaslight and stone-flagged floors. I used to go there as an art student in my teens and have also visited it several times with my brother in the past. After the day's stresses and strains it was therapeutic to sit and eat and drink together in this old haunt with its history, both local and personal. My little grandson Luke, with his positive, wide-eyed wonder, inspired a smile for us amidst the sad recollections. I too, inadvertently provided some humour by accidentally setting my hair on fire whilst standing beneath one of the pub's wall-mounted gas mantles. The first we knew of it was when we smelled something burning. Then the top of my head felt very hot. I managed to move away from the gas light just in time. I could almost hear my brother Ian laughing at my folly.

That evening I sat up with Cousin Ian, talking about this and that. He's a lovely guy, good company, intelligent and knowledgeable (as is my other cousin, Walter). The next morning, Cousin Ian set off on the long drive back to Canterbury. We plan to get together again before too long. I went back to the cemetery last Friday with my mother. It was a warm, sunny spring day, a clear blue sky overhead, the trees leading to Ian's grave heavy with pink blossom. Such a contrast to the day of the funeral and so much new-life and fecundity evident in the immediate environment.

By coincidence, Diane had also chosen to re-visit the spot at exactly the same time. As mum and I arrived, Diane was just helping her mother and father from her car. Diane's mum and dad are lovely people and it's plain that they both were very fond of my brother. I was conscious that we might be intruding on their privacy but my mother said not to worry and we joined them at Ian's grave. Emi's flowers were still in place though the more delicate ones had either become wilted or blown away with the winds and occasional rain of the previous day. The floral saxophone, magically, seemed reasonably intact. I fetched water to nourish the remaining flowers in the hope of keeping them going a short while longer.

After a while, when Diane and her parents had left, Mum and I walked around the older side of the cemetery, looking at the old gravestones in the hope of maybe locating John Henry Griffiths. He was, in the 1920s and early 1930s, a lamplighter, going around the Wakefield streets at twilight, lighting the gas lamps, then going around again at dawn, putting them out and knocking on people's windows with his lamplighter's pole to wake them up to go to work in the local textile mills. My mother tells me that she sometimes accompanied him in the evenings when she was a young child. She has told me of walk-ing the rainy cobbled streets with him and watching the gas mantles burst into light as he switched them on, one by one. A poetic and beautiful image. However, his resting place still eludes us.

After dropping mum off at her home, I bought a copy of the *Wakefield Express* as I'd been told that there was an article in it about Ian's passing. Ironically, in another part of the newspaper (as I was later informed), there was a photograph of myself, printed as part of an article about a local radio station that was apparently planning to broadcast my instrumental recording *Radiant Spires*. How I wish that the only announcement in the paper could have been about Ian and myself performing somewhere together, as we'd done at the Wakefield Arts Festival at the end of the 1990s, instead of the sad news that Friday's *Express* carried. That we won't be able to share a stage again in that way is an extra blow for me, something that will hurt every time I perform solo from now on.

Since the funeral, there's been an attempt by us all at some kind of adjustment, an attempt to come to terms with things. Not at all easy. Impossible, right now. I travelled to London on Saturday to attend the London Guitar Show at Wembley Exhibition Centre where I'd promised to appear on the Campbell American Guitar stand. I picked up the prototype of the signature model and brought it back home, along with an intense blue 'Precix' model that has a vibrato arm fitted. It was actually the first time I'd met Dean 'in the flesh', (despite many emails and phone conversations) and I was made to feel very welcome by him. He's a warm, genuine, lovely guy and couldn't have been kinder to me. His care helped ease what was going on behind my smile and he, plus his colleague Dan, plus Music Ground's Rick Harrison (who travelled down on the train and back with Emi and I) helped me through what might otherwise have been a difficult day.

And so here I am, one week after the funeral, still in a dark cloud despite all attempts at moving on. Too soon, of course, but I have to try to pick up my workload again. The song *Steam Radio Blues* that I was working on just over two weeks ago needs to be finished. It's just a matter of the mix really. But then I have to write and record more songs for the 'jazzy' album. I realise that it will be impossible not to write something about this recent tragedy and sadness. In fact, it may be a way forward for me, an attempt to exorcise some of the pain. I also hope to make a special tribute album for Ian later in the year, something that might directly benefit Ian's family. I have some ideas regarding this that I need to work on, but will announce more about it when things begin to fall into place.

Meanwhile, the sun shines outside my window; the swallows have arrived from Africa and swoop around the rooftops of the house. A cuckoo can be heard in the distant yellow meadow and fat bumble bees buzz amongst the flowers by our front door, oblivious to human suffering. Next month, Emi and I will fly to Tokyo for two weeks to visit Emi's mum and two brothers. And the work of making music will continue. Life goes on, though much more tenderly and tearfully than before.

Finally, I'd like to thank all those good people, family, friends and fans, whose words and deeds have brought a measure of comfort and kindness to what has been an extremely difficult time. Everyone's life is a work of art and everyone's life is precious. Heartfelt love to all.

·

It's now just over a month since Ian passed away. I'd like to think that I've begun to accept the situation and am coping reasonably well but the truth is a little different. There's an underlying depression at work here, dark and muted but insistent, insidious. So, how does one deal with bereavement of this kind? What's the precise formula? I presume that there isn't one. It just takes time. Maybe several years. I'm still in shock. Was else can I say? I'm doing my best?

I've immersed myself in work this last week or so. Concentrating on the *Return To Jazz Of Lights* album. The hard work doesn't remove the sadness but at least temporarily distracts me from it. It has to be said that some of the more melancholy pieces on the album, even though they were written before the events of 23rd of April, seem remarkably apt with hindsight. There are several poignant, prescient moments. This album has been an unexpected struggle, perhaps even more so than *The Alchemical Adventures Of Sailor Bill*. Maybe it doesn't have *Sailor Bill*'s sense of absolute completeness or maybe I personally don't have a sense of completeness right now. The whole album seems to comprise one big fragmented statement and could be judged tenderly flawed, though for special reasons. Its subtle imperfections may be interpreted by some listeners as seductive come-ons (well, I *do* hope it slides the pants off you).

So, yes, it's another personal, unique thing, sentimental but with a dash more irony than *Sailor Bill*. It has a bizarre mix of inspirations and influences, containing elements of jazz, big band swing, jive, lounge, electronica, easy listening and Vegas show music, shot through with what, I guess, an objective ear might describe as archetypal Bill Nelson 'whimsicality.' It's somewhere to the left of post-modern; not easy to describe in precise terms at all. The truth is, I don't really know what to make of it. But it's finished, as of this last, exhausting hour. I've decided upon the final song selection and running order and now have to arrange time at Fairview to master the damn thing. It's gone through several mutations. It started life as a throwaway side-project, a light-hearted six song ep or mini-album, everything recorded quickly, something that I hoped might be reasonably painless to put together. But, despite those modest intentions, over the last few months it has taken on a peculiar life of its own and I've had no choice but to follow wherever it led.

The project grew from six tracks to 10. Then to 12 and now, this week, to 15. (Although I've recorded 18 songs for it in total.) Listening back to the 15 track version last night, I decided it was too long and have spent all of today re-working the running order to get it back to a more easily digested 12 track album. I think this latest 12 song version works better. The six songs left over from my final selection will be moved to the list of possibilities for this year's forthcoming Nelsonica fan convention CD. In that respect, the project has gone down almost the same path as *Sailor Bill*. Last year's Nelsonica CD, *Orpheus In Ultraland,* provided a home for tracks that didn't make it onto the *Sailor Bill* project. Ironically, people snapped that one up faster than the *Sailor Bill* album.

There will be a few more tracks to add to the convention album, including the song that proved very popular on last year's concert tour, *Snow Is Falling*. (But how that will fit with the above 'jazzy' stylings is another mystery.) So, for the moment, that is *all* the music I have to offer, other than the completed though not yet mastered *Neptune's Galaxy* album.

As usual, there are other concepts percolating in the coffee shop of dreams but I'm feeling genuinely tired right now and need a break. Perhaps the trip to Tokyo in June will give me a breather of some kind, though it won't be particularly relaxing. To be honest, I'm not looking forward to the journey at all. I don't enjoy flying, especially long-haul flights to Japan that involve several hour's stop-over, awaiting connections at some European airport or other (in this case, Amsterdam) but cheap tickets require one to endure such tedium. I'll take my camcorder, still camera and small sketchbook/watercolour set with me. Perhaps there may be a moment's grace during our Tokyo stay when I can capture the tranquillity of a Zen temple garden amidst the city's hustle and bustle. I fear there will hardly be time to relax though, as Emi needs to hook up with long-missed family and friends. It will be a very busy schedule, once we arrive.

I bought a book dealing with aspects of the history of Wakefield yesterday. In it there is a section dealing with the history of Wakefield's 'yards'. Amazingly, there is mention of Marriot's Yard, around which Marriot's Buildings were located. (I've searched for years to find reference to this personally important location.) Marriot's Buildings was where my grandmother lived and where I was born. (Now long since demolished.) The book quotes from an ancient report written by a medical official in the 1800s. He comments on the unsanitary conditions of the housing there and briefly describes the setting. When I was born there, in 1948, Marriot's Buildings and its yard had not changed at all from those dark Victorian times.

There was still no hot water, no electricity and only a communal outside privy with newspaper for toilet paper. An old tin bath for the once-a-week bath night and a stone floor that would later, briefly, receive the 'luxury' of linoleum. Unbelievable.

Nevertheless, I remember the place with clarity and great fondness. As I've often mentioned in these diary pages, my autobiography contains elaborate descriptions of that dwelling, exactly as it was when I was a very young infant, not yet able to walk but definitely able to retain strong visual impressions of my surroundings, albeit from ground level. How I wish I could trace some photographs of the building as it was around the time of my birth. Or at *any* time before its demise.

My old pal John Spence called me last night. We spoke for quite a while, talking about my brother (and life and its struggles in general). John has come to play an important part in my life over the years, not just because of his talents in the realm of studio engineering, but because of his understanding of me as a human being. I value his friendship tremendously and feel privileged to know him.

I'm still receiving kind messages of sympathy from various people. So many that it is proving difficult to answer every single one of them, although I'm still attempting to. I've certainly felt the spiritual embrace of many good hearted people these last few weeks. A lot of love has come my way and I'm very grateful. I've been reading some Buddhist texts before sleeping. In the mornings I've watched the clouds passing overhead, glimpsed through the bathroom skylight as I lie in the bath. I've also watched the recent torrential rain hitting the vast pool of water in our garden, making rippling circles of light on the driveway. Our garden and drive doesn't drain and becomes a virtual lake when the weather turns wet. One of dozens of flaws that this place has. It needs lots of money spending on it at the moment, but things are tight and it will have to wait.

I live in a perpetual state of 'make-do' and that includes the recording of my music. It's a never-ending compromise. But, isn't everything? I've been playing the first prototype of my Campbell American 'Transitone' signature guitar and have refined my initial ideas for the instrument's development which I'll be passing on to the Campbell company soon. It is, unsurprisingly, a very unique instrument and will become even more so as its development continues. Meeting Dean Campbell at the London Guitar Show a week or two ago was a real pleasure. I actually saw Bert Weedon there too, though just from the back as he walked the show's corridors with (I presume) his wife. He looked very frail. His *Play In A Day* book was purchased for me by my father when I got my first guitar. I did absorb the info in the tutor book about which way up to hold the instrument and how to attach the strap but, beyond that it was a mystery to me and remains so to this day. I have fond memories of Bert on *Five-O'Clock Club* on television in the late 1950s and 1960s. He used to have very thick, crinkly, shiny hair in those days. It's very white, faint and wispy now.

Well, nothing much more to add at this point in time. Whatever else I've got to say would only come across as even more melancholy than usual and I'm trying to fight such a temptation right now. Oh, I saw a film called *Northfork* on television the other week. It was marvellous, magical. A young boy goes to heaven in a silver Dakota aeroplane as a small American town vanishes beneath a man-made flood to make way for a new dam and its attendant lake. The film is filled with poetic and surreal images that sing from the screen.

Now that the new album's running order is decided, I may try to relax and watch an old Bing Crosby film tonight. Either, *Birth Of The Blues* or *Blue Skies*. My Mother and Father loved Bing when I was a little kid so I've sort of grown up with that kind of music and gentle sentiment. I also love the 'Road' movies with Bing and Bob Hope together. Happy, inconsequential nonsense. If only life could be that way.

·

MONDAY 5TH JUNE 2006

Spent most of today at Fairview studios with John Spence. We mastered my two newest albums in preparation for their manufacture. I'm hoping to release *Neptune's Galaxy* in July, although this has yet to be confirmed. *Return To Jazz Of Lights* will be held over until autumn. It's a relief to know that the musical and technical aspects of these two projects are finally complete. All that remains for me to do is work with David Graham on the tidying up of each album's packaging art. John was kind enough to comment on the quality of the recordings as he mastered each album. He's always positive and supportive and understands that, recording alone as I do, encouragement and appreciation of my work is very much needed. Sometimes I feel as if I'm working in a vacuum and that only a small number of people grasp the implications of the music I make. But that's partly a result of ploughing an individual furrow, or because I wilfully ignore pressures to either conform to my own past or to someone else's present. Occasionally it's tough but it's absolutely the correct way forward.

Ultimately, I have no regrets or qualms about any of the difficulties that this approach throws up. I follow where the muse leads and damn the consequences. Is this why the character of Orpheus has always fascinated me? Or Don Quixote?

My trip to Japan soon, very soon. In fact just over a week away. I have to start packing clothes. I'll probably take too much, as usual. (I find it impossible to travel light.) Like Don Quixote, I need my armour. I'm not looking forward to the flight. I don't enjoy flying at all; hate it, actually, so I'm now wondering whether I should have stuck to my original plan of staying at home. But, if I'd done that, I'd have been terribly lonely without Emiko and not taken care of myself properly. I'm hopeless at self-sufficiency, at least in real world terms. In creative terms, I'm the captain of my own ship, but that seaworthiness limits itself to the world of art and music. Elsewhere, I'm a fish out of water. Emiko has become my life support system as well as my wife, lover and friend. So, off to Tokyo I go! Actually, it will be good to see my mother-in-law and my two brother's-in-law. Plus my old friend Nick and his wife, Yoko. And there's bound to be a guitar adventure or two.

We're staying at an inexpensive business hotel in the Shibuya district of Tokyo. When I say 'inexpensive' I mean inexpensive by Tokyo standards. It's still a largish chunk of cash for Emi and I, even though it will be a room the size of a broom cupboard. At least I know the surrounding area like the back of my hand and will be able to find my way around. Shibuya is quite lively and we'll only need the cupboard for sleeping. We're planning a trip out to Kamakura and the Gretsch guitar company have invited me to visit their factóry which is about two hours out of Tokyo by train. (In Nagoya, I think.)

When I return, a long list of work projects awaits my attention — the EMI box set's live recordings need mixing. I also have a long list of Nelsonica 06 tasks to work my way through. (The annual conventions get more and more elaborate, partly my own fault for trying to raise the bar each year.) Then I have to seriously get down to business with the film I must make for next spring's contemporary music festival at Leeds University. Such a lot of work needed for that. I made a sort of start last week when I paid a visit to Wakefield Museum to talk about the possibility of accessing their archives for info and still photographs. The film is intended to be a poetic, autobiographical exploration of memory. Its working title is *Ghosts Etched On Glass*.

I've also discovered two film archives, one in London, one in York, that may be able to supply me with some historical footage that I'd like to weave into the film. At a price though, from what I can tell. When I get back from Japan, I have to make an appointment to see the curators of Wakefield Museum and also of the two film archives. Just researching this project will take time, before I even begin to deal with its creative practicalities. Nevertheless, I have an outline vision of how this thing should develop and I'm prepared for it to be a long and ongoing process. Its initial showings will be as a 'work in progress' rather than a completed film.

I've been speaking to Dean Campbell about my Transitone signature guitar. I gave him a list of my thoughts after working with the prototype model. The prototype plays extremely well but Dean tells me that the finished model will be even better.

He seems to think that he can accommodate the majority of things I've suggested. Looking forward to seeing the finished item!

Emi and I went to Whitby yesterday. It took ages to get there as a section of the road over the North Yorkshire Moors had been closed by the police due to an accident that apparently killed a biker. A large, yellow, air-sea rescue helicopter was brought in. It landed, just ahead of us, on the road at the site of the crash. After an extensive wait, the police directed us towards an alternative route, a long way round but picturesque. We eventually got to Whitby, only just in time for lunch at The White Horse And Griffin. But I couldn't stop thinking about the biker and how his family's life had been changed in the instant of that accident. After lunch, we walked out on the harbour walls to the very end, where the two small stone, lighthouses stand. The sea and sky blurred into one another, a smear of pastel pink and hazy blue, small white-sailed yachts floating in the early summer Sunday luminescence, big blue sky arcing overhead. It was blissful, transcendent. And I hadn't brought my camera.

Then, on our way home, we stopped off at Robin Hood's Bay and marvelled at the view from the top of the hill that leads down to the old village. Again, absolutely sublime, so magnificently beautiful, the cliffs of the far coastline framing the bay, the sea stretching out to horizon. I turned to Emi and said, "This is what makes life worth living. A place like this and someone to share it with." Emi said, "That's the important thing, someone to share it with." We both treasure the times we can get out into the Yorkshire countryside together.

No surprise to us that North Yorkshire has just been voted

the most beautiful county in the whole of England. I'm intimately connected to this particular landscape. My heart beats in it.

Visited my brother's grave last week with my Mother and Emi. We laid flowers. I need to speak with Diane about our plan to raise a headstone for Ian. I must call her before I leave for Japan. For now, that's all I can write. Tired. I'll try to write another diary entry before my trip to Japan.

Oh, still reading Lindsay Anderson's diaries and have four new books to take to Tokyo with me. (Or one if I can make up my mind which one to read first.) They are: *The Necropolis Railway* by Andrew Martin, (author of *The Blackpool High-flyer*), *The Mysterious Flame Of Queen Loana* by Umberto Eco. *Attention All Shipping* by Charlie Connelly and *Strange Angel* by George Pendle. But right now, I'm going to sit downstairs with my wife and eat strawberries and ice cream.

.

MONDAY 12TH JUNE 2006

Only two and a half days until the start of my trip to Japan and I'm feeling unwell. Last Thursday, I awoke in the middle of the night with an excruciatingly sore throat, really painful. This continued for three days before easing off a little but has been replaced by a flu-like lethargy and clamminess. My chest is a bit tight too, irritated but not a fully blown cough. It feels virus-like but is sort of veiled, fogged over. Maybe my system is trying to fight it off or maybe it hasn't yet fully developed. Whatever it is, it's come at a bad time as I have had so much to prepare before we leave for Tokyo. I've been taking my usual daily multi-vitamins and have supplemented these with Echinacea which is reputed to boost one's immune system. I just hope that I can shake this thing off before Thursday. All those hours cooped up in an aeroplane won't help matters at all.

I've put a few things in place before we leave. Album artwork for *Neptune's Galaxy* and *Return To Jazz Of Lights* has now been fully completed and signed off. I need to speak to Paul (Gilby) before leaving to let him know that *Neptune* is all ready to go to the pressing plant. *Jazz* can go a little later, once *Neptune* has been available for a while. I've also made an image for the central 'logo' of Nelsonica 06. It's a fairly free-handed drawing of a satyr-like creature with ram's horns and goatee. I've framed the original. Not sure if I should keep it for myself or offer it for auction at Nelsonica.

Further refinements to my Campbell Transitone signature model guitar and another drawing sent off to Dean. Maybe there will be something solid for me to look at when I get back from Tokyo.

I've packed everything, suitcase-wise, now. Just a few final toiletries to cram in on the morning of our departure. I had second thoughts about some of the clothes I'd packed and did a bit of a swap around. A token attempt to cut back on the bulk. I think I've got fractionally less in there now but it still feels damn heavy. Emi's case is smaller. (But then she's a lot smaller than me anyway. Her clothes take up less room, even when the quantity is the same as mine.) Have also packed my carry-on bag. I need to charge my camcorder batteries before packing that though. All that boring waiting around at Amsterdam Airport will give me plenty of time to wander about the concourse with video and still cameras. See if I can come up with images that could be used in future creative projects. I have two pairs of trousers to collect from the alterations shop this afternoon. Damn! Does this mean I'll have to find space in my case for them? Probably. Have been trying to catch up with emails again but with only partial success. People must think that I don't care to respond but I'm actually full of good intentions to do so. It's just that my life is so full of distractions. One has only to look at my creative output to understand that.

Went over to Wakefield to visit my sister-in-law Diane last week. Life has hit her hard again. Her mother has just passed away, only six weeks after she lost her husband. I couldn't believe it or come up with anything to say that would have been of any solace. I just felt absolutely inadequate. It's mind-numbingly sad. Her mother was buried at the weekend in a plot directly behind Ian's. Diane's mum and he were actually very fond of each other, not at all the clichéd comedy relationship of 'mothers-in-law' perpetuated by the likes of Les Dawson. I'd last seen Diane's mum two days after Ian's funeral. I'd gone with my mother to visit Ian's grave and, by coincidence, Diane and her mum and dad had also chosen to visit the cemetery at the same time. Diane's mum was in a wheelchair and she'd shed a tear at Ian's graveside. She spoke warmly of him. My generation has reached an age when the harshness of mortality is brought home to us on a fairly regular basis. Knowing that doesn't make it any easier to accept though. Diane told me that she missed Ian even more at this sad time. He would have been a pillar of strength for her in such a situation. After years of marriage, he understood her emotional responses more than anyone and knew exactly how to steer Diane away from too much despair.

Other, less depressing news: Emi and I took my son Elliot

out for a meal last week. A local tapas place. We sat on the roof terrace surrounded by sun-tanned girls in skimpy vests. A bit of a cleavage exhibition. Of course, I'm far too old and decrepit to notice such things (but Emi sometimes points them out to me — she knows I'm an art lover). Got an email from my daughter Elle in London. She's picking up some work designing websites at the moment.

The plan to license my *Getting The Holy Ghost Across / On A Blue Wing* album from Sony is going ahead. It's ironic that I have to pay them an advance and a royalty share as part of the deal for them to give me permission to re-issue the album on my own label. But that's what happens when you dance with the galloping majors. I just hope that enough people want to buy it to warrant me paying out so much to Sony. Still, it will be the first time its officially been available on CD.

I really want to start work on *Romance Of Sustain* volume two. I have several unreleased guitar compositions that I've been performing live over these last two or three years. They should be put onto an album. I still need to dub the lead guitar parts onto the backing tracks, though, and mix them carefully. It shouldn't be too difficult a process as most of the 'writing' is done and the basic recording too. (Nevertheless, I'd like to write at least a couple of brand new pieces for the project.) I'm thinking of calling this album, *The Last Of The Gentleman Rocketeers*. (Or perhaps have one of the instrumentals called that.)

But, before I can even contemplate starting on the project, I have to mix the ancient Be Bop Deluxe live recordings for EMI Records' forthcoming box set. And begin work on my *Ghosts Etched On Glass* film. Plenty to do.

Now I have to attempt to weigh our suitcases. Emi called

from work just now to say that she'd heard that new airline regulations restrict the weight of individual cases, rather than the collective weight of the total. If this is so, there may be a last minute frenzy of re-packing to distribute the tonnage between both our cases. As if the trip to Japan wasn't difficult enough already. I do get so stressed out by travel these days. I'll try to take a notebook to Tokyo to jot down some day to day happenings so that I can write them up in this diary when I return.

•

THURSDAY 29TH JUNE 2006

Returned from our trip to Tokyo last night. A long journey and a busy, exhausting time in Japan. Far too fraught and intense to be called a holiday but we were not really expecting it to be anything other.

I'm feeling jet-lagged and sleepy but Emiko went to work at the flower shop this morning so she's had a much tougher day than me. I spent the day unpacking suitcases and gifts for friends and family and then headed off to town and later to the supermarket to stock up on food and other essentials. It now feels as if we've not been away at all but while we were in Tokyo it felt like we'd been there for at least a month, so much activity did we cram in to our stay. There's too much to tell in a single diary entry and I'm too tired to tell it all in one attempt anyway, so I'll spread it out via two or three entries over the next few days.

I returned to find dozens of emails and Dreamsville Forum private messages awaiting my attention. And a pile of posted mail in the letterbox. (Various bills, unfortunately.) I will only be able to deal with the most pressing correspondence as there is a long list of work-related projects to catch up with. My list of 'things to do' seems to have doubled since I've been away. The most recent of these is the task of photographing my musical instrument collection for a Japanese magazine called *Player*. This magazine, one of the largest musicians' magazines in Japan, interviewed me whilst I was in Tokyo for a six page feature which will appear in an autumn issue. They arranged a two hour photo session along with the actual interview. Emi acted as translator. It was the first time I'd been in a proper photographer's studio for several years and I wasn't really looking forward to it (nor was I 'sartorially prepared') but, as it turned out, it was reasonably painless. The most difficult part of the *Player* magazine feature is the photographing of my musical instrument collection.

The editor wants me to take individual photos of every guitar, mandolin, banjo, ukulele, keyboard, amplifier etc, etc, that I own. The magazine also wants a list of all the serial numbers of the instruments (a typically Japanese thing, detail being everything) and would also like photos of my recording room from various angles. The individual items must each be photographed against a plain background, keeping the proportions identical. As there are no plain backgrounds in our house (due to shelves of books, ceramics, paintings, prints, etc) I'll need to go out and buy a roll of plain coloured cloth to pin and drape from the house's ceiling beams to provide a suitable backdrop to photograph the instruments against. Once the photographs are taken, I have to get them burned to a CD to post to Japan, and they must have them by July 10th if the feature is to meet their autumn schedule/deadline. It looks as if I'll have to make a start very soon as it will take at least a couple of days to photograph everything, if not longer. On the positive side, it will provide an opportunity for me to catalogue my collection and will also double up as source material for the Dreamsville site's 'Guitar Arcade.'

As my computer doesn't have a disc burner, I'll have to enlist the help of a more technically articulate friend to get the pics stored to disc for posting to Japan. I desperately need a more up-to-date Mac but can't afford it at the moment as there are so many other, more pressing, domestic problems around the house. Both Emi's car and mine are in need of repair too and I've just booked them in for servicing, repairs and MOT examinations. They have to go in to the garage next week, one at a time so that we're not without transport.

Of course, the Tokyo trip has been mind-numbingly expensive. Despite talk of the Japanese economy being less strong these days, we were horrified by how much things still cost. A small glass of fresh orange juice, an iced-tea and an iced-coffee at the hotel cafe came to just over £15. A two-hour trip from Tokyo to Nagoya to visit the Terada guitar factory cost us £100 each. A similar length trip from here to London and back can be had for around £30 each, so we were shocked by the quite dramatic difference

Nevertheless, the Japanese Shinkansen is a superb way to travel and makes our British rail system seem antiquated and slow. The trains in Japan are marvels of engineering, clean, fast, smooth and silent. I was seriously impressed. I was also tremendously impressed by my visit to the Terada guitar factory, a family business begun back in 1915. I was expecting something very high tech and modern but it's a very old-fashioned set up and labour intensive. This factory is number one in Japan for building artchtop guitars. They build for Gretsch, D'Angelico, D'Aquisto, Sadowsky and some other makes. The quality and attention to detail is remarkable. I took some camcorder footage of the craftsmen at work which I'll try to assemble into a little video documentary—a souvenir of my Japan trip to show at this year's Nelsonica convention in October (another addition to the day's events. It's going to be a jam-packed convention this year).

Tomorrow I have to hunt for plain fabric for those magazine guitar photograph backgrounds so I'll keep this diary entry brief. But much more to follow over the next few days. Stay tuned.

·

FRIDAY 30TH JUNE 2006

Perhaps I should start at the beginning of my recent trip to Japan, see if I can recall all the relevant details. It seems to have already become a distant blur but this may partly be due to my jet-lag and low energy level.

As noted in my diary entry of 12th June, I wasn't feeling well two days prior to leaving. This was due to a virus I'd picked up and, in fact, I was feeling even worse the night before we were due to leave (so much so that I seriously considered not going at one point). I couldn't imagine how I could endure the long journey. I'd been dosing myself with all the usual remedies but to little avail. I felt weak and decidedly virus-stricken. Nevertheless, I decided to pack as much 'medicine' as I could, Night Nurse tablets, vitamins, sore throat tablets, pain killers, etc, etc (my carry-on bag resembled a mobile pharmacist's shop) and made the effort to get myself half-way around the world to Japan, for Emi's sake, if nothing else.

I hardly slept the night before the flight, a combination of anxiety and sickness. Our friends Steve and Julia had generously offered to drive us to the airport but we still needed to be up early to get there two hours ahead of our scheduled take-off time. When we got up at the crack of dawn, I was in grumpy old man mood from lack of sleep. My mood didn't improve when we arrived at the airport to find that the airline had seated Emi and I in totally separate parts of the aeroplane, on both legs of the journey (we were flying first to Amsterdam's Schipol airport, then transferring to another flight to travel to Tokyo). On top of this, due to new cabin baggage restrictions, one of our carry-on bags was deemed too heavy so some items had to be taken out. During this messing about, my electric razor fell on to the floor and broke. Time for a beard development fortnight, I thought. Eventually we made it through to the departure lounge and grabbed a light breakfast from the cafe before boarding the plane to Amsterdam. Luckily, we were able to wangle two seats together which cheered me up a little.

The trip to Amsterdam was short, around 55 minutes actual flight time, but we then had a long wait in the transit zone of Schipol Airport before boarding our Boeing 777 for the connecting flight to Tokyo. We passed some of the time sitting in one of the airport's many cafe bars. I nursed a glass of red wine which, in turn, nursed me. By the time we boarded the aeroplane, I was feeling pleasantly, er, shall we just say 'vague?'

Once again, we negotiated to obtain seats sitting next to each other and finally succeeded, though it was in a row of three. As it happened, our third party companion spoke nary a word throughout the 12 hour flight.

After taking off, I had my customary Bloody Mary cocktail, something that I only ever seem to drink whilst on long-haul flights. It's a habit going back to the days of Be Bop Deluxe touring America in the 1970s. Anyway, it did the trick and my virus-stricken discomfort was slowly buried under a rapidly increasing alcoholic haze.

I looked through the list of movies available on the in-flight entertainment centre, a surprisingly large selection covering several tastes. Of course, each seat has its own integral video screen nowadays and each occupant their own individual selection of films and entertainment but I can recall when things were somewhat different. On those long-ago Be Bop Deluxe US tours of the mid 1970s there was just one solitary screen at the head of each section of cabin and an equally solitary RGB projector suspended from the cabin's roof. As far as having a choice of films goes, there simply was no choice at all, passengers just watched whatever was selected by the air-line. Usually, there was a main feature plus a supporting one. (A bit like the old, early-1960s days of British cinema minus the ice-cream lady, the cinema organist and the agonisingly slow attempt to slide your hand beneath your new girlfriend's angora sweater, then under her bra. Oh, what sweet joy when the target of one's lust was reached.) But even those 1970s Be Bop American tour long-haul single screen flights seemed high-tech to us back then.

I can recall an incident when Charlie Tumahai, a little 'worse for wear', decided to start up a running commentary on the film being shown. He did this in a loud, pantomime 'Aussie' style accent, shouting out perceptive phrases such as 'He's behind ya, yer dim-brained bastard!!' and 'I'd shag the arse off that Sheila, mate!" He was always ready with a sophisticated turn of phrase.

When the cabin staff asked him to stop spoiling the film for the other passengers, he sulked for a couple of minutes before coming up with the idea of using his hands to cast shadow puppet images onto the screen. These hand shadows, representing birds, elephants, foxes, etc, interacted amusingly with the various characters in the film, although the other passengers seemed to think otherwise for some reason. Eventually, cabin staff and the rest of Be Bop Deluxe had to persuade Charlie to cease and desist. It wasn't easy to get him to stop but eventually, with the aid of a trip to the toilet for him to smoke a clandestine 'jazz woodbine', he'd settle down and eventually drift off to sleep for the remainder of the trip. A right card was our Charlie. I still miss him.

Back to the 21st century and our KLM flight to Tokyo. I decided to watch the recent re-make of *King Kong* which was listed on the in-flight movie menu. I hadn't gone to the cinema to see it when it was released (last year?) as I'd always been fond of the black and white original with Fay Wray, and didn't feel that a new version would add anything to that. However, after watching the first 15 minutes or so, I was sufficiently impressed to decide to rent it out on video when I returned to the UK and view it on a larger screen, rather than watch it on the tiny one built into the seat on the aeroplane. So I stopped the playback and selected *Wallace And Gromit And The Curse Of The*

Were-Rabbit instead. Well, in the absence of *Meshes Of The Afternoon* or *The Testament Of Orpheus*' what did you expect? After an amusing chuckle at the wayward adventures of the much celebrated animated plasticised man and his dog, I settled down to read *The Necropolis Railway* by Andrew Martin which turned out to be not too bad at all. (Now there's a riveting, perceptive review-cum-advertising quote for you, "Not too bad at all" – Bill Nelson, KLM Airlines. The author skilfully evokes a vivid picture of the sooty, grim, steam-driven London of the early 20th Century. The fact that the central character hails from Robin Hood's Bay, just outside Whitby, is an extra bonus for me. At this point in time, I'm just over half-way through the book, having found little time to read whilst in Tokyo, but I've been gently entertained by the story so far. Perhaps Mr. Martin and myself have some interests in common.

The flight to Japan seemed endless. I slept fitfully, sporadically. Actually, it wasn't sleeping at all, just a semi-unconscious state, the Boeing's engines droning like a million bees in a metal hive, a constantly humming background to the half-stupor I found myself in. The in-flight meals were slight and inconsequential but the little bottles of wine that came with them found whatever edge I had left and hammered, then smoothed it into a rusty bluntness.

After what felt like an eternity, we landed at Tokyo's Narita Airport. Emiko, because she is still a Japanese passport holder, was able to go through passport control/ immigration like a knife through butter. Myself, being a foreigner (or 'Gaijin') went through it like a feather through stone. I joined the back of a long, long line of non-Japanese and awaited my turn to be given entry to the country. After such a long flight, this long wait proved difficult. I felt dizzy and exhausted but eventually I reached the head of the line and presented my passport to the immigration officer. After a few moments of checking on his computer screen to make sure that I wasn't on any list of known terrorists, football hooligans, drug smugglers or people who cross the road whilst the little walking-man signal is still on red, I was waved through to the baggage reclaim area where Emi was waiting patiently for me.

But our journey was not yet over. We now had to haul our luggage onto the Airport Limousine. This vehicle is actually not nearly as glamourous as it sounds. The 'limousine' is nothing more than a plain old bus that ferries passengers from Narita airport into Tokyo. We bought our tickets and climbed on board and found two seats at the back, settling down for the two-hour drive into Tokyo itself. Not exactly Tokyo airport at all, really, as Tokyo is a two-hour ride away. But that's Japan. I dozed as the bus swept along the motorway but woke as we hit the first traffic snarl-ups that signalled that we were entering the city at last. We finally, gratefully, got off at the Hotel Excel (one of the bus's several scheduled stops) and wearily hauled our luggage to a taxi to drive to another, much less expensive 'business hotel' that we'd pre-booked from England. The taxi driver, much to my annoyance, stood by and watched me struggle to load our heavy and bulky cases into the boot and the back seat of his cab. Not once did he offer to help me. I was, by this time, beyond verbal complaint and felt like a mere robot switched to automatic; a suitably appropriate condition for Tokyo life.

Our cheap business hotel was in Shibuya, up a little hill on a small side road, not too far from Shibuya station. The hotel was due to close down three days after our check-in, but for now, it was to be our home. The room was tiny, the bathroom even more so, almost microscopic but we were too exhausted to care and simply unlocked our cases, took a bath and wandered out into the neon Shibuya night. It was as if I'd never been away from the place. Tokyo is a kind of glittering hell, a consumer orgy lit by advertising signs, giant video screens and scored by dozens of discordant broadcasts from loudspeakers situated on every building. The message is simple, "Buy me! Buy Me! Buy Me!" It is, as so many first-time visitors say, 'just like *Blade Runner*'. But the more often you visit, this romantic, futurist impression is diluted and then replaced by something far more mundane. In fact, Tokyo is neither *Blade Runner* nor *Lost In Translation but instead* a city of millions of lives banged up together in a desperate fight for either survival or acquisition. In many ways, it embodies everything that has gone awry with human society, even though, as the tour salesmen say, there is much less crime than in the West.

In Tokyo, to one degree or another, nothing is as it seems and almost everything is fake, simulated or appropriated from somewhere else. I've known this from the beginning of course but, with each subsequent visit, it becomes more and more apparent, less interesting, less humorously ironic, less 'post-modern'. Eventually, it simply becomes something to be endured. A candy-coloured purgatory that can only be safely navigated by a wallet full of cash and a credit card willingly sacrificed to the max.

Outside of Tokyo though, Japan has its compensations, its unique solaces. Emi and I spent a day with two of her Tokyo friends visiting Kamakura, a not too long train ride out of

Tokyo, near the coast. Kamakura has become a kind of spiritual theme park. It has what seems like an endless collection of old temples which one can visit. A tourist thing, not just for westerners but for the Japanese too. We crammed several of these into one day and it became something of a blur. I can't recall the various names of them, though I paid attention to each one that we visited. Each temple seemed to involve the climbing of a hill. In the June heat and high humidity, this was even more strenuous than normal for me. But there were one or two brief moments of grace and beauty. And some very good, locally brewed Kamakura beer. No wonder those Zen monks were looking so blissed out.

At one point on our tour of the temples, I got Emi to take a snapshot of me standing in one of the Zendo rooms, where the monks would sit in meditation. I wanted to climb up onto the sitting area mats and pose in Buddha fashion but Emi said I'd better not. Perhaps I would have profaned the space with my lazy Buddha posture. But this opportunity to behave like tourists was an anomaly as the rest of our time in Japan was taken up with a punishing schedule involving meetings with Emi's relatives and friends, plus the *Player* Magazine interview and photo session and my visit to the Terada guitar factory in Nagoya. (Actually, this last was the highlight of the entire trip for me.) Now I'm tired again so I'll continue with the story in a day or two's time. Meanwhile, don't touch that dial.

.

As previously mentioned, our trip to Japan was dominated by an intense schedule of meetings, mostly connected with Emi's family obligations and with her friends. Her diary was crammed with appointments throughout each day and we hardly had a moment to ourselves. These meetings were sometimes difficult for me as, due to my small grasp of Japanese, I couldn't really join in the various conversations and so had to politely sit there smiling, offering an occasional "Domo Arigato" when someone would re-fill my beer glass. I did, however, appreciate that this was a rare and important opportunity for Emi to meet up with her old friends and I felt content to just sit on the side-lines and allow her as much time and space as she needed to talk with them. She bought a mobile phone as soon as we got to Tokyo (at under £20 pounds it was actually cheaper than renting one) and within a few hours had set up a network of connections.

We were deluged with invitations, so much so that we couldn't fit them all in to our 12 day schedule so some meetings had to be politely declined. Of course, one of the most important reasons for our trip was for Emi to see her mother and two brothers. She hadn't seen them for three years, the last time being when her father died. Emi's mother is in her eighties now and looks frail although her health is reasonable at the moment. She was, naturally, extremely pleased to see Emi. Emi's family have always been very good to me and they all made me feel very welcome. Food and eating plays a central role in Japanese family and social life so there was lots of sitting around tables sampling various delicacies and much uttering of the word 'Oishi', which means 'delicious.'

I do enjoy a lot of Japanese food but there are a few things that don't particularly appeal to me. These tend to be things of the glutinous variety, certain sweet things and, whilst I'm a firm lover of seafood, I'm not a fan of the eel-like fish that are sometimes served up and which Emi adores. Not because of their flavour but because of the tiny bones one must encounter whilst eating them. Good wine tends to be very expensive in Japan and cheap wine is, to western tastes at least, almost unpalatable so I contented myself with Japanese beer which was very clean and refreshing, particularly with all the heat and humidity that we encountered.

Every day required us to do a fair amount of walking and also to take train rides on the busy Tokyo local railways and subway systems. At rush hour, these trains are crammed full of commuters. It's amazing how many people are compacted into each carriage, squashed up together like sardines in a tin. It can be a little disturbing to the unwary 'gaijin' such as myself. I'm sure that, in this country, such intense overcrowding would break all safety regulations but no-one seems to think anything of it over there. There are even uniformed, white gloved platform staff who help push people through the doors, squeezing as many of them into the trains as possible. This makes for some rather intimate physical encounters between the passengers. For a still red-blooded male like myself, it can provide one with a pleasant few minutes of travel if one is lucky enough to be crushed up against an attractive Japanese lady or two. (And yes, I really should feel guilty about admitting that!) Less so if it happens to be halitosis-stricken Japanese businessman bearing down upon you.

But my, oh, my, aren't the girls out there skinny? It's kind of worrying. Many give the appearance of being virtually anorexic. There seems to be a widespread obsession with being super-thin. I get the impression that this is connected more to fashion's dictates than anything else. One of the first things I noticed upon returning to the UK was that women here have dangerous curves and full breasts. Of course, these variations and sexual preferences are cultural inheritances as much as anything else, though it seems that many Japanese men hanker after a more 'meaty' physicality and fantasise about western women quite a lot. But then, we English men often find the Japanese female face and form beguiling, so maybe it's our perception of 'difference as exotic' that makes the grass appear greener on the other side of the fence. Oh dear, I fear I'm beginning to sound like a stereotypical, old-school, un-reconstructed, politically incorrect male here (or one of those cartoon randy old-goats of the Leslie Phillips variety). Perhaps I should change the subject!

Not all of our time in Tokyo was given over to Emi's busy schedule. I was allowed a couple of indulgences of my own. One of these was to accept an invitation to visit the Terada guitar factory in Nagoya. We were met at Nagoya station by one of the factory's executive staff, Mr. 'Chet' Nakagawa who turned out to be a lovely guy. Chet treat us to lunch at a small restaurant that served one of Emi's favourite Japanese dishes, 'Unagi' (the eel-like fish I mentioned earlier). She was very pleased to have an opportunity to eat this. I ate some very good Sahshimi (raw fish) washed down with Japanese beer. Chet then drove us to the guitar factory. The Terada factory makes guitars for Gretsch (which is how I came by my invitation) but they also build guitars for D'Angelico, D'Aquisto and several other companies. They seem to specialise in building archtop style guitars. It began as a family business in 1915 when the company made violins and it is still a family run business today.

The tour of the factory that we were given was fascinating. I'd expected something very high-tech and modern but was surprised to find a series of quite modest, semi-dilapidated buildings that looked as if they were at least 50 years old. Each building dealt with different stages of a guitar's construction, from stacked piles of raw wood to beautifully finished, shiny instruments. The craftsmen building them are mostly young guys, all with university degrees in guitar-making. Everyone who works there is a guitar player too and they take a tremendous pride in the high quality instruments that they create. I was impressed by the obsessive attention to detail and obvious care that went into each guitar. I was introduced to Mr. Terada who runs the factory. Terada-San was very gracious and told me a little of the company's history. He also let me in on some new work the factory is planning to undertake but that's to be kept under my hat.

Unfortunately, I didn't take any still photos of the work being done there but I did manage to shoot some camcorder footage which I hope to incorporate into a little documentary video about my Japanese trip which, all being well, I'll screen at this year's Nelsonica. After the factory visit, Mr. Chet Nakagawa became our tour guide and generously took us to see the impressive Nagoya Castle which looked like something from the animated film, *Spirited Away*. He kindly took a photo of Emi and I standing in front of the castle. Afterwards, he drove us back to Nagoya station for our two hour trip back to Tokyo on the bullet train. We invited him to look us up if he should visit England in the future. We'd be very happy to put him up and show him the beauty of Yorkshire's moors and coastline. A very nice, warm man.

Another guitar related event on our busy schedule was my interview and photo session for *Player* magazine. As mentioned in an earlier diary entry, I wasn't expecting anything more than a brief interview and therefore hadn't prepared clothes for a photo session but, as the magazine said they wanted to create a six-page feature about me and my guitar collection, it seemed churlish to complain. The photo session and interview was held in a professional photographic studio in Tokyo. No-one complained when I kept my dark glasses on, so I was reasonably happy. Actually, from what I've seen of the Polaroid roughs, taken as the shoot was being set up, the end results shouldn't be too bad at all. But I genuinely do dislike being photographed these days. I much prefer being behind the camera, rather than in front of it.

Another enjoyable part of our trip was the evening when we had dinner with my good friend Nick James and his wife Yoko. Nick has, astonishingly, been living in Tokyo for 17 years now. He originally hails from Selby in Yorkshire, which is where we first met. He was a young guy trying to get into the music industry at that time, his main interest being in studio engineering. But Nick is also a fine musician who plays keyboards and, in recent years, some guitar too. He owns a beautiful Martin acoustic which I envy. Nick and I have worked together in the past, most notably on my old Cocteau Records single *Life In Your Hands*. Nick engineered that and played piano on it, too. These days he's in demand in Tokyo as a producer and composer as well as an engineer and has created musical scores for films and television. His wife Yoko is a talented singer and they have a very comprehensive home studio set-up that makes my own equipment seem quite minimal and humble.

When Nick and Yoko were married, back in the early 1990s, I was proud to be asked to act as Nick's best man. They married in England at Brayton Church on the edge of Selby. My after dinner speech was pathetic. I developed food poisoning at the after-reception party and ended up in a bit of a state, but it was still a memorable day and the only time I've ever worn the traditional full tie and tails regalia. I seem to recall that I looked rather smart, quite the gentleman toff in fact. Anyway, on this latest visit to Japan, Nick and Yoko took us to a little Italian restaurant where it was good to enjoy a meal without requiring the public display of my rudimentary chopstick technique. (Actually, Japanese people always seem to compliment me on my use of chopsticks so maybe I'm not quite as clumsy as I think I am. Either that or they're just being typically polite.) Of course, I once lived in Tokyo for almost a year so it was a matter of 'chopsticks or starve.' Well, I soon got the hang of it.

Another evening was taken up by a re-union party of Emi's old workmates. When I first went to live with Emi in Tokyo, she was in charge of Kenneth Turner's flower shop. Kenneth Turner is a renowned English floral designer who is highly respected in Japan. The flower company that Emi used to work for (Floral Vision) was chosen by Kenneth Turner to manage the Japanese branch of his business and Emi was chosen to run his shop for him. I was always impressed by Emi's efficiency and professionalism when I dropped into the Kenneth Turner shop, close to Tokyo Tower. Her staff showed an obvious respect to her and Kenneth himself thought highly of her. Her floral designs were regularly featured in interior design magazines in Japan and I'm pleased that she's kept a number of these magazines for her archives. But it's been several years since the company staff has been together in one place, many of them moving off to start their own flower businesses or going into teaching. On this latest trip though, a special party was arranged to honour Emi's visit to Tokyo and I found myself the only westerner amongst 11 Japanese girls and two Japanese males. There was much warm humour and (unsurprisingly) lots of good food and drink. Once again, I found myself disadvantaged by my lack of conversational Japanese but everyone was extremely good to me and it proved to be less of an ordeal than I'd expected. What I love about these situations is that Emi is able to converse naturally in her native tongue. She seems quite different from her UK persona, when she has to carefully consider how to translate her thoughts into English. Even though she's made great progress since coming here to live with me as my wife, she still feels that she lacks confidence in speaking English and is often hesitant or uneasy about the matter. We understand each other in ways that only two people who love each other can, so the technical side of any language problem is not such a big deal for us. But in Japan, Emi's steady, considered speech changes to rapid fire, energetic conversation, filled with laughter and sparks. I get a real pleasure from seeing her freed from the constraints of the English language.

On another occasion we had lunch with a different set of Emi's friends, one of whom, Gan-chan, turned out to be a collector of vintage Japanese toys. When I spoke to him about my fascination with an early 1950s Japanese cartoon character called 'Atom' (or, as he is sometimes known, 'Astroboy') he immediately left the table, hopped on his pushbike and cycled off in the direction of his home. Ten minutes later, he returned with two gifts for me from his private collection. One was a vintage plastic figure of the Astroboy/Atom character, the other was a now 10-year-old reproduction of an almost two-foot high statuette of the same character. I couldn't believe he was giving me these things as they're quite rare and therefore, I presume, quite valuable. I'm very pleased to have them on display here in my home. I'll try to take a photograph of the big one for the diary pages soon. There's still more to tell but it will have to wait until the next diary entry. Once again, exhaustion is taking its toll and I'm losing concentration. The heat here today hasn't helped much either, nor the running around getting Emi's car repaired, serviced and M.O.T.'d. My car's turn tomorrow.

·

FRIDAY 7TH JULY 2006

One of the duties/perils inherent in any trip to Japan is the buying of gifts to bring back for family and friends. This time, because of the crowded nature of our schedule, there was only a little time available for shopping, though I managed to grab some extra time whilst Emi dealt with other matters. I put in a lot of walking — hard work, due to the humidity. Nevertheless I managed to grab quite a few things to take home as gifts. The problem with Tokyo is that the city is virtually one giant department store and there's so much on offer. Seeking out things that are suitable for a wide range of friends, not 'over the top' expensive things but sensible ones, practical for packing into suitcases is not an easy task. It's all about context. The shops in Tokyo are so beautifully designed, carefully lit and laid out that even the most mundane goods take on the glamour of jewels. Things that, in the UK, you would normally pass by thinking them frivolous or slight, become super-stylish objects of desire. The background music in these shops is equally evocative and sleek. No Brit-pop lads with lagers, monkey legs and 1970s guitar re-treads here, just spare, minimal, ambient backdrops. Clear notes hanging in the air like chimes from heaven, subtle beat manipulations, all discreet, knowing, swish, elegant and elite. The carefully sculpted sounds add to the sense of exquisiteness in the stores. In some ways, it's style taken to extremes, artificial, phony, far too obviously studied and mannered. But it does the trick.

Some of the things we bought, when we got them home, looked far less impressive in the cynical light of a Yorkshire living room. Of course, there are less sophisticated shopping areas. There are back streets around Harajuku that cater to a very young generation of Tokyo shoppers. Here the music is a Japanese interpretation of rap or reggae, sometimes hilarious in its misappropriation of those particular genres. The street fashion is often a meaningless mix of styles, no coherence, no awareness of the negative effect that certain combinations of clothes have on the wearer's body. There's one very odd (though tackily interesting) trend that I noticed. I saw several girls dressed in what I can only describe as 'Kate Greenaway' chic (though it's far from 'chic' in reality). These girls look like something from a vintage English nursery rhyme, Little Bo Peep perhaps, all layered lace, bibs and pinafores and mop hats tied under the chin with pink ribbons. When encountering them in the street, it is as if the cast of an English pantomime has left the theatre in full costume. In some ways, it's quite perverse. There's a knowing hint of fetishism in the eyes of the wearers. It's like an inverse 'Goth' look. For all its super-tweeness, there's something dark and sinister about it. But 10 out of 10 for bravery. Japan is full of these surprises and contradictions. For someone such as myself, a person with an interest in trash culture, fine art and the blurred boundary in between. Walking down the street for an hour or two can cause one to re-think the world.

Whilst we were in Japan, I deliberately severed all connection with the western hemisphere, apart from a couple of phone calls to my mother. At the same time, I was wondering what would await me on my return. I knew that there was a long list of projects requiring my attention. These days, being a cottage industry type of chap, music is only one of my pre-occupations. As regular readers of this diary know, my work doesn't stop there. I personally oversee every aspect of what I create. It's very hard work and often deeply frustrating, but it's the path I've chosen so I shouldn't complain too loudly. Not so much a control freak but more of a 'vision freak'. I suppose, ultimately, I'm the only person who knows what my work is about. I spend a lot of time trying to explain it to others in the hope of some fortunate connection or other.

I *did* try not to worry about the project list in the UK But my thoughts strayed across the oceans to England and the next few months busy schedule. (and beyond). I've commented on it before, but it is often quite a struggle. Earning a living from my music, and earning the right to make more albums, is a precarious thing. My age, my personal musical preferences, my refusal to deal with the industry on its own terms, all these things, well, they often work against me. Still, I continue to try it on. To bang my head against that old brick wall. Maybe it's a habit.

Eventually, we had to pack and prepare to leave Japan. It was hard, particularly for Emi, to say goodbye to her mother and brothers, but, if truth were told, we were not sorry to leave Tokyo itself. Yorkshire and its beautiful moors and coastline beckoned us and promised us a spiritual sense of space denied to us in our temporary hole in Shibuya. Quality of life, I guess. At least Emi and I are able to recognise the difference and appreciate our luck at being able to access those places and spaces within our Yorkshire habitat. Beyond price, really.

The journey back was longer than the outward one. I drowned myself in alcohol again. After a seemingly endless flight we arrived in Holland. The hours that we then spent at Amsterdam's Schipol airport were hyper-boring. We holed up in a cafe called 'Sandwich Island.' It was dreadful. The staff were hopeless, got conversion rates wrong, short changed us, served up poor food. Then, as we sat at a table finishing our meal, two rats ran across the cafe's floor and between our legs. And all this in a shiny, chrome, steel and glass airport that prides itself on its modernity. We were not impressed.

Eventually, Emi and I boarded our transfer flight to England and soon found ourselves flying over the coastline of Yorkshire, just above Spurn Point on the Humber estuary. Spurn Point is one of those special places for me. A place I've visited since childhood. It's magical and romantic, sand dunes, sea grass, shells, wild birds and an old lighthouse. It reminds me of my father and three or four romantic relationships from my haphazard past. To see it from the air, particularly after two weeks in Tokyo, was a wonderful 'welcome home' treat. I watched the Humber estuary twist and flow into the river proper, saw the city of Hull and the elegant Humber bridge pass by below me, and then, in what seemed like a few scant minutes, the pilot announced our descent into Leeds-Bradford airport.

There is only one place in the world I'm reluctant to leave when I fly abroad, and that is the South Coast of France. Villefranche-Sur-Mer and its environs is the only place where I would be happy to stay, to settle, if, by some miracle, I could afford a home there. Anywhere else on this planet, no matter how interesting or entertaining, I can generally leave behind without a single tear. But, the Cote d'Azur aside, Yorkshire claims something of my soul and I have no qualms in surrendering to its charms.

Our neighbour Steve was waiting for us at the airport. A good and true friend. We were both pleased to see him. I was by now, of course, inebriated in a haphazardly loquacious fashion. Part articulate, part incoherent. Babbling like an idiot but pleased to be home. Steve put up with this obviously overtired tirade and drove us quickly and safely home.

A stack of bills awaited us and a house that smelled damp and unlived in. Our neighbours, Jim and Claire, had kindly watered the plants for us and kept their eye on things. Suitcases were opened, clothes assigned to the washing machine and gifts checked for breakages. In a very short space of time, it felt as if we'd only been away for a day or two. Then the jet-lag. Several nights of sudden awakening, bedside lamps being switched on and reading glasses donned. Now it feels as if all this happened months ago. A vague memory, a dream. But, that's life. Now, the usual stresses have returned. I'm inundated with emails. There's a 'to do' list that freaks me out every time I think about it.

I've been to visit my brother's grave in Wakefield Cemetery. I laid fresh flowers. Oh, dear, how I miss him, want to see him, hug him. I dreamt about him again. (Last night was the third or fourth time since he passed away.) I visited my mother last weekend but not have yet found time to see Elliot, (though we met in the street just over a week ago.) Elle is due to visit from London soon, so maybe then. I have gifts from Japan for them both.

I managed to get both Emi's car and mine through the MOT, (though not without expense). I've photographed almost my entire guitar collection for *Player* magazine (with the generous help of Jon Wallinger and Paul Gilby). A three day job in total. Had dinner out at a brand new restaurant in town (with Paul,) though it was a restaurant that was suffering from teething problems. (Wrong food arrived, etc, etc.) Spoke with Dean Campbell about the next stage of my signature guitar and am looking forward to seeing what may turn out to be the final design soon. Dean called me 'Gretsch boy.' (He'd read my diary.) Well, maybe I'm just a guitar-whore and he's jealous! All I can say is that it's a good job it's guitars and not women, otherwise I'd really be in trouble!

Today I posted a CDR of photos of my guitar collection and home studio to *Player*, arranged emails of a couple of extra photos for their forthcoming feature on my work (including a Martin Bostock portrait). I also spoke to Opium Arts about the go-ahead on my deal to licence my *Getting The Holy Ghost Across* album for re-issue later in the year. (First official release of the album on CD.) Various details discussed regarding distribution, review copies, release dates, etc.

I now need to speak with my graphic art buddy Dave Graham about various things, including a new design for the *Holy Ghost* album's re-packaging.

Spoke with my good friend John Spence about mixing the Be Bop live tracks for the EMI Records box set, studio time pencilled in for next week. Will I remember what I wanted to do with this material? It seems unlikely. I listened to it months ago and made mental notes. All lost in fog now. (I also need to talk to John about booking some time at Fairview to remaster *Holy Ghost* and *soon* too as I need finished copies of the album to put to the media for review by the start of September.)

Today I took delivery of a lovely little Greco L-10P archtop jazz guitar that I bought in Tokyo. (Can't wait to use this on something. In fact, more than anything right now, I'd like to start work on a new album but there's no time available. And I have such a lovely list of titles to inspire me at the moment.) I also need to do more preparatory work for this year's Nelsonica convention, make a start on the *Ghosts Etched On Glass* film, attempt the *Romance Of Sustain* volume 2 album, work on the 'Arcadian Salon' convention album, create some drawings for the convention, and several more things that I either can't recall or am recklessly trying to avoid. *Neptune's Galaxy* is due for official release soon too, maybe next week although no-one should attempt to order it until the official announcement is posted on the site.

The Dreamsville/Sound-On-Sound store can't deal with pre-orders due to the nature of the computer system used but, once the album is in stock, there will be no problems and people can order at will. It's a superbly apt album for this time of year and will complement a relaxing day in the garden or by the sea. It also has the power to transform a cold autumn-winter night into something more balmy and paradisiacal.

Despite the work pressures, I've managed to write a few diary entries, answer several emails (but still more to deal with) looked through some household bills (but not paid any yet), made another couple of trips to the supermarket for domestic supplies and am duty bound to help Emiko with a freelance flower job tomorrow. There is, as diary readers may have noticed, nothing 'nine-to-five' about my life. Only one week returned from Japan and I'm even more exhausted than before I went there. It's a kind of endurance test. Why do I do it? Because I have no choice. The luxury of leisurely contemplation is denied me. It's simply all action, compulsion. Nervous energy, empty mind. Orgasmic Zen. Now I will open the case of my little Greco guitar and play some blues in the heat of my tiny recording room. Summer hums in the dark outside my window.

•

TUESDAY 11TH JULY 2006

Tokyo has now faded into the mist of memory and I've picked up my workload with a vengeance. It's been almost non-stop since returning home. It seems as if something new appears on the horizon every day. The latest development concerns a deal with Sony Records to license my 1980s album *Getting The Holy Ghost Across* from them. The terms of the deal, which will allow me to re-issue the album on my own Sonoluxe label, have finally been agreed. When the album surfaces it will be the very first time that it will have been officially available on CD. I'm looking at late-October as a possible release date. Of course, I have to pay Sony a cash advance and a percentage of the album's sales as part of the deal (ironic, as it's my own damn music and it's normally the artist who gets an advance) but those are the terms Sony have laid out. I must comply if I'm to be allowed to re-issue it. (And even then, it's for a limited time only.) Sony do not seem to have any interest in releasing it themselves, though. I also have to pay the costs of transferring the original tapes to the digital domain from the analogue masters. Then I will re-master the tracks at Fairview and create (with the assistance of my pal David Graham) a brand new visual package for the album. I also need to write some new sleeve notes, setting the album in its historical context. Then, once all that is done, the album and its artwork can be manufactured. Putting all this together isn't cheap, in fact the whole process is much more expensive than usual. If I rely on website sales alone, I may well lose money on it. The amount of albums I sell via the site is so small that, if my usual album sales figures were applied to *Getting The Holy Ghost Across*, it simply wouldn't be worth doing. The production/licensing costs add too much to the equation. However, if I can sell some copies of the album, through a distributor, to record shops, I may be in with a chance. (Or at least, hopefully, break-even.) The album really needs to come to the attention of those people who are unaware of my *Dreamsville* site or who may be newcomers to my music. So, the distribution route is being looked into at the moment, as is the possibility of getting review copies to various magazines. It's all a bit of a financial gamble. Let's hope that the regular fan requests for this album to be re-issued are followed up by firm orders.

One of the problems of being an independent artist is that it is impossible not to have to deal with these things. Music is the starting point but the process doesn't stop there. There are so many other things to consider and to work on. It's extremely time-consuming and often frustrating. But perhaps that's the price of artistic freedom. I've also been debating the title of the re-issue. Its original title in the UK was *Getting The Holy Ghost Across* but this was changed for the USA release. The package design was changed, too. CBS Records (since bought out by Sony) who originally released the album was concerned that several right-wing Christian fundamentalist-owned record stores in the US wouldn't stock the album due to its 'controversial' title and mystical-alchemic-occult art work. It seemed that there was a paranoia about anything that might smack of 'magick'. So, in America, the album was re-titled: *On A Blue Wing* and an entirely different package was designed, one that could not possibly cause offence to anyone. (Except the artist, of course. I was not particularly pleased about it at the time.) But with the re-issue, I really want to re-think the packaging, bring it up to date. I intend to reproduce both the UK and US front cover art on the inside of the jewel box insert, just for the sake of the album's history, but I do want to try and create something to set the re-issue apart from the original. The *'Holy Ghost* title is quite restricting in some ways. *On A Blue Win*' is much more flexible in terms of visual interpretation. On the other hand, the *Holy Ghost* title was my original title for the project, back in the 1980s. However, I am no longer involved with the various occult orders that I belonged to back then and, whilst my personal experiences within them were appropriate for my development at the time, that particular path has, in recent years, become overgrown with weeds and I feel less comfortable signposting it for others. But one can't re-write one's own history. (Unless one happens to be a mega pop star with an appetite for fame and fortune outweighing one's integrity. And there are plenty of those around without me adding to the myths.) But it's up in the air at the moment. My starting point is the original title and I'll only revert to the secondary title if the first one doesn't inspire a suitable visual style. I've already searched through my old alchemical books for something that might work, but in a 'lower key' than the original art. I want it to be somewhat more subdued and enigmatic. It's needed quickly though, if the deadline for media copies is to be met.

The songs on the album are less 'occult' than they might seem, once the listener has the key to their true inspiration. They are, in the main, about my first romantic encounter with Emiko, long before I was in a position to marry her. We had an intense but brief relationship the year before I started work on the album. Because the situation wasn't yet right for us to be together, there was a lot of tears and heartache. The music reflects that, particularly the song, *Because Of You*. In many ways, it's a typical 1980s album in style, all post-modernist funk, some tracks veering towards a hard, jazzy blues. The late Dick Morrissey plays sax on the album, as does my much-missed brother Ian.

Some great bass playing from Ian Denby, too. But it is, for me, perhaps the one album of mine that declares the era of its creation. It is unmistakeably a product of those Linn Drum-driven 1980s.

Studio time at Fairview has been confirmed for next week, but in connection with an entirely different re-issue project. This is to mix the unreleased live concert Be Bop Deluxe tracks for the forthcoming EMI Records Be Bop Deluxe complete recordings box set. I start work on this project on Monday. I can't say it's something I'm particularly excited about (regular diary readers will know how, er, 'amoral' I am about dealing with old material beyond a certain point) but ... better that I personally mix it, rather than a complete stranger to the band's history. Nevertheless, I'm very much looking forward to spending a few days with my friend John Spence who will be working with me on the mixes. John transforms even the dullest task into a pleasure. His engineering skills are second to none so I'm certain that the tracks will sound fabulous when the two of us are done with them.

Enough of all this' re-issue' stuff. It makes me feel so pathetically old. But, there's *new* music afoot! Much more satisfying. I heard, an hour or so ago, that stocks of *Neptune's Galaxy* have finally arrived at the Dreamsville Department Store and are available for ordering with immediate dispatch. I've limited this one to 500 copies. If the demand is there, I may press up more, but *Sailor Bill* has still not yet sold out so I'm being cautious. I'm glad that *Neptune's Galaxy* has become available before the summer expires though. It's a perfect complement to an afternoon on the beach or a picnic on the clifftops. Or even a barbeque by the garden pond. In winter, a bath with aromatherapy oils whilst listening will provide the listener with an equally blissful experience. Is this a soft hard-sell? Maybe

I should have been a salesman (but maybe not). As I've mentioned before, the album is a companion piece to *The Alchemical Adventures Of Sailor Bill* but it sails on a purely instrumental, drifting, ambient tide. It's a mellow, relaxed seascape of an album and sits comfortably alongside my *Dreamland To Starboard* and *Crimsworth* projects with a hint of 'Rosewood' thrown in.

Another recently completed album, *Return To Jazz Of Lights*, is waiting in the wings for its own debut but *not* until autumn. This is a vocal-based album and quite different to *Neptune's Galaxy*. Its release is definitely being held back for a few months, though it's champing at the bit.

I now really feel the urge to start something new, as noted in a previous diary entry, but there are several other projects clamouring for my attention. I have no idea why there is so much music in the air and why my internal antenna seems so eager to beam it down. I seem to exist in a permanent monsoon of sound. It's always stormy weather, but of the most beautiful, ravishing kind. The view from my window is of lightning dancing over hills and valleys, illuminating tiny details normally invisible to the naked eye. Lovely.

I received confirmation today, via email, that the CDR containing photographs of my musical instrument collection and my studio arrived safely at the headquarters of *Player* magazine in Tokyo. The magazine also confirmed that my photos were of good enough quality to be used in the article they are planning for an autumn issue. The magazine's visual standards are high so it's a relief to know that everything has worked out fine. I couldn't have faced another attempt at photographing everything again; it took me so long to do it the first time.

It hasn't all been work, though. On Sunday, Emi and I drove out to Nunnington Hall, a National Trust property with 15th century rooms. It isn't too far from Helmsley, north of York. The weather was good too. Our visit wasn't purely to see the lovely old house but to also take in the exhibition of photographs of Bob Dylan that were on display in the house's upper rooms. It was a very good exhibition. I would have dearly loved to purchase a print for myself but they were too expensive for me, averaging about £900 but the more expensive ones nearer £3,000. I still adore Bob Dylan. I first found his music when I was at art school in the 1960s. He's a hero of mine. I did spend a small amount of money though (£7) on a book in the shop in Nunnington Hall. It was a book about Christies' pop memorabilia auctions with photos of various items that have passed through the Christies' auction rooms over the years. The real reason I bought it was that it contained a picture of the first guitar I ever played (not the *actual* guitar but an identical one). This was a plastic, toy instrument, made by a company called 'Selcol' and had an Elvis Presley theme. It was originally bought, in the late 1950s, as a Christmas present for my brother Ian but he was a bit too young for it at the time and, fatefully, it ended up in my hands. It was made from brown and cream plastic and had a picture of Elvis Presley on the headstock. I figured out how to play the *Third Man* theme on this guitar, then my dad taught me three or four banjo chords on it. And that was how I began a life-long love affair with the guitar. I would dearly love to get my hands on one of those old Selco Elvis Presley toy guitars again. One really should be in my collection. It's where it all started for me and even seeing the photograph of it in the Christies' book flooded me with a deeply emotional nostalgia. Perhaps I should ask the Dreamsville site's citizens to keep an eye out for an example. There may be one out there somewhere, just waiting for me to claim it.

Driving back from Nunnington Hall, Emi and I stopped off at a hotel in Hovingham for a drink before heading home. All in all, it was another of those really nice days that we try to spend together at weekends. Emi is not just my wife but my best friend and I treasure the times we share travelling around our beloved North Yorkshire. She's the perfect companion for me.

Last night provided us with another social occasion. Jane, a good friend of ours, celebrated her 50th birthday. She, her husband Mark, Emi and I, were all invited to the home of our mutual friends, Steve and Julia. Julia had prepared a really excellent dinner for us all. As usual, I ended up merrily mellow.

A phone call this evening to Dave regarding artwork. Some emails sent to various people (including Dean Campbell regarding the actual written signature to go onto my signature guitar) but more still to write. And more work to deal with tomorrow. Tired now though. Maybe enough for today

·

FRIDAY 14TH JULY 2006

Tomorrow is the 15th of July. Approximately 33 years ago, events transpired that gave birth to the song *15th Of July, (Invisibles)* This song was part of Be Bop Deluxe's live performances at the time but the song was not included in the recording sessions that produced the band's first album *Axe Victim*. The only evidence that the song ever actually existed (apart from fading memory) is provided by Be Bop Deluxe's very first BBC radio one session on the late and much missed John Peel show. I don't think the band had even consolidated its deal with EMI Records at that time. Thankfully, the BBC kept a recording of the show in its archives and the track was eventually immortalised on CD when it appeared, a few years ago now, on an album called *Tramcar To Tomorrow*, which focused on those long ago John Peel sessions. Some fans may already know about that particular song's origins, how it sprang from a relationship that I had with a certain girl, a girl who inspired the song *Teenage Archangel* (Be Bop Deluxe's first independently made single) and who also inspired *Love Is Swift Arrows* among several other later titles.

Be Bop Deluxe had a regular monthly gig at The Duke Of Cumberland pub in North Ferriby, near Hull in the early 1970s. The band were young and naive and we met girls, as young bands do. I was married to my first wife (Shirley) at the time and shouldn't really have been looking for romance, but I was. It hadn't turned out to be the ideal marriage, either for me or for Shirley. Not Shirley's fault at all really, just me and my usual saying 'yes' when I really meant 'no.' I'd plunged into it far too young and hardly knew what I was doing, though as a result, I have a wonderful, intelligent daughter that I couldn't live without (Julia Tuesday Nelson). It was, as the old cliché has it, 'just one of those things.' Nevertheless it has become a vital part of my history and an important, formative, invaluable experience. In those days, I had a day job working for the West Riding County Council's 'Supplies Department,' a miserable enough job that offered no real future, other than a daily shuffling of papers from one desk tray to another until old age and retirement when I could look forward to a mantelpiece clock and a briefcase full of good wishes. I tolerated it as cheerfully as I could, along with the well meaning but relatively unambitious people I worked with. No, let me be honest here: I hated the damn job, grateful as I was to have enough income to maintain my two-up, two-down, industrial-age terrace house, nestled just outside Wakefield's high security prison in an area known as Plumpton (In fact, just across the road from the one-time site of Mariott's Buildings, my grandmother's house, where I was born). I felt like a man from Mars in that rank and file environment, and people treated me as if I *was* from another world. I was greeted with a mixture of suspicion, derision and thinly disguised prejudice. My liberal, non-conformist attitudes were seen as threatening by some of my fellow workers. I was an enigma or a curiosity to them. My enthusiasm for art and music was simply their confirmation that I was weird, oddball, maybe even slightly crazy. I did my best to live with it, believing, somewhere inside, that my instincts were right and that it was they who were odd, mutant, deviant almost, and that I had a much more healthy, broad and open attitude towards life.

My life and its daily grind were in some ways responsible for my dreams of an idealistic, romantic, creative lifestyle. Anything to escape. Under all the paper-filing, telephone-answering mundanity lurked the ecstatic, melancholy, heart of a poet. Let's not be coy here, that is what I was and what I still am. (And always have been since the day I was born, despite my occasional protests and faux-modest denials.) I still believe that everyone is a poet, given the right situation, environment, opportunity to express themselves, or whatever. (And poetry, as I've said so often before, is not a 'form' but a quality.) But ... blah, blah, blah...easy to say or think this back then in my youth, with no evidence of very much at all. No visible track record, very few marks in the sand. Not like now. Song after song after song, still yearning, searching, harvesting every last straw for the thatched roof of my own private cottage museum. The proof, for what it's worth, is there. Thirty-three years worth of proof or more if needed. I'm 58 this coming December. Actually, all taken into account. Undeniable then ... A life devoted to it, whatever IT is. But, yes, I was right, THAT is what I am, for better or for worse. Poet, artist, imaginer. How wonderful, how privileged, how highly UNLIKELY! Regardless of good, bad or indifferent. I can't judge what it's worth and ultimately don't care. (Or do I?) But there's something there, an integrity of sorts. Maybe nothing more.

Around 33 years ago, on the 15th of July, Be Bop Deluxe's gig at The Duke Of Cumberland was cancelled due to summer thunderstorms that caused an electricity cut in the North Ferriby area. The band had made friends with various locals since first playing there. Instead of jumping in our van and heading back to Wakefield, we were persuaded to spend the rest of the day with various locals. We were adored by our regular audience at the Duke and there was no shortage of offers to go and relax with them. I'd fallen head over heels in love with a beautiful, intelligent, dark haired, half-Jewish girl called Lisa. We'd met at one of the earliest of Duke gigs. She was stunning and I was smitten. It was as if I'd been granted a miracle. I couldn't believe my luck. Why was she interested in me? An unhappy, married man from a working class background with nothing but a pocketful of dreams. Her family was wealthy, sophisticated, everything that I wasn't.

On that 15th of July, Lisa invited me to go with her in her car to her parents' house in Kirkella, an upper class village not far from North Ferriby. I worried about the fact that they did not know that I was married, though Lisa was aware of this from the start of our relationship and accepted it. She said not to worry and off we went to her home. The house was called 'West Acre' and was, by my standards at the time, almost a palace. Her parents were gracious and her home was large and luxurious. I recall it vividly; it made such an impression on me. Lisa cooked me lunch, Steak and chips, if I remember correctly. Her father proudly showed me his hi-fi system, built into an expensive antique cabinet and Lisa showed me her bedroom. She kept a photo of me pinned to a set of drawers next to her bed. The house was filled with expensive furniture and objects d' arte. Maybe I wouldn't be so impressed now, but then: I was stunned.

It was raining, though warm. Some of Lisa's friends called around to see her and we all sat in a lounge at the front of the house. I could see the lane outside the front garden's perimeter with its line of green trees and an old fashioned lamppost a few yards or so away. It reminded me of an illustration in an old children's book from my childhood, sort of 1930s or 1940s upper class, 'proper' English society. I'd grown up on a council house estate and this was magic to me. I felt out of place, though I was desperately glad to be sitting next to Lisa, who I adored. One of Lisa's friends commented on how bad the weather was, with the rain and everything. Lisa just smiled, squeezed my hand and said, "It couldn't be better…" And that was the exact moment that the song, *15th Of July, (Invisibles)* sprang into being. Perhaps it was the painfulness of our situation that was 'invisible.' Only she and I knew that I was married, her friends and parents being unaware of it at the time. The song's lyrics start like this: 'It rained all day across the world, and turned the dark trees deeper green ...' It goes on to portray the house, Lisa's friends and quotes her comment and plainly states my yearning for her. For all its innocence and naivety, it's one of the purest, most heartfelt love songs I've ever written. And it's 33 years old tomorrow

I received CDR masters of the *Holy Ghost* and *Spangled Moment* recordings from Sony today. When I played them back, I was shocked. I haven't listened to these recordings for many years (apart from the song *Contemplation* which I had to reference for the band tour of 2004). My first impression was that I'd dearly love to get my hands on the original 24 track tapes and completely remix them, get rid of that terribly dated 1980s crashing reverb snare drum sound. Too much reverb overall in fact, and not enough bass. It all sounds very brittle and insubstantial. Ironic that the majority of it was recorded on what was then considered to be state-of-the-art early digital equipment. My current home studio mixes are infinitely superior. But it would be too expensive and time consuming to remix the album, so I will have to content myself with simply re-mastering it. Try to add some weight to the overall sound. Good songs, on the whole though. Better than I'd remembered. If only I could remix them to bring out the vocals more. The vocals are really quite good, though at the time I tended towards the opposite opinion, making them subsidiary to the instrumental mix. More fool me. If I could do it all again (mix the tracks that is) I'd make the entire thing much dryer, more focused, more vocal centred, and feature the bass guitar of Ian Denby more, *and* my late brother's saxophone and clarinet too. One thing I *can* do, and *will* do, is re-think the track listing, especially as I am now able to integrate the eight-song, *Living For The Spangled Moment* mini-album into the project. The running order would definitely benefit from the years of experience granted to me since the original album's release. I need to bring the entire project into the 21st Century, at least in its presentation.

Next week I'm in Fairview, mixing the EMI Be Bop Box Set live tapes, so I'll have to put *Holy Ghost* on ice for a short while. But it needs to be worked on very soon if I'm to keep things on schedule. So busy.

Work on my Campbell signature model guitar goes on apace. I got photos of the naked, carved mahogany body last night. I also emailed Dean Campbell regarding some cosmetic details and gave him a title for the red paint colour that will be used. I've called it Rocketship Red. There will be 'atom' style fret position markers at the 12th fret too. The model will be known as a 'Nelsonic Transitone.' Looking forward to seeing the final version. I need to approve it before production starts. *Neptune's Galaxy* finally going out the door of the Dreamsville Department Store. People already posting their response to the album on the website forum. I think that the music is low-key but beautiful. Gentle tides and drifting clouds. Perfect for a summer afternoon. Perfect for dreaming. Now it's the weekend. But no rest. I need to think about the revised *Holy Ghost* running order. *And* new artwork. The weather is so nice outside my window.

Today was the first day of work at Fairview Studios, mixing the previously unreleased Be Bop Deluxe live recordings. John Spence and I managed to get one track completed and in the can. (*Swansong*, originally a track from the *Futurama* album but, for the first time ever, now presented in its live performance state). It feels a little strange, working on these 1970s live recordings after such a long time. The mixing process dictates that the individual components of the recording are listened to in great detail, each instrument or voice isolated from the others whilst sound is adjusted and a proper relationship between the parts established.

Listening to Simon Fox's drums without the rest of the instruments took me back to those days in Abbey Road Studios or to Villa St. George in Juan Les Pins, near Antibes, in the South Of France, when John Leckie and myself would spend hours trying to get the drum sound together, microphones moved from one position to another on each drum, equalisation tweaked until a 'good' drum sound was arrived at. Thud, whack, bang! Listening to the drum parts on *Swansong* today reminded me how complex some of our arrangements were. The songs were much more puzzle-like than I would accept today. My current song writing is leaner, more focused, less inclined to show-off. But I was young back then and had the hapless energy and naivety that youth inevitably entails. I'm not favouring one approach over another here, just noting that sensibilities shift with age and experience, for everyone. We have little choice in the matter (unless we are complete fakes).

There was a problem with the recording of the first opening verse of *Swansong*. Microphone/monitor feedback ruined almost every line of that particular verse. It screeched, squealed and howled in a very unpleasant way, right through it, burying the vocals, and there was nothing that John nor I could do to get rid of it. The more we listened to it, the more unpleasant and ugly it became. In the end, we decided to copy the final verse of the song and paste it in place of the first one. This may be seen as technical trickery by some purists, but it is infinitely preferable to listening to several bars of high pitched microphone feedback at a level that would induce migraine in most listeners. Maybe on the first two plays it might be accepted as part of the scenario, but it would soon have everyone's teeth on edge and their hand reaching for the skip button on their CD player. So, with a little digital sleight-of-hand, the offensive verse has been banished and a more palatable one substituted.

A particular treat for me was being able to listen to Charlie Tumahai's voice in isolation. He was a very good vocalist and had been the lead singer in bands previous to Be Bop Deluxe (and in bands afterwards, I think). Charlie sadly passed away several years ago which is why there will never be a re-formed Be Bop Deluxe. Even if Simon, Andy and myself unexpectedly felt the urge to get together again, it simply wouldn't be the same without the happy fountain that was Mr. Tumahai. And that 'if' is a fairly big one, for I can't imagine that Andy would be in the least interested in such a thing. As for me, well, I was fortunate enough to get my retro-band fix in 2004 with the Be Bop and Beyond tour. I'd love to assemble a band again but it would have to be one that could play a lot of new material created specifically for it. Even if it did dip into my song-writing treasure chest for some 'vintage' material here and there. But, as my friends all know, despite my somewhat, some-times, nostalgic tendencies, when it comes to music, I just love the smell of fresh paint.

Anyway, back to Fairview tomorrow to continue working on the live track mixes. *Forbidden Lovers* and *Terminal Street* up next. Not the best time of year to be stuck in a windowless studio all day, though. It's been blisteringly hot out in the sunshine today. More heatwave to come too, apparently.

Yesterday (Sunday) I decided to make the most of the weather before confining myself to the studio control room for the rest of the week. I bundled Emi into the car and we set off for the East Coast of Yorkshire, driving to Bridlington and then up the coast to Sewerby, then to Flamborough Head, then Filey, Scarborough, then past Robin Hood's Bay and on to Whitby where we had dinner at our usual favourite seaside restaurant, The White Horse And Griffin. Unfortunately, the food wasn't quite up to the restaurant's usual standard, nor the service, I thought. Maybe this was because of the summer seasonal rush, or new staff? I really have no real idea. Still, it wasn't terrible either, so I'll give them another chance, next time we visit. I *did* have a positive moment though, when I found a copy of the third part of John Betjeman's biography, written by Bevis Hillier. I'm a fan of the late Sir John B. and of Bevis Hillier's writing too. In fact, my son Elliot's full name is Elliot Walter Bevis Nelson. Walter after my father, Bevis after Bevis Hillier. Visiting Flamborough Head was a treat. Incredibly, I haven't been there since the mid-1960s. I fondly remember reclining on the cliff's edge with my then girlfriend, Lynne Holiday, listening to my little red and white plastic transistor radio. It was playing the latest songs of the day (*San Francisco* by Scott McKenzie.) There was also a Frank Sinatra hit, either *Send In The Clowns* or *Strangers In The Night*. Plus some other half-straight, half-psychedelic pop from various artists trying to catch the wave that was beginning to break on these shores — the kind of music that turns up on those 'Remember the Sixties' compilation CDs these days (every supermarket has them). It seems that my generation has, in recent years, become a prime target for that style of marketing. But what excuse do I have? Damn it, I'm mixing material more than 25 years old! Give me strength! But on that warm summer day back in … 1966 was it? Yes, give or take a year. Well, all seemed wonderful with the world. We youngsters had found our voice, our cause, our raison d' etre. An all-inclusive, arms-held-wide, big welcoming peaceful hug for everyone, regardless of age or background. We'd swallowed that San Francisco, West-Coast, peace and love ideology lock stock, barrel and flowers. We looked the part, we walked the part and talked it, 10 to the dozen. And the amazing thing is, we actually felt it. We thought we could bring it about, turn the world around, ring the changes. And in a positive, non-violent fashion, everyone included. So, where did all that hope and love vanish to? Look at the world outside our window now. See the horrific hatreds that poison our planet. Even on a basic, local level, it's hard not to be aware of several generations of cynical, negative, heartless chancers, grasping, filching, fiddling while Rome burns. What have we lost? What have they missed? Well, hell, yes … I'm a cynical old bastard. Maybe it was nothing but naive optimism. Still, despite all that: yesterday afternoon, a clear blue, BLUE sky stretching down to a blue, BLUE sea. A pure white lighthouse gleaming against all heaven. A skylark singing fit to bust somewhere so high in the blue beyond that I couldn't even see it, but, oh! How I could hear it! White-capped waves lapping far below the yellow-white chalk cliffs, coarse grasses swaying in the sea breeze. Man, it just doesn't get much better or more blissful. I was gone, sent, away with the birds. I WAS that skylark, that little winged insect with bright red wings flitting from wild flower to wild flower. I was every one of those cricket-like bugs rubbing their legs together in some summer-fuelled mating song. I was so HERE and THERE and EVERYWHERE, so deeply in tune with it all you wouldn't believe. I had a ball simply looking and feeling. Wow! And I remembered Lynne and our youth and those times and that music and I was grateful to be alive and to have lived through those times. And AMEN to that then and AMEN to this now. Despite the terrors we endure, despite all that. Ain't life grand when you're in the mood for it to be so?

·

SATURDAY 29TH JULY, 2006

The heat goes on, externally, internally and weather-wise. Just returned home from an evening out with Emiko. A meal at Ceasar's restaurant, the best value-for-money Italian in town. Nothing too fussy, just down-to-earth cooking and warm, friendly staff who always recognise us and treat us well. I generally try to put a little time aside for Emi at the weekends. She patiently puts up with me working long hours in my studio during the week, so, as much as possible, I give my weekends over to her. I think I'll drive her out to Castle Howard tomorrow afternoon. It's not far from here and a late lunch at the Castle Howard cafe, followed by a gentle stroll around those magnificently landscaped grounds will be a nice treat for both of us. Especially under these big blue summer skies we're being blessed with right now. But, my, oh my, it has been so HOT! The summer has baked our day-to-day lives without mercy these last few weeks, a heatwave that now seems to have stretched on forever. Nights have been sticky and interrupted by bouts of insomnia and perversely lusty dreams. Apparently these are a result of the sun shining on the pineal gland on the top of one's head. It's maybe why Mediterranean men and women are so erotically charged. Well, I don't know about that but something's up in the land of nod.

My studio room has felt like a sauna lately. Or an oven set to 'roast'. Impossible to work during the day, at least from 12 noon until early evening. The sun beams down through my skylight window and fries everything to a crisp: me, the guitars, the mixing desk, my imagination and anything else that I need to make music. I can't open any windows for fear of annoying the neighbours. Haven't got air-conditioning, so I either have to work stark naked or abandon recording completely until things cool down a little during the evening. The latter, these middle-aged days, is generally preferable I'm sorry to say!

I *have* managed to finish mixing the Be Bop Deluxe live tracks for the forthcoming EMI box set. These mixes were made at Fairview Studios, not far from the river Humber, rather than at the Abbey Road studios of the band's heyday but the results are equal to anything from the past, if not better.

John Spence has helped me to bring about what I think will be universally accepted as an absolutely classic set of Be Bop performances, none of which have been previously available to the public. There's no doubt that fans of the band will be extremely excited when they hear these live recordings. The memories that came flooding back to me were poignant. Despite my reservations about this old material, there's nothing for me to be ashamed of. And what a band! Listening to the individual parts in isolation brought home just how distinctive and sympathetic my three fellow musicians were. *Swansong*, *Forbidden Lovers*, *Terminal Street* and *The Modern Music Suite* have all been mixed to bring out their naked beauty. They sound wonderful, even though the technical aspects of the performances are raw and bleeding. But I'm so glad that they've been preserved for posterity.

It's been incredibly moving for me to work on these rare recordings after all these years. Part of me was smiling, part of me was lamenting, but all of me was proud. It was also lovely to hear John Spence say that he was thrilled to become part of Be Bop Deluxe's legacy, too. Our collaboration (and John's experience and technical expertise) has served the band's history well. Since completing the Be Bop live mixes, John and I have been working on the re-mastering of the *Getting The Holy Ghost* Across album, also at Fairview. I've added the *Living For The Spangled Moment* mini-album to the disc, too (*and* an obscure track called *The Yo-Yo-Dyne*).

Dave Graham and myself are still working on the repack-aging of this album and have now found a suitable starting point to build the design around. Dave's close understanding of my visual style will, once again, contribute towards a highly appropriate layout. It will look quite beautiful when it is completed.

I've been having a very nice, surprising guitar week (or two) lately. I won't go into details for fear of embarrassing a couple of 'super-fans' who have been incredibly helpful in helping me acquire a new instrument or two but, well, a childhood dream of a flamingo pink Fender Stratocaster (via a Rickenbacker 12-string) has come true, as has a 'full-circle' situation regarding a toy Elvis Presley guitar that once, long, long ago, was responsible for capturing my pre-teen imagination and putting my feet on the path to a lifelong career in music. I don't think I'm permitted to name names here but the people involved will know that it is they of whom I speak. All I can say is that I'm blown away, deeply grateful, totally amazed and sincerely moved by their generosity.

I'm blessed with some tremendously loyal and kind fans. They sometimes take on the role of theatrical 'angels' or art patrons. Their involvement often goes beyond basic 'fandom' and enters the realms (and ideals) of a long-ago Golden Age when aesthetically refined connoisseurs once helped artists to bring their work before a wider world. Or is that just me being romantic again? Nevertheless, these instances prove that that spirit of patronage and support is not dead, and that it *is* possible to produce a music that does not need to bow down to the rigid limitations of the mainstream music industry. I'm eternally grateful that there are several special people, (some are fans, some are friends, some are business people) who help to create an atmosphere of freedom and creativity around me, within which I'm able to achieve my life's work. Without their support and generosity, I'm lost.

I noticed, in the latest issue of *Mojo*, reference to two new albums (by other artists) themed around sea-going concepts. One is called *Rogue's Gallery: Pirate Ballads, Sea Songs and Chantey'* (odd spelling of the latter word?). This album is apparently co-produced by Johnny Depp, the well known Keith Richards impressionist. The album actually features my Channel Light Vessel dreamboat, Kate St. John, as well as the somewhat less erotically-charged, Bryan Ferry. It also features Sting, Nick Cave, Jarvis Cocker, Rufus Wainwright and various other poptastic media stars, the most interesting and worthy of which are David Thomas of Pere Ubu, Van Dyke Parks and Mary Margaret O'Hara. The *Mojo* reviewer says that the album will 'shiver your timbers in the most rewarding of ways'. The other album is *Ocean: Songs For The Night Sea Journey* by Jennifer Cutting's Ocean Orchestra. The review says it employs synths and samples alongside accordions, pipes and strings. Well, well, it looks like I've been rolling along on the crest of a wave but, of course, my 'Lighthouse Signal Mechanism Orchestra' came into that particular harbour almost a year ago now. Perhaps my ship is equipped with a more finely attuned compass. Oh, well. But what a pity that *The Alchemical Adventures Of Sailor Bill* didn't receive the media attention that the above two albums seem to be currently enjoying. I may be ahead of the wave but I'm under the radar, or so it seems.

I went to see my friend John Foxx last week. He was playing at Fibbers in York. Haven't had chance to meet with him since we both took part in Harold Budd's 'farewell' concert at the Brighton Dome last year, though we've exchanged several emails since. John braved the heat of summer (and of Fibbers) to give a vibrant, almost 'electro-punk' show which delighted his audience. He got a great reception, not least from my neighbour and good friend Steve who has been a big fan of John's since the early Ultravox days. And I gained brownie points from introducing Steve to John after the show. It was really good to see John enjoying himself and celebrating an energetic 'roots' approach to performance. He and I still plan to get together, both with Harold and with each other. The only thing slowing us down is lack of time. One of these days though ...

This coming week, I must seriously try to overcome the heat (and my exhaustion) and finish recording the *Arcadian Salon* album. Then I must decide upon a track running order and master the album as soon as possible as there is no time available for me in Fairview Studio from the middle of August on. This thing *has* to be ready for the convention in early October. It's rushing up like a runaway express train, as usual more than ever. I'm way behind schedule.

Haven't begun to make any in-roads at all into the autobiographical film *Ghosts Etched On Glass* (an excerpt from which I'm supposed to present at Nelsonica 06 as a 'work in progress'). In fact, the list of jobs I have to tackle for the convention is becoming an increasingly scary and, maybe even impossible, task. How on earth can I get all this stuff together in the scant time remaining to me before the convention date? Yes, okay, I always panic but, it seems that each year I take on more and more work, projects that, despite all good intentions, are increasingly difficult to complete without tremendous effort and sacrifice. I guess the recent tasks I've had to undertake regarding re-issues and associated items have thrown the proverbial spanner into the works. I have to admit that my trip to Japan robbed me of two weeks working time, also. But there's nothing left for me but to plough on, to do the best I can under the circumstances. No point in working myself up into a paranoid, desperate panic about it all. After all, I love it, don't I? And it usually works out okay. Doesn't it? Well, too hot right now, even though it's late evening. Can't sit here typing. I'll continue this in a day or two when I'm less exhausted and there's more progress to report. And less sweat dripping onto my computer keyboard.

·

SUNDAY 30TH JULY 2006

Went to Castle Howard with Emi as planned. Lunch was good, sitting in the grounds of the house, watching white fluffy clouds drift by in a high blue heaven. Apparently, Jools Holland and his pals played at Castle Howard on Friday (I think), a big outdoor bash or something grand. Emi and I are thinking of attending the annual classical 'Proms' concert at Castle Howard, in August. It's a picnic hamper/champers type of affair. Maybe even grander than Jools' big do. We could dress up in our summer finery, get completely, joyously blathered, then slip away into the woods to frighten the peacocks. Pan chasing his favourite nymph through a sylvan glade, and that sort of thing. Libido a-go-go. Let's hope the weather holds up.

Last ever *Top Of The Pops* on television tonight. Caught the back end of the final show (when I switched on the television during dinner). It seemed to have been full of clips from across the ages. Don't know whether they showed anything from the time when pop music actually resembled pop ART, when it genuinely had something to say for itself (Jimi Hendrix, Syd-era Floyd, etc, etc). Whatever, the last five minutes illustrated perfectly why it has finally been axed by the BBC. Pop music has become irrelevant, hollow and dull and is, to all intents and purposes, dead.

I met Jimmy Savile once (Be Bop Deluxe were on *Top Of The Pops* at the time, drooling over Pan's People backstage). I also saw Jimmy standing at a bus stop across the road from the Music Ground guitar shop in Leeds, maybe only a year ago at most. Perhaps I was the only person in the street who noticed. He was nice enough to us when we were on *Top Of The Pops*. He may even have played our records on his radio shows. Sooner or later, though, we all come to resemble decrepit old age pensioners. No pop star remains unscathed. And thank goodness for that. Insufferable narcissists, the lot of 'em.

•

MONDAY 7TH AUGUST 2006

Made the mistake of presuming that I'd finally completed the track running order for this year's Nelsonica CD but I was wrong (and after I'd announced it on the Dreamsville Inn Forum, too). The first two versions proved to be far too long to fit onto a CD so I had to drop three tracks and record two shorter, brand new ones to get the total running time to just under 80 minutes in length. The revised, (and hopefully final) track listing looks like this [list or tracks].

The three tracks that I couldn't fit on to the album are: *Rail-*

way across the Roof of the World; *Pilgrim* and *This Sky, This Sea, This Summer*. These leftovers will either go towards next year's Nelsonica CD or appear as bonus tracks on any re-issue projects that I might undertake next year. It all depends on context and mood.

Arcadian Salon has been a tricky album to put together as the music on it covers a quite diverse set of styles. The first six tracks are all from the *Return To Jazz Of Lights* sessions and have a very jazzy feel. I couldn't find space for them on that album so they are presented here instead. Track 7, (*Spaceport*) whilst not from those sessions ALSO has a jazzy influence and features my recently aquired Greco L10P archtop guitar. Track 8, *Superadventure (Sound-On-Sound)* is the epic instrumental piece that originally appeared exclusively on *Sound-On-Sound* magazine's DVD, an item that was attached to the special anniversary issue. It appears here on one of my own albums for the very first time. This piece covers several of my musical acres in one single composition; it almost constitutes a potted history of my instrumental work. Tracks 9, 10 and 11 continue in an instrumental vein and act as a bridge between the CD's earlier jazzy feel and the 'rockier' tracks that appear on the latter part of the album. Having said that, tracks 13, 15 and 17 are also little instrumental interludes and serve to break up some of the vocal tracks. The entire CD is now just a few scant seconds under 79 minutes long, making it a somewhat longer listening experience than the *Return To Jazz Of Lights* album.

I now have to try to get some mastering time booked at Fairview so that it can be manufactured in time for the convention. (Actually, after writing that sentence, John Spence literally just called me to say he can fit the mastering session in at the end of this month, so manufacturing should be on schedule if the master goes straight off to the factory, once we've completed the process.)

Yesterday afternoon brought a meeting of the Nelsonica Planning Department, which I was invited to attend. Always a pleasure to meet the members of the convention team, they're so enthusiastic and creative and always make me feel rather special. And this particular meeting was made extra special by Ian Haydock who gave me a gift of a 1950s Selcol Toy Guitar (which may well make an appearance at Nelsonica this year.) Actually, this is the second Selcol guitar I've been given. Long-time fan Scott Tiggert sent one to me by post a week or so ago. Suddenly, I've been re-connected with the very roots of my guitar playing. In the late 1950s, this plastic, toy instrument introduced me to the delights of the guitar for the very first time. I'll relate the story of my guitar beginnings at Nelsonica as part of my presentation. The toy Selcol Elvis Presley guitar I was so generously given yesterday actually has an 'autochord' unit with it, a small box with buttons. This fixes on to the neck and produces a few simple chords when each button is pressed. These Selcol guitars are very rare and, being a collector of retro design items, I'm thrilled to now own two of them, thanks to the generosity and thoughtfulness of my kind benefactors.

At the Nelsonica meeting, the team and I talked through various details regarding this year's convention content. It's going to be a non-stop delight if all goes to plan. Fitting everything in to a single day is the hardest part. There's certainly no lack of content. Apparently, the event has already sold out and there is a waiting list for any tickets that might become available.

Now I have to start making a list of the pieces of music I want to include in my Nelsonica 'radio show.' I also would like to create a couple of new pieces to play as part of my live performance, too. So, perhaps I should park the diary for a little while and get on with some work.

On the domestic front, not much to report. With all the work on my plate at the moment, there's not a lot of time available for socialising, though Emi and I are attending our friend's 40th Birthday celebrations soon and also going to a little art gallery party north of York later this week. It would be nice to find a little more time for relaxing though. But work is a pleasure for me. How can music making not be?

Saw a beautifully coloured bird outside our house a couple of days ago. Couldn't identify it but we certainly hadn't seen one like it in our garden before. Perhaps it was a finch of some kind. I wonder if it's the result of this particularly warm summer? There seems to have been a few more butterflies in our garden this year, too, and bumble bees. The English summer of childhood fantasy, right here and now. Wish I had more time to enjoy it.

Attendees certainly get value for money as the ticket entitles them to a copy of the limited edition *Arcadian Salon* album (these things tend to become valuable collector's items); a live performance of instrumental music by myself; a 'meet and greet' session; a live on-stage interview between Leeds University School Of Music lecturer Simon Warner and myself; a separate talk about 'guitar philosophy' including the importance of the instrument in my life and some technical hints and tips; a question and answer session; an exhibition of several special items from my guitar collection; an exhibition of some early artwork; rare video footage presentations of Be Bop

Deluxe and Red Noise; a special tribute to my much-loved and missed brother Ian featuring rare Fiat Lux videos; a 'Dreamsville Radio Show' with me acting as presenter and DJ; a video presentation of some of my own musical inspirations; a selection of my self-created videograms; a preview of the re-mastered *Getting The Holy Ghost Across* album; exclusive previews of unreleased recordings from the 1980s; an auction of artwork and memorabilia; a raffle with some impressive prizes; a preview of work-in-progress on the *Ghosts Etched On Glass* film (if I can find time to take it beyond the opening title sequence which is all I've completed so far!); a preview of the previously unreleased Be Bop Deluxe live tracks AND a merchandise stall that will have advance copies of *Return To Jazz Of Lights* for sale, amongst other things. How we'll fit all that into the day is a mystery but there certainly won't be a dull moment.

·

SATURDAY 30TH SEPTEMBER 2006

Okay, I know. I've been absent. From both this diary *and* the Dreamsville website. Had to hide away and concentrate on the intensely time-consuming work that will hopefully provide this year's Nelsonica Convention attendees with something very, very special. No choice really, it was a matter of 'head down' or 'off with his head'. I would have been for the proverbial chop if I hadn't got everything together in time. Maybe I still haven't, despite all efforts.

It's been a tremendously long haul, this one, and not 100%

finished yet. Some things still to complete. But, I've finally got close to seeing it all through to its conclusion. The amount of work that goes into these annual events is staggering. Impossible for someone viewing it from the outside to appreciate just how much effort is needed. Not just the input from myself, (though this year's Nelsonica has a more direct, personal touch than previous years) but from the dedicated, talented and loyal Nelsonica team whose enthusiasm and expertise helps to make the day so unique. Although the convention lasts for just one single day, there have been several months of constant, concentrated, hard work from all sides to make it a day to remember.

As noted in earlier diary entries, my own schedule has been dominated by the wide-ranging creativity that this year's Nelsonica has demanded. I'm shattered by it all at the moment. It's required a daily effort to pull it all together. I don't know whether my age makes the going harder each year or whether it's just that I've attempted to give even more of myself to the various projects than before. I definitely think that my standards are higher, though perhaps I'm far too obsessive about minor details (even though it could be argued that I've always been that way).

Ultimately, I have no idea how much of this fanatical attention to detail will become apparent at Nelsonica. I guess that it will look pretty much effortless on the day. Nevertheless, the bite that this thing has taken out of my life is quite something. No one to blame for these struggles but myself, of course. I don't really need to put quite so much into it, it's just that I feel compelled to do so and am subsequently exhausted by it.

Here is a list, of things achieved, giving an idea of some of the preparatory work of the last few months:

1. The writing and recording of a limited edition Nelsonica album, *Arcadian Salo*, and its cover art and packaging. (*Lots* of tracks on it, too.)

2. The creation of an autobiographical video-film presentation, (*Memory Codex Number One*) exclusive to Nelsonica, lasting almost 40 minutes and capturing in images, text and music the essence of my early life. It is a 'sketch' or preliminary draft of what will eventually be a much longer and more complex work. It is also quite likely that this special screening will be the only time that this particular version of the film will be seen in public. Of course, this version is not perfect but I just hope that people will sit and concentrate on it, try to follow its drift and not treat it as a background piece. It took almost four weeks of long hours per day to get this finished for the convention, preliminary work or not. Perhaps it deserves attention for that reason alone.

3. The creation of a continuous musical soundtrack score to the above film. This will appear on an album in the earlier part of next year, along with some other recently recorded but previously unreleased material. The soundtrack occupied a great deal of my time too.

4. The creation of an hour-long, pre-recorded radio show featuring myself as presenter and DJ, playing and talking about early musical inspirations from my childhood and teenage years. I've chosen some very early musical memories to present to the listeners, from Freddie Gardener, through Danny Kaye to Chet Atkins and Johnny Smith with lots of stops in between. This will constitute part one of 'Radio Dreamsville' and will eventually be available as a

Dreamsville website broadcast, though aired for the first time ever at this year's Nelsonica.

5. The preparation of a live instrumental performance, lasting approximately 90 minutes. I've just settled on what will probably be the final choice of tracks and running order for the set. Nineteen pieces of music in all. Now I have to start checking through equipment and getting repairs done, then pack it all ready for transportation. I also still have to write out my 'charts' to guide me through the various pieces of music. This takes time.

6. The creation of several brand new pieces of music to be included in the above performance. Nine of which made it to the set. I've still been working on this aspect of the event today.

7. The involvement, in the above live performance, of Theo Travis and Dave Stuart, (who sometimes operate as the duo Cipher) who are planning to join with me in an improvisational trio, to which I've given the name 'Orchestra Futura.' I've created an almost ten-minute long 'foundation' track for us to play over. The piece is titled *Fever Dream of the Starlight Man*. It's a compelling, complex, modal, polyrhythmic piece. It may not frighten the horses but it may bewilder the artistically faint of heart. At least, that's my intention.

8. A special section of the convention will be given over to a tribute to my much loved and deeply missed brother Ian who passed away in April of this year. There will be rare video presentations of his work with Fiat Lux and a chance to hear the last music he ever recorded, a CD of original material by Ian and his musical partner and good friend, John Nixon.

9. A 'live on stage' interview with myself conducted by Leeds University School of Music's Senior Lecturer, Simon Warner. Simon's appearance at last year's Nelsonica provided the audience with an insight into the pop-cultural inspirations and influences that underpin my work. This year's interview will deal with song writing and it's methods and inspirational energies. Maybe I'll learn something. I've often wondered how I do it.

10. I've yet to prepare (but will, in the end, probably improvise) a free-ranging talk about guitar philosophies and inspirations. This will include video illustrations and an audience question and answer session at its conclusion. I've already chosen some video illustrations for the talk. Not sure how wise my choices are though as they will definitely make my own guitar playing appear quite amateur by comparison. Impossible to compete with the likes of Joe Pass, Wes Montgomery and Charlie Bird!

11. I've created and framed 16 original artworks for the traditional annual Nelsonica auction. Along with these, there will be a rare electric guitar of mine and some Red Noise memorabilia offered for sale.

12. I've yet to create any ambient video projections for my live performance. This visual aspect may, due to the above heavy workload, end up being somewhat compromised (or even missed out altogether) but no-one can say I've not tried my best under the circumstances, particularly considering everything else I've attempted to achieve this year. Ultimately, there's only so much one person can do, no matter how stubborn my persistence. Still, I have to sympathise with those who may regard the ordeal of just looking at me, sans projections, all alone on stage, as somewhat de-

pressing. Believe me, even I'd prefer something projected behind me to distract the audience from the ugly old creature clinging to all those beautiful guitars. You know: "What's a lovely guitar like you doing hanging round that old goat's neck?"

But, luck being on my side, it should fall in place on the day, even though, as you can tell from this diary entry, dear reader, that it's been a long hard slog, one way or another. Oh, the above list doesn't take into account things such as the *Return To Jazz Of Lights* album which will, I can confirm, be available for the very first time at the convention, before its 'official' release (once the convention is over, it will be available for general purchase through the Dreamsville Department Store). As regular diary readers know, I'm proud of this album and, along with *The Alchemical Adventures Of Sailor Bill*, *Dreamland To Starboard* and the two *Rosewood* albums, I consider it one of the more personal and satisfying achievements of my recent solo career. And you know that I'm a difficult cove to satisfy.

Then there is the forthcoming re-issue (first time *ever* on CD) of the 1980s *Getting The Holy Ghost Across* album, which, for a limited period only, I've managed to license from the mighty Sony Records (mighty maybe but virtually oblivious to my musical worth). There will be a unique chance to hear a preview of this re-issue at Nelsonica, time permitting. The album will be officially released in November on my Sonoluxe label.

There will also be an opportunity to hear my recent mixes of some extremely rare and previously unreleased Be Bop Deluxe live recordings from the 1970s which are scheduled for inclusion as part of an EMI Records special boxed set next year.

There are a few other surprises in store for convention attendees. Those who secured tickets as soon as they became available will be glad that they did so. The event was, amazingly,
sold out within a couple of weeks of its announcement and
there has apparently been a waiting list of people eager to gain
tickets in the event of any cancellations. Does all this lovely and
loving interest in my work make me nervous? Damn right it
does! It's 12 months or so since I last appeared or performed in
public and I'm definitely feeling slightly freaked out about playing live again (the word 'slightly' reveals an attempt at under-
statement). I have, however, chosen to focus on instrumental
works for this convention, not being in a vocal mood at the
moment, for various reasons too complex to go into here. So
the first person to shout out *Ships In The Night* will be taken
out back and his underwear searched for signs of boorish
insensitivity. And if it happens to be a female person, I'll
undertake the search myself. (Did I really say that?). I've just
been reading George Melly's wonderful, *Slowing Down* book
and have gained encouragement from the revelation that even
at an advanced stage of decrepitude, it's still possible to have a
scandalous moment or two in the, let's say, 'erotic' department
(third floor, ladies corsetry and gentlemen's relish). Of course,
Emiko has been instructed to pour me a cup of medicinal
libido-suppressive tea if I become a little too frisky at the
thought of this. Failing that, a stern look and a slap on the
wrists will suffice. All in the interests of my blood pressure, you
understand.

But back to the music. Rest assured, I'm gearing up for a
major vocal/song-oriented project for the coming year (appar-

ently, the 'chicks' go for that sort of thing). Can I take my tongue out of my cheek now? (Oh, sorry, dear, didn't realise it was in *your* cheek!) What *am* I like? This Nelsonica concert, the only live performance I've agreed to during 2006, will be centred on the instrument that has fuelled my imagination for so many years: the electric guitar. As will several aspects of the rest of the convention. The performance itself is called *Guitar Dharmas And Bleeping Electricals*, a whimsical title but, as attendees will discover, a perfectly apt one.

I've actually included several new pieces created especially for this performance. There are now more new backing tracks than I can practically incorporate into the set, but, even so, I've managed to squeeze *nine* of them, all brand new, into the already-packed concert agenda. This still leaves some further unheard tracks waiting in the wings for the *Painting With Guitars Volume 2* album which will be completed early next year, all being well. So, here is a preview of the Nelsonica Concert set [list of tracks].

Other things that have occupied me of late: the final stages of the development of my Campbell American Signature Model 'Nelsonic Transitone' guitar (including the signing of the limited edition certificates that will accompany each guitar sold). Dean Campbell has been trying to get a completed guitar over to me in time for the convention but has been held up by a couple of outside suppliers, mainly the case manufacturer and the supplier of the custom made 'Atom' symbol 12th fret marker (cutting these atom inlays is a skilled job and it takes a while to get them perfect). As a compromise, the guitar he will send me for Nelsonica will be missing some minor cosmetic details but I'm assured that I will be able to exchange this for a fully completed production model in a month or so. Dean called me the other week to ask if I could let people know, via the Dreamsville site, that these production models are not yet ready but, as soon as they are, an announcement will be made (both on the Campbell Website and here in Dreamsville). Apparently, Dean has been getting swamped by calls from people who have either ordered the guitar in advance or who would like to order one. His message to customers is to please be patient and wait for the official starting gun. We will inform potential buyers and those with a deposit as soon as things are ready to roll. Not too long now though, all being well

The guitar is looking fabulous in the photos that Dean has sent me of the partially assembled instrument. The colour is super-vibrant. I've christened it 'Rocketship Red.' With its cream and smoke grey pickguard and gold hardware, the guitar should be both beautiful and unique to behold as well as sonically exciting. Guitars still bring sunshine into the dark corners my life. I received a great new model from Eastwood Guitars a few weeks ago, their re-issue of the early 1960s Airline 'Town And Country' model. Three pickups, more controls than Dr. Who's Tardis and a retro-art-deco design that wouldn't look out of place in a classic Flash Gordon Saturday matinee cliffhanger. It will also be making an appearance at Nelsonica, along with some other favourite guitars of mine.

For all the stress that live performance brings, playing in public does allow me to take my guitars out for a 'proper run' and it's satisfying to share their sound and visual charms with an audience, rather than keeping them selfishly to myself in my recording room. I'm just as excited about the visual aspect of guitars as I was as a beginner, all those long, lost years ago. I sometimes sit contemplating my favourite instruments, hardly believing my luck. What a wonderful thing, what a privilege, to be able to dedicate one's life to something so musically rewarding.

Of course, all this creative activity has its downside. As mentioned above, I really *have* been pushing things too hard and I've definitely felt the consequences of this, health wise. Some worrying issues which, with my usual paranoia concerning all things medical, I've ignored, avoiding seeking a doctor's advice. Thankfully, most of these have improved of their own accord and I think it is mainly stress and tiredness that is affecting me at the moment. Nor do I suppose that much will change until the convention is over and I can ease off the fast pedal for a little while. I do need to recover from this year's exertions though. Nevertheless, projects are already stacking up for the post-Nelsonica months. Hopefully, I'll be able to deal with them at a more leisurely and humane pace than recent months have allowed. But I must try to take a little break before starting again, if only a weekend away somewhere with my patient and loving wife.

Working on the live set list for the Nelsonica performance has also held an emotional impact for me. My brother Ian was originally planning to join me on stage for much of this year's Nelsonica set and the concert in Leeds next spring. The two of us spoke about this, the last time we saw each other, just two weeks before he died. He was looking forward to it as much as I. This last week, whilst going through some of the older material to select pieces for the performance, I was forcefully reminded of previous concerts where Ian and I had stood alongside each other on stage. There will be difficult moments during this year's Nelsonica set where his spiritual presence will be tangible but his physical loss deeply painful. It's something that I won't be able to avoid, other than by giving up playing these pieces altogether, but Ian, I know, wouldn't want that. He'd tell me to get out there and play. And so I'll try. But I'll be missing him so much. Forgive my melancholy mood. It's unavoidable, I suppose.

On the domestic front, there have been repairs to external windows and doors and, finally, the completion of the house's exterior paintwork. The new colour scheme I've chosen, of Buttermilk and Peridot, really suits the old brickwork and ivy clad walls (the ivy goes a spectacular shade of red in the Autumn too). This renovation/repair work has required me to be constantly present at the house so I've had to forgo aspects of my creative work that might have taken me away from my recording room for a while. I now have to catch up with that side of things. Guitar repairs and so on. It will feel a little bit like being let off the leash. The house's interior needs attention too, and in more than one area. One of the house's two bathrooms (the en-suite one) has been out of commission since our ill-fated brush with MFI and is still in need of renovation. The kitchen is now seriously ready for an overhaul. It's starting to look like a 19th Century cow-herder's hut, with dripping tap and lime encrusted walls. All I need is some straw on the floor and a few chickens.

Actually, our neighbours already have the latter. A 21st Century version of *The Good Life*, though Emi and I are more of the Margot and Jerry type (were those their names?) than the Barbara and Tom couple's 'back-to-the-land' pseudo-rusticism. Perhaps I've got their names wrong. It was a 1970s television series, after all. Actually, I'm probably more like Margot than Jerry, being insufferably snobby at times and just as partial to low cut dresses and canapés. More tea vicar? And more household problems: our living room television set has been broken for several weeks now, the Sky digi-box has packed in completely, the hi-fi has given up the ghost long ago and both Emi's car and mine are virtually on their last legs, or wheels. But I've had no time spare to deal with organising repairs due to the long hours I've been putting into the music. My mind gets focused on work and everything else is forgotten. Perhaps, once Nelsonica is over, I can attempt to tackle some of these domestic issues, one at a time.

A headstone has now been ordered for Ian's grave and should be in place by Christmas. Despite moaning about my workload, I have managed to make fairly regular visits to the cemetery in Wakefield to place fresh flowers and to quietly remember our years together as brothers. The *Memory Codex* video I've made for Nelsonica contains some very touching images of the two of us when we were just innocent kids. It's terribly poignant in places.

One thing I've had to acknowledge is that a certain amount of my health problems of late have been caused by a kind of suppressed, internalised grief. The truth is, I've been and still am suffering from depression over Ian's loss. It's a submerged anguish, the silent cry of an angry creature gripped by tentacles of despair. Black, green and dark. I've tried to help my mother deal with her own deeply-felt bereavement but, underneath it all, despite my own advice, I guess I'm struggling, too. I'm not putting on a brave face so much as wearing a mask. The plunge into such an intensely self-punishing work schedule has, in part, been a desperate attempt to escape the reality of what has happened. But sudden awakenings in the middle of the night have brought a confrontation with the finality of it all, cold realizations that have been difficult, sad and painful for me. It's impossible to accurately put these things into words. I just don't have the language for it. Nor does anyone else suffering bereavement. There's a hopelessness at the bottom of this particular emotional pit that I find extremely debilitating.

I just need to work my way through it to something approaching equilibrium. Right now, it's all mood swings and extremes. Lots of well-meant advice from people and, of course, lots of well-meant advice from myself to my mother. But it's all noise and static at the end of the day. It can be tuned out. In truth, Mum, Diane and Ian's children, Ian's friends and myself have no option but to walk on these burning coals until we feel their pain no more. One day, I'm told, the coals will become just glowing embers, warm — happy memories of Ian's life and a final acceptance of its outcome. Right now though, it's something else entirely.

More future projects for me: I also had an offer from Sound-On-Sound publications to publish my autobiography. This isn't complete yet so I need to spend a large part of next year working on it. I've completed the period from birth to leaving school but that still leaves an enormous amount of writing and research for the rest of the book. It will be a large publication and, all being well, may have an accompanying DVD documenting parts of my earlier life.

Still no definite news regarding the Paul Sutton-Reeves authored biography *Music In Dreamland* but I understand that there have been some behind-the-scenes proposals to try and get it finally into print. It's been a difficult time for Helter Skelter as the company's guiding light and main man has become seriously ill. His health is of much more concern to me than the book though and I accept that patience in needed. It will surface when the time is right for it to do so.

There will soon be discussions regarding the content of the EMI Be Bop Deluxe box set, mainly in terms of my contribution to its booklet text and images. Mark Powell, the independent researcher whom EMI employ to remind them of what treasures they have in their back catalogue, is planning a visit to interview me for the project. I also have to make a start on the *Ghosts Engraved On Glass* video-film that I'm to present at Leeds University's School Of Music next spring. The *Memory Codex* video I'm presenting at Nelsonica is, as already noted, a kind of rehearsal or dry run for that project. It's enabled me to see what material I have already and how much more I need to locate to bring the project to a fuller conclusion. A lot of work to do here.

There is review of the forthcoming re-issue of *Getting The Holy Ghost Across* album in the latest issue of *Record Collector* magazine. Not a bad review at all but (and Mark P should really know better) the album wasn't produced by John Leckie, as Mark's review states, but by myself. It says as much on the tin. Credit where credit is due and all that. Actually, there was a similar error from Mark P a while back when, in another review for *Record Collector*, he stated that I'd worked with Ryuichi Sakamoto on my *Chimera* album when in fact it was Yukihero Takahashi. Next time he visits our house, I'll give him a gentle refresher course! He's a nice guy though and wrote a very good book called *The Ambient Century* in which I feature alongside some of my contemporaries. For those new to this kind of music, it's an enlightening read.

Time is passing and here I am, still typing. There are other things that I'd like to deal with in this diary entry but, already, I'm feeling guilty for spending so much time writing it when I should really be working on the final details of Nelsonica. So, I'll turn my attentions back to the job in hand. Nearly there now. Lord, I hope it all comes together on the day.

·

THURSDAY 5TH OCTOBER 2006

The weather has changed quite dramatically, cold and wet today, the Indian Summer banished overnight. Emiko's 58th birthday yesterday. Despite my constant work on the Nelsonica material, I managed to get into town for an hour and find a gift and a card. We actually went out together for a meal last night. My own 58th birthday coming up in December, not far away now. Can't believe that we're both so close to 60. When I think about how rapidly the last 10 years have flown, and how quickly a week passes these days, it's difficult not to get into a state of panic. So much still to achieve in both creative and personal terms. Life's too short when your mind is buzzing like a hive full of idea bees.

Into the last stages of pre-Nelsonica work now. The main things are all in place but still a few details to attend to. Mastering the new backing tracks next Tuesday, the earliest Fairview could accommodate me. A rehearsal room now booked for Thursday to set out my equipment and wire it all up, attend to any repairs needed and try to get to grips with the new material and re-acquaint myself with the older pieces. I've made my 'charts' for the musical aspect of the set but can't make notes about the effects unit changes and which guitar goes with which number until next Thursday. Friday will be packing up other extra bits of gear, choosing, ironing and packing clothes for stage and the rest of the event and, hopefully, trying to get an early night (probably sleepless). It's going to be an extremely busy Saturday. Whilst the attendees will have approximately 11 or 12 hours of unique entertainment, I'll be there sometime before the doors open to sound-check and generally try to get my act together. Jon Wallinger and the dedicated Nelsonica team will actually be there even earlier, on the Friday night, making a start on some of the preparatory tasks. Their organisational work is, as always, carefully considered and meticulous. Each year, the project becomes increasingly more complex but also equally more professional. I'm deeply touched by the team's dedication to the music and filled with admiration for their expertise. Their vibrant enthusiasm and love shines through every aspect of what they do and guarantees that the day will be special. I'm very lucky to be surrounded by such genuine people. I hope that they realise how grateful I am.

As always, we have visitors from overseas but, this year, they'll have the wonderful City of York to enjoy during their weekend, as well as the live music, videos and other presentations. An exciting change from the village of North Ferriby no doubt, even though I have many happy past associations with that place.

I've had news from Campbell American guitars that my Nelsonic Transitone prototype 2 is winging its way across the

Atlantic and should be here for me to play (and unveil in public) for the first time at Nelsonica 06. Dean (Campbell) has sent me some new photographs of the instrument. It looks great and I'm eager to get to grips with it. Once I've assessed it and made any final suggestions, and the proposed minor cosmetic details are added, it will go into production, my first signature model! It's like giving birth but, I'm sure, somewhat less painful. There's some work to do towards an extra, unadvertised item on the Nelsonica agenda, but I won't spoil it by giving details here. It should, however, add further interest to the day. I'm also planning to bring Lost Satellite Steve Cook on stage with me for an improvisational piece. He may end up being part of the Orchestra Futura feature, too. We'll see. He and I are getting together this coming Sunday to work on some ideas. And he'll cut my hair at the same time (no, not on stage, here at home!).

I do find the current juggling of one thing or another diffi- cult, stressful. There seems to be so much going on at the same time. But then, hasn't that always been the case? I'm always trying to push towards, not the future so much, as the NOW, the instant moment when fresh possibilities arise and the past is left to the sadness of ghosts. The older we get, the more the tendency arises to perpetually dwell in what we perceive as our 'glory years'. Perhaps this is simply a sign of our increasing inability to keep up, not so much with the wider world (which often lags even further behind) but to keep up with the rate of our own inner mercurial change and progress. The artist must conquer such tendencies, such laziness, such temptation to be sweet-talked into servitude. He must constantly refuse the easy laurel, the placatory kiss on the cheek and renew his commitment to the visionary impulse that, unbidden, compelled him to embark on the work in the first place. There is no place for living art in the mausoleum of lost youth. But our maturity, our ever refined and re-defined adulthood, allows us bigger and greater adventures. Not that many people have the nous or guts to grasp this and run with it.

I'm sometimes guilty of being swayed by those who find change too challenging. It's purely a kind of insecurity on my part, a momentary lack of confidence that causes me to commit this error. But it's important that I do not give those weak impulses credence or grant them power over the muse that has accompanied me on my long creative journey. Sounds terribly pompous, this, I know, but, tough. To hell with those that think that's all there is to it. There's more things in heaven and earth ... etc, etc.

I'll be clearer: I know *exactly* what I'm about and exactly where I'm going. Those who lag behind are not (and, for art's sake, should never be) my problem. I never wanted to be in the business of selling soft soap for the sake of a few short-lived bubbles of adulation. And so I pledge a new commitment to forward motion. It will be bright, joyous, positive, enlightening (yes, *that* word again) and strong. The rest is merely dust and husks for the sweeping.

What brought this mood on, I wonder? Maybe the nostalgia that inevitably accompanies certain aspects of Nelsonica? A frustration with the pace of progress here in my little room, in my life? *Return To Jazz Of Lights* was finished several months ago but won't be heard by my audience until the 14th of this month. I'm already thinking about the next step, where I should go from here. Is this part of the problem? That I'm in some sort of hyper-speed realm whilst the 'real' world inevitably drags its worn-out heels? Or am I just bored and disgusted with the dull, tired conservatism that seems to permeate 'pop' and 'rock' culture in general? Maybe the latter, maybe all of the aforementioned. I actually haven't a clue. Or if I have, I'm not telling here.

Well, that's it. A cutting of certain ties, a new freedom, a new resolve. Bob's your uncle and the world's your oyster. This is where it begins. Yet again. One of the things I'm looking forward to, once the pressure I'm feeling eases off, is to sit down and listen to some music, other than my own. I have a pile of CDs that haven't been out of their jewel cases yet, some Lennie Tristano, some old recordings of John Cage's piano sonatas, the latest Bill Frisell album, some Derek Bailey, a little bit of Charles Ives, some Nino Rota. Then there's the new Madeline Peyroux album that I'm eager to buy and hear. Oh, it goes on. A long list of lovely sounds and none of them remotely connected with what some people might think of as Bill Nelson's music. But then, they're not listening hard enough and so, as far as I'm concerned, their opinions don't count. Talking of Nino Rota, I've been reminded of his work by the score he created for Fellini's *Juliette Of The Spirits* which I've managed to watch late at night on DVD (though not all the way through yet). I first saw this film in the 1970s, I think, and loved it.

Almost finished the fabulous George Melly's *Slowing Down* which I've been reading when I wake up in a cold panic in the middle of the night. It calms me no end for some strange reason. My brother Ian once spent a little time with George. When Ian worked at the Yorkshire Sculpture Park, he was once assigned to collect George from the station and drive him to the park. It must have been a special visit or something. I can't recall the exact circumstances now but, sadly, Ian isn't around for me to call him up and check. Anyway, Ian was apparently quite impressed by George, particularly his apparent ability to allow himself the vigorous consumption of the kind of food, drink and cigarettes that were not perhaps wise for a man of his age. Somehow, George, despite various medical issues, appeared to be immune to these transgressions. My mother once commented that Ian took this as an example of the possibility of his own immunity to such things. Ian thought quite highly of George, as do I, but everyone's physical constitution is different. Not that I am particularly wise with my own health. Far from it. but, there you go. I'm reading a book by the man my brother once drove to the sculpture park. Life's like that, isn't it? Sitting here surrounded by several bright guitars. A kind of sculpture park here in my room. They're beautiful, colourful, inviting. But I'm avoiding dealing with them and their demands. It's an ambivalent relationship sometimes. I'll have to face the music tomorrow though as I still need to run some of the Nelsonica concert set through to try to grasp the shape and form of it. It's getting closer and closer. The clouds are parting and the stars are rising, a theatre of possibility. And myself alone and trembling, moving on.

•

Spent much of the day at Fairview studios with engineer John Spence, mastering the new instrumental pieces and assembling the final backing tracks for my live performance at this coming Saturday's Nelsonica convention. No second guessing now as the set list is finally 'written in stone.' After a quick run-through (and a haircut) with Steve Cook on keyboards on Sunday, I've decided to add *Nebulous Trolleybus* to the list, so there will now be 20 instrumentals performed at the convention. It makes for a quite sophisticated set lasting around one and three-quarter hours. Ten of those 20 numbers are brand new, receiving their premiere live performance at Nelsonica. The other 10 include some pieces that are also relatively new, so everything should sound nice and fresh. Some of it so fresh that I'll be struggling to remember it.

As always, it was a pleasure to sit with John as he mastered the backing tracks for me. This process makes a noticeable difference to the sound of the performance, ensuring that each piece sits at the correct level with the other pieces and that the sound is uniform and as punchy as possible. Not only does this provide a better listening experience for the audience but it also allows me to more clearly pick out the details within the backing tracks and thereby play in the most appropriate manner. I need to feel inspired by the on-stage sound if I'm to be at my best.

John was planning to visit Hull's annual autumn fair this evening. I would have loved to tag along with him but there's too much to attend to here, not least this diary update. The autumn Hull fair, John tells me, is the largest in Europe and has been a regular fixture for many years. I really would have enjoyed taking my camcorder along to grab some footage for possible use in one of my videograms, but time doesn't favour this. Maybe next year. Actually, I'll probably be just as busy with Nelsonica then, *and* there's the possibility of an American Nelsonica right after it Have been speaking with Simon Warner about our on-stage interview. Sent him some albums to fuel his questions. Should prove to be an interesting talk for those fans who take an interest in the subjects that have inspired me during the last year or two. Simon called me a few minutes ago to confirm some of the pieces to be discussed. We will have one more conversation on Friday to tie up any loose ends.

I still haven't prepared any thoughts or words for my Guitar Talk though (a separate thing from the Simon Warner interview). Perhaps time is against me now. I'll have to rely on my wits on the day. If the weather favours my imagination, it may yet turn out to be an interesting talk.

Before I could go to Fairview this morning, I had a diversion. I received notification that Parcel Force was holding an international package for me. It was prototype 2 of my signature Nelsonic Transitone guitar. I called John Spence to delay our starting time at Fairview and drove out to the Parcel Force depot on the edge of the city, paid the import duty on the guitar and brought it home. I took the guitar case from its exterior packaging and opened it up. A stunning colour, the red and cream and gold make for a very rich and warm looking instrument. I bundled it back into the car and headed off towards Hull and Fairview, eager to try it out against the soon to be mastered backing tracks. There are a few minor cosmetic details still missing on the guitar, but these will definitely be present on production models. Even without these, it's a striking instrument, as John noted. It sounds excellent. I specified a Seymour Duncan jazz pickup in the neck position which provides a glowing, warm tone to contrast with the bridge pickup's wiry twang. One thing that is remarkable about Campbell American guitars is their consistency. The quality standards are always the same, from one instrument to another. So often, you have to sort through a batch of supposedly identical guitars to find what might be considered a 'good' one. No such problem with these instruments. The three Campbell guitars I own all perform to the same high standard. As noted in previous diary entries, this year's Nelsonica will be very much a guitar-centred affair. I'm taking several favourite instruments to Thursday's rehearsal to decide on the final allocation of which instrument fits best with which track. There will be another special treat for guitar fans at the convention too but I'm keeping that as a surprise.

An enthusiastic and positive reaction on the Dreamsville site to the announcement about the forthcoming Dreamsville/Nelsonica Art Awards. I'm hoping that the standard of entries will be high and that the work submitted will serve to demonstrate the intelligence and imagination of those fans who appreciate the potential of art to enliven and enlighten our lives. I have to admit that I've always felt a little uneasy using the word 'fan' to describe those people who find enjoyment and information from listening to the music I create. I tend to think of fans as being young teenagers with little experience of life and not much sophistication, cannon fodder for the big bad music industry's marketing machine. My own experience, as regards my 'fans', is more complex than that and far less easy to define. Two things seem to emerge from my experiences of meeting them. One is their clearly evident warmth, good judgement and humanity. The other is their wide-ranging cultural appetite (not the best phrase but the closest to what I feel, especially at this hour of night).

Music seems to have informed their lives to a tremendous degree. Many of them regularly demonstrate an awareness and depth of insight that an intelligent exploration of the creative arts inevitably brings to those who care about these things. There often seems to be what one might refer to as a 'spiritual dimension' too. Certainly, my personal encounters with my audience via my concerts and the Dreamsville website bears this observation out.

So perhaps there's another word, one less loaded with notions of immaturity that might apply to those who share and enjoy my musical output with me. But I'm damned if I can come up with something appropriate. 'Connoisseurs' comes close but doesn't completely hit the spot. The word 'patrons' could be considered as part of the equation, too. It's both these attributes but something more, several things more. So, out of sheer frustration at a true definition, maybe for now, the epithet 'fans' has to suffice. Nevertheless, the word belittles the actual deed. Perhaps something as plain and simple as 'friends' comes closest. If there's one thing I should be proud of it is that my music has attracted, in the main, people of this calibre. Or am I just imagining that this is so? No matter how hard one tries to communicate, there will always be a minority who, from no great fault of their own, nor mine, misunderstand the work in one way or another. This is, as in other aspects of human interaction, inevitable. One has to accept that such confusions will be part of the scenario, no matter how hard one tries to aim for clarity. This can, for any artist driven by his or her creative forward momentum, prove to be frustrating. I've jumped through this particular hoop over and over again during my life as a musician and no doubt will be forced to do so again and again. This is part of the 'job', I suppose. But, as painful as it feels sometimes, it has to be done. There is no choice, other than to give in to things that one instinctively rejects as alien to one's sensibilities. It's a compulsion, in the end. Not everyone will feel like keeping pace, no matter how hard the artist pushes. But that too is the way it should be. Things eventually find their own level. For every thing left by the wayside, a new thing is gained. I'm more than happy with that. It seems natural enough to me.

Whilst on the subject of art (and I *was* on that subject, somewhere further back in this diary entry) I'm intrigued by Carsten Holler's work currently on show at Tate Modern. It's a kind of conceptual, futuristic fairground slide, taking up much of the vast space of Tate Modern's Turbine Hall. I plan to travel to London at some point during the next few weeks and will definitely be paying a visit to see this. Whenever I go to London, I make a habit of visiting one or other of the Tates (more often than not Tate Modern) where I browse in their bookshops, have lunch in their cafe and generally try to resist spending money on books that I can ill afford. But I do so much enjoy the experience of visiting these galleries and wandering amongst other art lovers. (There's now't more civilised than an art gallery, tha knows!) How I'd love to be able to create an audio-visual piece for the Turbine Hall. Or for York Minster, or the Cocteau Ampitheater just outside Monte Carlo, or, well, the list goes on and on. A series of concerts-come-installations at beautiful or inspiring locations around the world, maybe with a documentary film crew in tow to document it. A celebration of the sound of special places, the resonance of travel.

In today's *Independent*, an interesting article about Facel Vega cars. A company long defunct but, if I were able to indulge myself along the lines of a super-rich pop star, a company whose elegant and stylish automobiles I would enthusiastically collect and drive. 'Automobile', so much more evocative a word than 'Car', I think.

The real news, in the REAL world, really ugly and worrying, is that North Korea has tested its first nuclear weapon. A country ruled by what appears to be a very unpredictable fanatic has now become a serious threat to its Asian neighbours and the rest of the world. As if there wasn't already enough bloody-minded insanity on our own doorstep.

Bought a copy of *The Oldie* this week. Much more provocative and stimulating than the average rock rag or whatever. What will folks think? But then, I'm getting to that age when I'm damned if I give a bugger what folks think! One of the benefits of maturity is the ability to absolutely disregard the timid mediocrity of youth, my own youth included, by the way. We thought we had the world in our pocket but all we actually had was a soiled Kleenex and a copy of *Spic and Span* (look it up on the web if you weren't a male teenager in the early to mid 1960s). Late middle-age allows us to behave disgracefully whilst maintaining an annoying air of knowing nonchalance and crotchety grace. If there is such a thing. Well, there IS in MY book. But it's only valid when backed up with a certain savoir-faire (or something or other) but definitely not the loutish, beer-soaked whinging that some oldies carry over into middle-age from the cultural desert of their lost youth. I'm back in the last diary entry's territory here, by the sound of it. Railing against the dying of the light? No! Quite the opposite, trying to shield my eyes from its brilliance so that I can see my way forward. Sometimes, I'm deeply dazzled. Sometimes there's a headlamp that sees through the over-bright darkness as if by magic. Torchy The Battery Boy. A sky full of brilliant stars, obvious if you've got a telescope, less so if you're shoe-gazing.

It's autumn and the leaves are soon to be swept aside. A new broom, clear days ahead. Always looking forward to tomorrow. Saturday soon and nerves of steel. Ready, willing and able!

·

MONDAY 23RD OCTOBER 2006

Sometimes I wonder. Reading back through the most recent diary entries I can sense the pressure and stress of the last few months. There's much that I would (and should) change. My choice of words or phrase is sometimes ill-considered or untypical. At worst, totally off-target. A head spinning and dizzy with, if not euphoria, then ecstatic panic. Yes, Peter Panic, my alter-ego, a stretched-on-the-rack-of-existential-angst Cliff Richard, a dark shadow of the boy next door. Or maybe just the village idiot, the one who raided the local library and stole all the weird books that no-one ever read. (And then scribbled in their margins, slightly obscene doodles, fingerprints, ejaculations of dissent.)

I'm exhausted but buzzing with new ideas. Spinning.

Nelsonica 06 went pretty well last Saturday. Already over a week ago but still a blur for me as I was 'on tap' virtually all the time. Lots of people there, the best attendance yet, I think. The Nelsonica team had done a fabulous job of tricking up the venue with huge posters depicting various aspects of my work, including a magnificent one for the Dreamsville website. A tremendous effort all round. I exhibited part of my guitar collection. First time I'd seen these particular instruments out of their cases all at the same time. They looked beautiful. I took my Carlsbro Nelsonic amp to display too, although I went 100% digital with my live on-stage performance as I generally do at solo concerts these days. Prototype number two of my signature model 'Nelsonic Transitone' guitar had arrived at Nelson Acres a few days before the event and I was able to give it its first proper airing during the live performance. It sounded great and there are just a few minor tweaks that I've suggested to Dean Campbell before it goes into production. The guitar caused quite a stir amongst the players in the audience during the performance. It looks striking too, the colour has turned out just as I'd intended.

My live set wasn't strictly solo. This time, I actually had other musicians to share the stage with, at least for three numbers in the set. It was a pleasure to work, during the encore section of the live set, with Theo Travis, Dave Sturt and Steve Cook who joined me for three numbers under the alias of Orchestra Futura, an improvising ensemble of some considerable skill and imagination. We had no rehearsal, just dived in and swam for it. An ocean of sound but strong swimmers all. Theo played impressive flute and saxophone, treating his flute via a delay-looper. Dave played bass, using an unusual Viger fretless bass guitar with a metal fretboard, going via processors and a lap top. Quite a few people in the audience were intrigued by this instrument, judging by comments made afterwards. Steve played his keyboard, sticking with piano and Fender Rhodes sounds. The entire ensemble had a beautifully fragmented jazz-electronica sound. The feedback on my website about this ensemble has been very encouraging, though, as might be expected, it was seen as a little too left-field for some of the more traditionally minded fans. For me, it was a positive step towards another bright horizon. I'm rather keen to see where this might lead. A stimulating side-project with potential for both recorded and live music and an opportunity for me to stretch out and enjoy playing unshackled by people's pre-conceptions about the kind of music I'm 'supposed' to make.

None of this should come as much of a surprise to those fans who have been aware of my long-time passion for slightly more esoteric music. There have been plenty of precursors to the Orchestra Futura approach over the last 26 years or more, so it's not as if it's a newly acquired taste on my part. The 1980s saw me virtually abandon anything connected with straight rock music, apart from a few diversions. Works such as *Sounding The Ritual Echo*, *Simplex*, *Trial By Intimacy*, *Crimsworth*, the two Orchestra Arcana albums, amongst others, explored avenues flanked by a noticeably different musical architecture from the old Be Bop Deluxe sonic suburbia. In more recent years, I've re-introduced some familiar (to the older fans) elements to the mix. Perhaps the vocal approach has opened out a little and the music has assumed a broader, more general appeal. Even so, I've kept elements from the left-of-centre material and incorporated them into the straighter pieces.

Nothing I do is ever quite as straightforward as it might first appear. I think that, after all these years, it's fair to assume that the average listener has grown less Luddite about my music. After all, I'm not exactly known for sticking with the same formula for very long. Even Be Bop Deluxe rang the changes. It's amusing to note that the style of electronica-based music that I adopted in the early 1980s, a style that seemed somewhat controversial to many Be Bop Deluxe fans back then, has since been absorbed into the mainstream and is now perfectly ordinary and acceptable, cropping up in everything from television advertising to movie soundtracks. Minimalism, sampling, digital glitches, sonically 'distressed' sounds, modal music, drones, poly-rhythmic beats, artificially created timbres and post-modernist, conceptual ideas are just as familiar to the general public as guitars were back in the 1969s and 1970s. Cheaper technology has made that kind of music even more common, especially now when computer sequencing software has enabled almost anyone to try their hand at it. Not only has yesterday's Abbey Road become every man and his dog's home studio, yesterday's avant-garde has become today's popularist music too. What was once an outsider form has been embraced by the herd.

Of course, there's no reason why all these different 'genres' can't happily co-exist. To the open mind and ear, not only do they already co-exist but they mingle, mix and match also. The barriers have been down for some time and, for those of us who scraped away at them in the first place, the future is a wide open space. If the sound of dragging heels can sometimes still be heard it's probably from those who still locate their listening pleasure in the sphere of adolescent nostalgia. Now, don't misunderstand, I have a tremendous respect and love of the music that I grew up with and it naturally and unconsciously informs and inspires a lot of my contemporary output. Nevertheless, I'm constantly trying to widen my horizons. It's an approach I've nurtured almost from the beginning, a vigorous curiosity, a hunger for more. I'm just not one of those people who stopped listening to music post-Elvis, post-Hendrix, post-Sex Pistols (or post-Be Bop Deluxe for that matter). Life's too short to impose those kinds of limits when there's so much more to get to grips with, explore and enjoy. But that schoolboy 'either/or' situation where one has to join one tribe or another (but never both), that thing of never stepping over the line, of always having to wear the correct uniform, when music becomes a 'my favourite band is better than yours' slanging match, where there's no opportunity for forward movement, where musical taste becomes a closed shop, well, I don't really go for that. What causes such a dogmatic, narrow attitude? Fear of the unknown and the security of the familiar? Aesthetic timidity? It's sad how many people live in fear of Art with a capital 'A'. The one thing that might brighten and enliven their lives, more so than religion or politics.

Back to Nelsonica. There were lots of other things for the audience to enjoy: an onstage interview with myself conducted by Simon Warner, Senior Teaching Fellow at Leeds University's School Of Music, was well received. I've known Simon for quite a few years now and have contributed to his classes at Bretton Hall College in the past. I've also given talks with him at Wakefield's Unity Hall (the latter place filled with memories for me. It was here that I first recall seeing my father play his saxophone with his own band at the silver wedding anniversary ball of Ada and Herman Ackroyd, who were good friends of my parents back in the 1940s and 1960s). Simon's interview this year centred on the topic of songwriting. It was relatively stress-free, perceptive and a real pleasure to take part in. I also improvised a talk about guitars and guitar playing. I managed to do it without the list of prompts I'd prepared the night before, which, unfortunately, meant I missed some of the topics I'd intended to cover, but I just let it ramble wherever it needed to go and all seemed to work out okay in the end. I can't recall much of what I said now, but I did manage to show everyone a video clip of Joe Pass playing in concert. This seemed to blow a few minds in the audience, particularly those who hadn't pre-viously come across Joe's work. It felt like my younger days, when I'd turn friends on to my latest musical discoveries by lending them albums I'd found.

The hardest part of the convention, or at least the most emotionally testing part, was the little tribute to my brother, Ian, that I'd arranged. Again, I had not written anything down or rehearsed a speech; things just happened on the spur of the moment. I tried to talk about the childhood that Ian and I had shared, about how much I missed him, how much I wished I could talk with him. I wasn't particularly articulate, I fear. Afterwards, I realised that there was much more that I'd intended to say about him, but, due to nervousness and an inner struggle not to let my emotions run away with me, I didn't quite manage to include everything I'd hoped to get across to the audience. But at least I managed to say something, which is more than I could manage at Ian's funeral service when words would have been impossible and only tears articulate. My mother (and her husband, George) and also Ian's two sons (my nephews), Julian and Louis, were in attendance at the convention. I hope they felt the high regard the audience demonstrated for my much-missed and loved brother. I know he would have been deeply touched by it all.

At Nelsonica, I placed two framed photographs of Ian (playing his saxophone) on a little table next to me on stage. Emi had made a flower arrangement which was displayed in a vase next to the photos of Ian and I brought a small Buddha figure from my home studio, with a tea-light illuminated in it, to sit on the table too. It was symbolic of the fact that Ian had planned to share this year's Nelsonica stage with me. We'd discussed it just two weeks before he passed away. There were times during the performance that I felt his presence. Ian was once part of a group called Fiat Lux, back in the 1980s, and the band's vocalist and songwriter, Steve Wright, kindly agreed to come along to Nelsonica to talk about his memories of Ian. We also showed some Fiat Lux videos and played some of Ian's last recordings (made with his friend and musical partner John Nixon) to the audience. There was a wonderfully warm response from everyone.

Later on in the event, I had scheduled two separate 'meet 'n' greet' sessions of one hour each, where attendees could sit down, have a photograph taken with me by official Nelsonica photographer Martin Bostock, and get their Nelsonica album signed. As always, we'd underestimated how long this would take and the reality was that I ended up having one very long, continuous session of over three hours without a break. It's always nice to meet the people who enjoy my music and I'm always happy to make time to chat with them but, towards the end of this long, long signing session, my brain was less than sharp, not helped by a magic wine glass by my side which, amazingly, always seemed full! It was a very exhausting experience, not just for me but for the people at the back of the apparently infinite queue. In the end though, I think everyone went home happy, despite the fact that we'd been given less than enough seating arrangements by the venue itself. Most people had been on their feet all day (as had I), something we must guard against at next year's event.

One new feature of the convention was the presence of the rather lovely 'Nelsonettes', a group of young ladies decked out in specially made 'Nelsonette' T-shirts. They added a much needed feminine touch to the event as they moved amongst the attendees with camera and microphone, interviewing willing participants for a little souvenir audio-visual piece that we're hoping to assemble soon. Actually, there was a much higher number of females in the audience this year. A good thing in my book. I hope this trend continues! One of the sweetest aspects of Nelsonica is the unexpected giving of gifts that some fans bring. They're very generous and thoughtful with their choices, too. This year, I was given two extremely special and valuable books, one dealing with Chet Atkins' life and one with Les Paul's. The Les Paul book is a limited edition publication, hand-numbered and signed by Les himself. It's a superbly produced book and, for me, a huge Les Paul fan, it is something that I'll always treasure. I was also given a book dealing with Jean Cocteau's *Testament Of Orphee* film, which is my favourite Cocteau movie, though not necessarily, in critics' eyes, his best. Cocteau himself 'stars' in it though and it is clearly personal and autobiographical. I find the film very touching. Other gifts: a vintage style tin robot-spaceman; a copy of Madelline

Peyroux's latest album (excellent, by the way); a sailor's Theodolite (fascinating!); some CDs of fans' own music; a bottle of wine; some photographs of myself at previous year's Nelsonicas; a set of American Hot Rod and Custom Car magazines from the late 1950s and early 1960s (takes me back to my early teens and the model car kit mania I had then); a set of CDR copies of vintage radio shows and interviews with Derek Bailey and Bill Frisell; some video CDRs and even a 'Jesus Soap On A Rope'! (And there were more besides.) It felt as if my birthday had arrived two months early.

A really nice touch was when the Nelsonica team presented Emiko with a large bouquet of flowers (for putting up with me, I suspect!). She was completely taken aback and genuinely touched that the team had thought to do this for her. After a very long day, we eventually got home in the early hours of Sunday morning, slightly worse for wear but relieved that all had gone reasonably well. Mission accomplished, at least until next year.

On Sunday, I had to be up early to get all my equipment back into the house. My guitar tech, Pete Harwood, who had done a super job of looking after my on (and off) stage guitar needs, brought everything back in a large van. We stacked the guitars and other equipment in the dining room and hall. I wasn't in the mood (or energetic enough) to deal with the task of carting it upstairs, item by item, and trying to fit it into the limited space I have available for storage. I made a start at this on the Monday but it was Wednesday morning before absolutely everything was tidied away. Paul and Ian Gilby called around 1 pm on the Sunday and we went to a tiny village pub a few miles from where I live for a traditional Sunday roast. It was such a pleasure to be able to relax amongst genial company after the long, stressful build up to the convention. Ian and Paul have been such good friends in recent years and their help and support is something I appreciate very much. Sitting in the little pub allowed us time and space that, due to our various workloads, would usually be at such a premium for us. A very pleasant, civilised afternoon.

Time still runs fast however and already more than a week has flown since Nelsonica 06. I've been trying to catch up with various domestic duties that had been pushed to the back of the queue due to Nelsonica's demands, but I'm still behind. Thought I might get a proper break but that seems out of the question, too. I tried to book a cottage on the end of Whitby's harbour, part of my plan to have a three or four day 'mini-holiday' with Emi. However, the cottage we wanted was fully booked apart from the week around my birthday in December. This actually would have been ideal for me, a terrific birthday present but, unfortunately, Emi has to work during that week as it is one of the flower shops busiest periods (being Christmas) so we've had to give up on the idea of a break altogether.

Maybe I'll just book an overnight stay, one weekend, at the White Horse and Griffin hotel and restaurant. Better than nothing. I was really looking forward to the view from 'Captain's Cottage' though. It has windows overlooking the harbour, the harbour mouth and the ocean. It would be cold, dark and wild in December but I love Whitby out of season and the winter weather and early nights suits it somehow. So much more atmospheric than summertime when it's crowded with tourists.

A very good documentary on the Artsworld TV channel

the other night, dealing with Miles Davis' electric period. It featured several celebrity guest musicians talking about him, as well as interview clips and performances from Miles himself. I was amused when reminded of how some critics and many of Miles' fans reacted negatively to him introducing electronic keyboards and amplified guitars into his music, back in the 1960s. It caused something of a stir. As did Bob Dylan going from acoustic folk to electric rocker, Joni Mitchell adding jazz elements to her music etc. (On another level, Be Bop Deluxe to Red Noise, Red Noise to *Quit Dreaming*, and so on. Familiar reactions for me too but I've come to expect it and shouldn't be too surprised). The documentary's interviews emphasised one major point: a true artist can't stand still. It was also stated that Miles, and many other creative musicians, are not in the business of being entertainers. It was inspiring and encouraging to hear these attitudes and sentiments (which I've held since the start of my 'career') being confirmed by artists whom I deeply respect. I caught this programme halfway through but the timing was perfect as I'd just come down from an evening of trying to explain, on the forum of my website, why I can never look backwards for too long. I was feeling a little marginalised for sticking to my ideals and had been suffering some mild despair. The comments from Miles and fellow artists gave me some much needed confidence. At times, there is a sense that one is a small part of a bigger picture and, no matter how meagre, that one's own contribution is both worthwhile and honourable. How I would have loved to have played alongside Miles and others of that calibre. Perhaps that's an over-ambitious wish, in musical terms. But, hell, I'd have liked to try.

Just finished reading Frank Letchford's biography of Austin Osman Spare which throws light on the more human side of his life. So many of the (very few) books about AOS focus on his esoteric magical theories. It was good to read, in Mr. Letchford's *Michaelangelo In A Teacup* book about the sensitive and perceptive character behind the magical image. Frank Letchford was a long time friend of Austin's and has written very much from that privileged perspective. Another book about Spare is waiting on top of my bedside pile. So many books to read.

My scanner has broken down. First it kept quitting on me and now it's packed in altogether. It's not even switching on: completely inactive. I need it for album sleeve artwork and for website/diary images. I went to buy a new one but they all seem to require much more recent Mac operating systems than the one I use. I could, of course, install a newer OS but then my other software programmes wouldn't work. And I need my Final Cut Pro for the development of the *Ghosts Etched On Glass* film. It's a love and hate relationship, computers and me. What I *really* need is a NEW computer, even though mine is only six years old. The new Mac pro dual core G5 tower would be like a breath of fresh air. My current G4 is ancient in computer terms. What a game this computer lark is.

Autumn now has a firmer grip. Red and gold and brown, though there's still more green on the trees than is usual for this time of year. Not particularly cold either. Lots of Canada geese wheeling over the river in town today, great screeching circles of them. A girl lifted her tourist map over her head in self-protection, frightened of being dumped on.

Had one of my apocalyptic dreams last night. Extremely realistic. High tech Eurofighter style planes with the ability to hover, flying low and slow over English villages pumping hot lead and rockets into crowds of running, screaming people. A rain of metal and fire. I was there, trying to dodge the deadly hail. Got hit though. Who were these people, glimpsed through jet plane canopies, crystal clear, strange insignia on their craft? The machinery was awesome in its efficient beauty, bright light glinting from metal surfaces. Designer fighter aircraft, their pilots tricked out like military fashion plates, but merciless, trigger happy, ruthless. Why did I dream such a thing and why was it sharper and more vivid than my usual dreams? I've had far too many disturbing dreams of late.

I'm thinking of buying myself a new bicycle, my old one being a bit heavy, a bone-shaker. I could do with something lighter and more comfortable that would encourage me to get out of the studio more and take a little gentle exercise. Saw a nice one in a shop called Cycle Heaven the other day. Like most things that catch my eye, it was expensive. I'll search around for something more sensible. Actually, one of those 'electrically assisted' ones might be fun. Or a French Velo-Solex with the little petrol engine over the front wheel. I can just see me, putt-putt-putting along, from the village into town, dressed in my American newsboy's cap and steam engine driver's jacket, autumn leaves flying behind me. The neighbours would have a field day!

And now what? My 'to do' list is far from empty. Lots to tackle in the ensuing months. Difficult to know where best to start. Some much-needed household repairs first, though. Try to leave the guitars in their cases for a little while. Or am I asking too much of myself there? Enough diary, for now. I'm getting cabin fever. Time for a stroll around town.

·

TUESDAY 31ST OCTOBER 2006

I'm in a kind of limbo, a place when I've got plenty to do but little energy to do it. I feel as if I'd benefit from a week's holiday in Villefranche-Sur-Mer, strolling through the lamp-lit tunnel of Rue Obscura, or sitting in a seafood restaurant on the salty dog harbourside, taking a sneaky peek at the French girls' shapely legs whilst winking the tiniest hint of a twinkling eye, a salacious old Riviera goat, living the poet's life.

I've made a start on the 8 x 8 inch canvas artwork that I'm trying to create for the Stars On Canvas celebrity charity auction being held in Brighton in November, but I've thrown two half-completed canvases in the bin so far. I'm rushing it instead of considering what I really want to do. I've also wasted time trying to use oil pastels on a roughly textured and small canvas. Far too blunt an instrument. Despite this, I have managed to complete a very simple piece, almost minimalistic, using just a brush, black ink and the merest hint of colour. It's not really a painting as such, just a drawing executed on canvas. But it's not bad. It will be my failsafe if I don't come up with something better in time for the rapidly approaching November 10th exhibition date. I went out and bought four more blank canvases this afternoon though. So, even if nothing better comes down God's pipe, I can at least persuade myself that I've tried.

Attended a memorial service in Wakefield for my brother Ian this last Sunday. It was an emotional affair, fuelled even more by certain aspects of the religious ceremony. Perhaps that was the purpose of it, a deliberate and cathartic prodding of wounds. Although the vicar and his begowned acolytes were plainly sincere in their beliefs, I still couldn't help thinking that there was a frightening lack of light beneath all the ritual. Plenty of smoke and mirrors, though. I just instinctively felt that there was a catastrophic misunderstanding of what was really required in such a situation. There was some talk of healing; there was talk of solace, but also the usual evocation of the tortured and meat-racked Christ, the cannibalistic body and blood feast, a darkly guilty and sin-soaked ecstasy of gothic remorse. Not much sunshine or true celebration of Ian's life as it was actually lived. There was one aspect of the service though, that came closer to being universally appropriate to the situation and our love for Ian, and that was the lighting of a candle with his name on it, which we, as a family, were allowed to physically, directly deal with ourselves, with only minor assistance from the church 'staff.'

I guess the problem, for me at least, is that Christianity is shackled by the Bible and the history of the Church itself. It also makes me feel mean and churlish when I inevitably pick the fabric of faith apart, especially when so many good hearted people seem to gain something helpful from their involvement with orthodox religion. But it seems to me that much of religious thought and dogma is out of step with the true 'spirit' of the human condition. I know it is out of step with my own spiritual experience and I also know that my brother Ian had little time for religion in any form. He was a 'live-life-to-the-full' and 'damn the torpedoes' sort of chap. Any kind of religious or spiritual debate became an easy target for his scorn. Having said that, I do feel that he would have appreciated *some* sort of meaningful gesture, some declaration of love towards him from those of us left behind. He would also have returned the gesture with equal love. It was with that in mind that we, Ian's family and loved ones, gathered together at last Sunday's memorial service. I think he would have appreciated the lighting of the candle too. My mother, Ian's wife Diane, Ian's children, Emi and I and some close friends of Ian's all shed a good few tears in the more difficult moments of the service. The still unsettled grief, the emotional rawness, did somehow glue us together. I wish that I could spend more time with what remains of my family but I always seem to be caught up in a desperate, headlong rush to maintain what passes for my day-to-day existence. The curse of modern living? This fearful sense of time running out dissolves even the best of intentions.

Before the service, Emi and I had taken fresh flowers to Ian's grave. The beautiful spring blossoms that filled the avenue of trees near his grave not long after he was laid to rest have now given way to equally beautiful russet and gold autumn leaves. How quickly time has flown. Ian's headstone is being carved at the moment and should be in place by Christmas. It will be in light grey Indian marble with silver text. For now though, only the framework that held the flowers spelling out the word 'DAD' and a couple of rain soaked cards mark Ian's resting place. And three glass vases pressed into the soil, filled with flowers. Emi and I left just pure white ones this time. Ian's mother-in-law, who passed away only a few weeks after Ian, lies at peace in the plot just behind Ian's. Her headstone will be erected there soon also. It is being carved by the same person who is creating Ian's.

I've probably mentioned Wakefield Cemetery before in this diary, how, in the early 1950s, I used to visit it on Saturday mornings as a child with my mother and grandmother to place flowers on my great grandfather's grave, his location now long lost to me. How also, I used to visit the cemetery during my art school years in the 1960s, sometimes to sketch or photograph stone angels, sometimes just to wander amongst the Victorian graves and memorials, marvelling at the names and lives of souls who I never knew but, nevertheless felt some strange kinship with. An impossible nostalgia born of shared mortality perhaps? There was always an immense, overwhelming sadness in the air, but an aching, tender beauty, too. It was a place where people had been left behind, waylaid, abandoned by time and the world, yet freed from its ravages, despite the inevitable sense of decay. Those perpetual Victorians, eternal miners, frozen-in-time mill workers, industrialists, authors, artists, doctors and clergy, etc. Forever framed by and fixed in ancient Yorkshire landscapes of gas lamps, smoke and chimneys, cobblestones, dusty sash-windows, slate roofs and rainy, hooting, whistling railway sidings. Each and every gravestone marking an individual life filled with its own personal joys and sorrows, (and its own *universal* joys and sorrows!).

For some strange reason I felt more compassion, more connectedness with these distant, imagined lives than with flesh and blood passing strangers on the street. Perhaps, because death robs us of our insecurities, anger and greed, there is nothing to fear from the dead, only the living. Ghosts are our mortal fears made manifest.

After the memorial service at the church, Emi and I drove my Mum and her husband George up to the Kings Arms pub on Heath Common, just on the edge of Wakefield. It's an old haunt of mine from my 1960s art school days and also the early

1970s. It also holds some memories of Ian for me, (though not as many as the pub he and I used to meet up for lunch at when he worked at the Yorkshire Sculpture Park in the 1990s). It was here too that the Nelson family came after Ian's funeral service and reception last April. The Kings Arms and Heath Common itself form part of my own history. The food may be uninspiring but the atmosphere is special. Mum, George, Emi and I decided to have a meal there, nothing too fancy as George isn't a fancy eater, preferring what he refers to as 'traditional' food. Not that there was anything that he would have considered exotic on the menu anyway. So it was meat pie and veg for him and Mum and fish and chips for Emi and I. George did let me buy him a pint of lager, though. The Kings Arms ancient atmosphere soothed and charmed us. It is still lit by gaslight, a soft flickering amber-tinted glow. The pub has several small, nook-and-cranny wood panelled rooms, all crooked and tobacco stained and stone flagged. A *proper* pub and authentically old. Outside, the common stretched away in the clocks-just-changed darkness, the village of Heath quiet in the autumnal Sunday night air, a few lights visible from distant stone cottages. If I were ever to return to Wakefield to live, this would probably be my ideal location. But I can't see me returning for anything other than to visit family or to take flowers to Ian.

Car touble last week. Emi's car needed repairs. Costly but unavoidable. Fixed now but we need to seriously think about changing both our vehicles. Mileage too high and trade in value too low, but that's the way it goes with cars. Television broken in the living room, has been for months now. And I still haven't called a repair man. Communicated with Matt Howarth about our ever ongoing collaboration: *The Last Of The Neon Cynics*. Matt is looking for some more music from me. I got a disc from him with a full colour version of the story on it: looks great.

Too tired to write more now. I spend far too much time on website matters. It's surprising how much mail I get from fans and how often I feel compelled to respond to topics on the Dreamsville Forum. It does occupy a great deal of my time. Perhaps its just part of that impulse to leave footprints in the sand. Melancholia setting in. Time to go downstairs and watch television.

•

FRIDAY 10TH NOVEMBER 2006

After four attempts at coming up with a suitable 8 inch by 8 inch artwork for the Stars On Canvas exhibition and charity auction, I finally settled on the very first one I'd created. Two others went into the bin and a third I decided to give to a good friend. The canvas I've donated to the auction is called 'Starboy' and will be exhibited at the Julie-Anne Gilbert Gallery, Arches 283a, Madeira Drive, Brighton BN2 1PT, from the 18th of November. The charity auction (which is in aid of an organisation called Whoops-A-Daisy which helps children suffering from cerebral palsy) will be held on the 26th of November. Emiko took a photograph of me holding the artwork. As usual, I was horrified by my appearance which seems to get more wizened every time a shutter clicks in my direction. All is vanity, especially in this business.

Time still at a premium. I seem to be struggling to keep up, but that's always the case. I'm currently working on several pieces of art which I'm framing as gifts for the loyal and dedicated Nelsonica team who put together the fan convention every year. I'm taking them all out to dinner in just over a week's time and will give each of them an artwork. The table is booked for 10 people but I still need to complete a few more drawings to frame. I find I really have to be in the mood to come up with visual art, whereas with music, I *always* seem to be in the mood. In fact, I've got several musical ideas that I'd like to explore at the moment but no available time to do so. Perhaps I should list my plans for the coming months here, just to outline what I'm hoping to achieve. These are in no particular order but the future, at the moment, looks like this:

1. Repair and upgrade my Mackie hard-disk HDR 24/96 multi-track recorder and make a start on mixing the Be Bop Deluxe Decca tapes.
2. Work with Paul Sutton-Reeves towards establishing a 'coda' for his *Music In Dreamland* book, bringing it up to date. It isn't due to be published until early next year so there's now an opportunity to update the text to include more recent developments. The book was finished almost two and a half years ago but has been delayed due to the publisher's serious illness. The latest information I have is that it will see the light of day early in 2007.
3. Upgrade my computer and video editing software and attempt to make a start on my *Ghosts Etched On Glass* film autobiography. This will be a more sophisticated version of *Memory Codex Number On* which I screened at this year's Nelsonica convention. *Ghosts Etched On Glass* is planned to

be part of a special live event at Leeds University's School Of Music next April.

4. Transfer some of my more recent backing tracks onto my multi-track machine and overdub lead guitar parts, then mix and assemble a running order for *The Last Of The Gentleman Rocketeers* album that will constitute volume two of the *Painting With Guitars* series.

5. Go through several hours' worth of previously unreleased home recordings from the 1980s and assemble an album from the best tracks. An official title for this project has yet to be decided but working title possibilities are: *The Time Traveller's Companion*, *Electrical Goods And Knitting Yarns*, *An Imaginary History Of Magic* (*Music To Conjure The Ghosts Of The Past*), *Songs From A Secret Museum* or *Snowballs And Oranges*. As usual, it's quite possible that *none* of these titles will be used and something entirely different concocted, once I've selected the album's track running order.

6. Make a special compilation album using only the oddest, most 'psychedelic', trippy or eccentric tracks from my past home recordings and solo releases. Working title for this is: *Superheads Recommend*. I want this to concentrate mainly on vocal songs but with perhaps a few instrumentals thrown in. It should be compiled from obscure tracks that were originally hidden away in dark corners of earlier albums plus some previously unreleased oddities along similar lines.

7. Assemble Volume One of a series of compilation albums focusing exclusively on Nelsonica recordings. These would not be literal copies of the original albums but re-sequenced

tracks set in a different context and with new packaging artwork.

8. Re-release the *Noise Candy* recordings but as individual albums. Lenin Imports have not been in touch with me for a long time about the original release and have not responded to recent requests by my management for accounting so it's time I turned these recordings to my own advantage, rather than to anyone else's.

9. Attempt to write and record some brand new songs for an acoustic based vocal album. Possible working titles for the album are: *Songs Of The Blossom Tree Optimists*, *Every Blessed Thing Is So Damned Fragile* or *December Lane*.

10. Choose and assemble a compilation album focusing exclusively on past guitar instrumentals, choosing my favourite tracks from various albums. Working titles for this project are: *Great Northern Twang Magus*, *The Guitar Room*, *Six Lane Skyway* or *Like Time Machines*. Again, these are just initial titles. It could end up being something completely different.

11. Create some very short instrumental pieces, between one and two minutes in length which will become the basis of equally short video pieces. These to be made available as digital downloads from the Dreamsville Essoldo Cinema.

12. Work on the second volume of *Diary Of A Hyperdreamer*, to be published by Pomona.

13. Look at the possibility of a select series of live concerts for next year. My idea is to stage them in interesting or unorthodox venues.

14. Work on my autobiography, *Painted From Memory*, for publication by *Sound-On-Sound*. It would be nice to make

this a quite lavishly illustrated book, along the lines of an art book. It should also contain an accompanying DVD. It would need to sell as a limited edition expensive item to justify the time and cost involved in its production but I think something very special might come of this.

15. Create a new, commercially available DVD, following on from *Flashlight Dreams And Fleeting Shadows*.

16. Try to organise something around the 'Orchestra Futura' project with Theo Travis and Dave Sturt.

17 Work towards expanding the Dreamsville site, opening up the 'Museum Of Memory' and 'The Guitar Arcade.'

18. Choose certain tracks from my back catalogue to be made available as internet downloads.

19. Write and record a brand new instrumental album, placing minimalist guitar in a pure digital electronica setting.

20. Work towards an audio-visual exhibition/installation which would gather together drawings, photographs, album sleeve art and video work and present them in a gallery context with an accompanying soundtrack. This would depend on the help of fans who own some of my artwork. I would ask them to loan the pieces to the exhibition. The art would be returned to them afterwards and their names and help would be acknowledged in the catalogue and in the exhibition itself. The exhibition would need to find a sponsor to help mount it.

21. Find a choreographer/dance company who might be interested in collaborating with me in the creation of a contemporary dance piece. I've wanted to try something along these lines for many years but have never got around to finding out if it could be practically realised. I'm not getting

any younger, as they say, so I really ought to put the pedal to the metal and attempt the impossible. And that, for now, is enough. Plenty of goals to score, targets to hit.

Went to Whitby last Saturday, just for the day. An absolutely glorious, fiery sunset over the town as twilight flooded the opposite end of the harbour. A breath-taking, magical moment. Unfortunately, I hadn't taken my still camera with me but did have my camcorder so, thankfully, I managed to capture some of the dramatic and beautiful light. It will be used in one of the short video downloads I'm planning. Emi and I had dinner at The White Horse And Griffin, as is our habit when in Whitby. On the drive home over the North Yorkshire Moors, we could see firework displays ringing the horizon. Starbursts and rocket trails. I told Emiko about my boyhood experiences of bonfire night, treacle toffee and the selection boxes of fireworks manufactured by such companies as Standard, Lion, Pains and Brocks that my father used to bring home for our own back-yard display. Emi likes the idea of bonfire night, even though there's no Guy Fawkes equivalent in Japan.

Sunday we went to Salt's Mill at Saltaire, another fairly regular haunt for us. Emi managed a little bit of Christmas shopping. I guess mine will be the usual last minute panic, particularly as Emi will be busy at the flower shop until late on Christmas Eve. It seems like only yesterday I was taking down last year's Christmas decorations and packing them away in the cupboard under the stairs. And here it comes again, hurtling towards us, driven by hyper-speed reindeers.

Found some old photos of Emiko when she was a little girl, dressed in traditional Japanese costume for a school play. They are black and white photographs but I've messed around with them and got some nice colour effects happening. I may use one or two for a future instrumental album sleeve.

Went out with four of our best friends for dinner last night. A belated birthday celebration for Steve and for Emi. We went to San Martino in Harrogate, an excellent restaurant that was introduced to me by my friend Paul Gilby. A very civilised, convivial evening and a further respite from my work.

The last two days have seen another plunge in temperature. Feels quite wintry Big pullover time. I think I'll go set a log fire ready to light later this evening. Get the smell of wood smoke in the air.

·

TUESDAY 14TH NOVEMBER 2006

Spent the afternoon with Paul (Gilby) who is helping me to up-date my recording system software. He's fitted a new floppy drive and upgraded the memory of my Mackie HDR 24/96 multi-track recorder. Just a few more things to do to it tomorrow and then I'll be able to mix the Be Bop Deluxe Decca sessions for future release. Once I can set some personal time aside to deal with that, of course.

Went to London last Saturday, just for the day. Emi to her usual Japanese Buddhist temple meeting, me to the Tate and the usual round of bookshops. I bought several DVDs: the original BBC TV series of Dennis Potter's *Pennies From Heaven*, also DVD copies of films I have on VHS but wanted to secure as DVDs: *A Kind Of Loving* and *The Magnificent*

Ambersons. I also got *Hope and Glory* and a DVD titled *Legends Of Western Swing* which features vintage performances by Bob Wills and his Texas Playboys, Spade Cooley and several others. Finding time to watch all these is another matter.

It was the Lord Mayor's Parade and fireworks display on the Saturday too, something of which we hadn't been aware of. The city was even more busy than usual. Late afternoon, when Emi returned from her temple service, we met up with her friend Kyoko and had a drink at a Cuban bar in Wardour Street, not far from where the old Marquee club once stood. As Emi and Kyoko talked about this and that, my mind drifted back to the time when Be Bop Deluxe performed at The Marquee in 1974. We were booked to support a band called String Driven Thing. It was at that same Marquee Club gig that we were finally signed by EMI Records, an event which led to our first album, *Axe Victim*. In one of my ancient sketchbooks, I have a very rapidly executed drawing of the Marquee's interior that I scratched out under dim lights, whilst bored and waiting for our sound check (I think one of the figures depicted in the sketch is our then manager, Colin Mawston). I was thrilled to be playing there, on the exact same stage that my teenage heroes, such as Jeff Beck, Jimi Hendrix and The Who, had performed on in the 1960s. That creaky old platform held a special magic for me, as did the tiny, scruffy dressing room behind the stage itself. Several years later, when they demolished the club, I was saddened. It played an important part in the history of British pop culture and should really have been preserved. But so much that should be saved is lost (and so much that is preserved isn't worth the preserving).

One of the half-wild cats that live in the environs of our

house fell sick on Sunday evening. A tiny, lovely little kitten that hasn't yet been given a name by us but has become one of our favorites. There are five or six feral, or semi-feral cats sharing our garden with us. We put food out for them and provide a rudimentary shelter in the form of a plastic waste bin, turned on its side and placed under a garden bench. This particular, recently-born kitten is the tiniest of the litter, but the most affectionate and characterful. She is mostly a dark, cloudy grey colour with little patches of ginger and white. A little bumble bee of a thing. I took to her from first setting eyes on her when her mother, a gentle and elegant tabby we call Gizmo, carried her round to our front door, as if the kitten were an offering to us. The kitten was fine midday on Sunday, dancing around and mischievous, before Emi and I went into town for the afternoon. When we came back home, the other four feral cats all ran out to greet us, as is their custom, but the tiny kitten wasn't to be seen. After a few moments she emerged, painfully slowly, from the aforementioned shelter. She could hardly walk. We picked her up and took her into the house. There was fluid dripping from her mouth. We wrapped her in a thick towel and placed her in a shallow cardboard box and watched her anxiously. It looked as if she was dying.

I decided to call an emergency vet's number and made arrangements to take the kitten to a surgery not too far away from our home. I was informed that, as it was Sunday and an out of hours call, that it would be expensive. I couldn't have forgiven myself if the kitten had died without me giving it a chance of survival, no matter how slim, so I agreed to the fee and Emi and I drove to the surgery, the kitten still wrapped in the towel in the cardboard box. The lady vet, who was very sympathetic and pleasant, examined the kitten. She said that the poor little thing's temperature was very low and that she thought the kitten might not make it through the night. But she couldn't figure out what the problem was. One possibility may have been poisoning, she thought. She asked if we knew whether any neighbour might have left rat poison around or something similar. I couldn't see any reason for our neighbours to use such a thing as the cats normally take care of vermin and, as a result, we live in a rat-free environment. The vet gave the kitten an injection of antibiotics and anti-inflammatory drugs but said we should expect the worst. It sounded hopeless. We returned home with the kitten and kept her indoors, wrapped up in a towel and laid on top of a hot water bottle to try and get her temperature back up. We had to keep checking on her heartbeat and breathing as, at times, it appeared as if she'd given up the ghost. Two anxious hours later, she moved slightly, her eyes flicked open, then closed again. Emi and I knelt beside her, fearing the worst. A little while after that, she slowly appeared to be more alert, looking up at us with such a pitiful gaze. Then suddenly she sat up and, after a moment's hesitancy, hopped out of her cardboard box. Within minutes, she was playing with the fringe of a carpet, trotting around the room filled with curiosity. A miracle! We kept her inside overnight. She slept in the bathroom adjoining our bedroom, apparently content, even though she'd never spent a night inside before.

Now, two days later, she seems fine. We've been anxious to keep an eye on her, dreading a relapse, but, fingers crossed, she is surviving. Last night, whilst I caught a little bit of late night television, she slept curled up on Emi's bosom, as content as content can be. I'm in two minds as to whether we should keep her in the house as a domestic pet, or let her be part of the wild bunch who live outside in our garden. I have to think of a name for her, too. It's odd but I wasn't much of a cat person as a child. My parents preferred dogs. Cats were always dismissed as being 'not very nice' by mum and dad. But now, I really love cats. William Burroughs adored them too and Jean Cocteau said that 'cats contain the soul of a house.' Well, I'm in total agreement with that.

Looked through some photographs that Emi had taken of me at the Harold Budd farewell concert just over a year ago. I hate my appearance. That vanity thing again, I know but, I wish I could regain something of my younger appearance. Someone posted, on the website forum, an old picture of me when I used to sport dyed blonde hair. Wow! Couldn't believe it was really me. I should have been out chasing the girls looking like that instead of being Mr. Domestic (not that I've ever been particularly adept at the Mr. Domestic scenario).

I also found some photos from way back, taken when my brother Ian got married. We were both slim young things back then. One particular photo that I like from that wedding day shows just the two of us, me in the backround and Ian in the foreground, outside the register office in Wakefield, facing in different directions. It's only a casual snapshot but it has something that attracts me to it. Maybe it's my casual stance; I've got my hands in my pockets and one foot half off the ground. Or maybe it's my brother Ian's happy expression and the Polaroid sx70 camera that he's holding (which I think he'd borrowed from me as we had a Be Bop Deluxe sx70 club in the band in the late 1970s). Anyway, Ian and I both look fit, happy and healthy. And so damned *young*!

I had my Rolls Royce then and lived the archetypal rock-star life although I deliberately dressed as conservatively as possible 'off stage' to defuse people's expectations. I tried to avoid the rock gypsy vagabond look that was commonplace at the time and was attracted to the idea of looking as un-rock-star-like as possible whilst still being in a position to go on stage and take total command of a rock music audience. An audience which, at that time, was used to men wearing either denim, leather or glam satin. My rejection of this sort of signifying uniform was seen as a kind of inverse perversity, I guess. At least by those who measured authenticity by hair length and flared trouser width. I also recently saw some photographs of the Rolls Royce mentioned above, taken on the same day (Ian's wedding day). It was a pale metallic-blue Silver Shadow, unbelievably, the least reliable car I've ever owned, apart from the pre-VW era Skoda that I drove for a year or so after my divorce claimed everything of value.

I also have a photograph of the Rolls and my Panther Lima taken outside of Haddlesey House around the same time. There I stand, proud as punch, totally unaware of the tidal wave that was soon to sweep all that kind of thing away. I was apparently as unaware of the fact that such an ostentatious display was as much a sign of rock conformity as the tiresome heavy metal posturing I so despised at the time. But then, no one's perfect. But I digress: Wedding Days, Birthdays, Divorces, Solicitor's appointments and Funerals, the incandescent waystations of our lives.

I've said this before but when my brother Ian passed away on the morning of his 50th birthday in April of this year, an entire chapter of my life went with him. Just before he was buried, I arranged to have a little silver Buddhist medallion I owned placed in his suit pocket. It was in an envelope along with a farewell letter I'd written to him. The Buddha medallion had been a favourite of mine and, despite my current rejection of superstition, I wanted to give it to Ian to protect his soul and spirit in some way.

Last Saturday, when I was in London, I managed to find an absolutely identical medallion. So, I bought it to carry with me as a physical connection between the two of us. I'd looked for one on my previous visit, a few weeks earlier, but hadn't been able to locate one that was exactly the same as the one that I buried with Ian. But, almost miraculously, an identical medallion appeared. In Watkins esoteric bookshop in Cecil Court in London. I don't know — miraculously cured kittens and synchronistic Buddha tokens, it's enough to make me believe that there are more things between heaven and earth than I might suspect. If only in a moment of emotional need and weakness.

Meeting up with my good friend John Spence on Thursday. We usually only meet under 'working' conditions at Fairview studios. It will be good to take time out from our respective career pressures to relax and chat without any other distractions.

The Nelsonica team dinner coming up very soon, this Saturday. I've still got a drawing or two to finalise before then to give as gifts to the team members (as I mentioned in my previous diary entry). Jon Wallinger and Paul Gilby have already claimed their 'thank you' artworks and taken them home. They are local boys so have picked up their prizes during recent visits to Nelson Acres.

Reading a huge book about Edgard Varese at the moment, a massive catalogue from an exhibition held in Switzerland. Bought it second-hand locally. The pile of books by my bedside is now so high that I didn't bother to purchase a single book on my trip to London last weekend. And THAT is most unusual for me. I will now go downstairs and see if the kitten is okay. Nestled up to Emi's breast, no doubt. Lucky creature.

·

MONDAY 20TH NOVEMBER 2006

Some tragic news yesterday. Chuck Bird, who fulfilled the role of webmaster at the American Bill Nelson Permanent Flame website for several years, has sadly passed away, a victim of diabetes. I received an email from his brother Larry informing me that Chuck had died just one week previous. I was deeply shocked and saddened. Chuck was a genuine fan who ran the US website without any thought other than to provide fans with a facility worthy of them. Chuck was forever loyal to the music and myself, never allowing temperament or personal ego to enter the equation. He always came across as a modest man and an extremely dedicated and knowledgeable fan. I'm proud to have counted him amongst my friends and I'm still trying to come to terms with this unexpected and unhappy development. I know that fans will feel the same sense of loss that I do. On those occasions when I was able to meet Chuck, he was positive, optimistic and enthusiastic, always polite, respectful and kind. And when the urgent need to provide fans with a reliable UK website arose, Chuck was one of several people who gave me the personal encouragement and moral support I needed to go ahead with the Dreamsville project, particularly when I felt like giving up completely as a result of lack of support elsewhere. Chuck, along with a few other generous and far-sighted people (including *Sound-On-Sound* magazine, Jon Wallinger, Dave Graham, my management, my close friends and family) helped me to overcome any doubts and fears. They pursuaded me to go ahead and build a website to serve those people who cared about my work. It was thanks to their combined encouragement that the Dreamsville site has become so valued by fans.

An example of Chuck's generosity: Without any prompting from anyone, Chuck suggested that I might like to take on the bill nelson.com address that the Permanent Flame site had used since its inception. He offered to transfer the ownership of the internet address over to me for use by the Dreamsville site. He also passed on all the archived files that Permanent Flame had amassed since it was originally created by Mark Rushton, back in 1995. Mark also approved of Chuck's altruistic act and I am indebted to them both for their help and co-operation, along with Paul and Ian Gilby, *Sound-On-Sound* and the Dreamsville/ Nelsonica team, who all have had a hand in setting up and running the current official website. As a tribute to both Mark and Chuck, the original site that Mark initiated and that Chuck came to maintain has been archived as a fixed item in The Permanent Flame Museum on the Dreamsville site. It will remain as a historical testimony to their initiative and enterprise.

Once again though, for the second time this year, mortality has raised its spectre. Increasingly, I find myself experiencing personal bereavements. I accept that this is what must happen when one's friends and family enter a certain stage of life. But the knowledge that these things are inevitable does nothing to soften the blows when they come. When all tears are shed though, it's life we're left to deal with, and our own lives and personal ability (or inability) to face the future with equilibrium and hope. It's easy to lose sight of what matters, to become wrapped up in issues of no positive advantage to us. Maybe I'm allowing pessimism too strong a hand here, but the society we inhabit seems to have become an increasingly cynical and sick place. It's impossible to ignore the malaise that seeps into so many aspects of our daily life. I personally find myself struggling to deal with the general unfairness and moral ambiguousness of 'things', even though I'm sometimes unwillingly sucked into their twisted orbit.

But it still comes as a shock to me that some people seem incapable of grasping the bigger picture, the preciousness and fragility of life, whether it be theirs or anyone else's. It's as if some souls are born genetically immune to anything other than the most petty concerns and obsessions. Why is it that gentleness and sensitivity are in short supply whilst cynical spite and small-mindedness flourishes? It seems that it takes hardly anything these days to build an ugly monster from the most insignificant of human emotions. Perhaps we have only two choices, either to resist the route of spiritless ignorance, or to turn our hand to the wheel (the wheel of Dharma?) and steer away from the cheap and easy option, the tabloid mentality, the lazy temptation that leads to a profound loss of everything that might redeem us. But somehow, it becomes tougher than ever to resist the prevailing darkness and to shine our warm lamps into the cold, mean shadows.

I've been personally struggling with various similar issues of late. I feel as if matters should be directly addressed, that certain injustices need adjustment, that things that have been portrayed in a particular light should be revealed for what they really are. Then again, when I stand back and look at these things in context, they are so pathetic and trivial as to be not worth even the slightest effort on my part. Maybe I should simply let the rotten go to rot. Nature will take its course without any need of intervention by me or by others. No cause for concern. I must simply remember to get on with what experience has taught me to regard as true and real, no matter how meagre these experiences may appear in the overall scheme of things. But it's the only positive alternative and the only one I'm equipped to offer. The empty darkness is for those who have already shown themselves to be without a lamp to illuminate the way. Some might advise me that life is dark enough without straying into the shadows of others. But, it's not in my nature to be blind to those shadows or indifferent to those who are lost in them. As selfish and pre-occupied with my music as I often am, I find it difficult to stand back and let the suffering suffer, whether that be the runt of a cat's litter or an adult human being. It seems cruel to turn away from these issues. But I am, more often than not, ill equipped to do much about it. Whatever I do will be flawed and stricken by my own inadequacy. I'm not up to the task, nor do I pretend to be. But I do try.

Does that excuse me? Or simply place me among the ranks of those whom I despair of the most? Perhaps only the music I create stands a chance of offering something approaching the value of healing. Some people seem to assure me that it has that quality, or at least a potential to attain that quality. And that's why I am, and will remain, an artist first and foremost. Best to leave the argument and debate about such things to those with little else to do and even less to offer. An old cliché but a true one: a Daffodil doesn't have to agonise about being bright yellow. Nor should an artist worry about what he naturally is.

The kitten I referred to in my last diary has survived and seems fit and well, although she has continued to live the outdoor life with the other four cats that we feed. I was heartened by the response on the Dreamsville site to my telling of the tale in my previous diary entry. It says something positive about those people who appreciate my music that they are compassionate towards animals. There was such a warm response from cat-lovers on the site, many of them relating their own similar experiences and even posting photographs of their cats on the Dreamsville Forum. It was something I didn't expect but it was a pleasant surprise to get such warm support for such a simple act of kindness. As someone once said: 'Never trust a person who has no empathy with cats.'

Last Saturday's Nelsonica team official dinner was a happy occasion. Ten of us around the table (Jon, Dave Graham, Ian Haydock, Ged, Eddie, Paul Gilby, Duncan, Martin Bostock, Emiko and myself) even though one person (Ian C) couldn't attend as he was away on holiday. We all had a good time although I drank rather too much wine and felt a little worse for wear the next day. At the restaurant, I presented the team with framed artwork that I'd made for each of them. I'd been panicking, worried that I wouldn't get all the drawings finished and framed in time, so it was a great relief to finally give everyone their gift with no one left out.

There will be two new members joining the offcial Nelsonica team this coming year too. They have enthusiastically accepted the invitation that Jon Wallinger and the rest of us extended to them, amidst jokes about the strange initiation rites that they would have to undergo. Maybe I really *should* devise something along those lines, turn it into a quasi-Masonic, mock-esoteric secret society, just for laughs! On a practical note, the new team members will prove extremely helpful as the last couple of years has seen the annual convention becoming more complex and better attended than ever. The original team has expanded to deal with the increased content and organisational skills involved and they make a great job of it, which I know the convention attendees appreciate.

This last week, my studio equipment software was updated to deal with the proposed mixing of the ancient Be Bop Deluxe Decca sessions. Paul came over to install new software and replace an ailing floppy drive. It took a couple of days but eventually everything was re-assembled, wired up and put back in place. I'm currently going through various old plug-in hard drives to convert and store specific multi-track masters that were recorded on the old operating system. They have to be put through a special conversion process, one by one, before I can use or store them on the new O.S. There are several pieces that I definitely don't want to erase, particularly the multi-tracks for the *Sailor Bill* album. That project took up so much time and energy and is so complex that it would feel like sacrilege to not archive the master tracks. I might even want to remix the album, (maybe as purely instrumental pieces,) at some point in the future. Who knows? Better not to lose them, I think.

I had a brief listen to the multi-track Be Bop Decca sessions too and was taken aback by how flat and dead the recordings sound, even though they were recorded in what was the classic

Decca Studios. When I put up a recently recorded piece along-side them, it suddenly became apparent how far recording technology has come since the early 1970s. My humble little home studio system sounds expensive, rich and three-dimensional compared to the Decca recordings, which sound like they were made in a fake-fur lined box. I'm increasingly less sure of the 'vintage is best' argument, though, to be honest, I've always been an early adopter of musical technology. In an ideal world, it's not about either/or situations. It's fun to combine the vintage approach with the modern and that's generally the way I work with my own recordings.

The cold weather back again today. Christmas stuff in town, everywhere you look. I ought to try and get an earlier start on the seasonal shopping this year. But it will probably be last minute, as always.

·

FRIDAY 8TH DECEMBER 2006

In 10 days it will be my 58th birthday. I've planned nothing by way of celebration so far. If I'm to have an evening out with friends, I should get it organised quickly. I tend to overlook the fact that, at this time of year, restaurants are booked solid with office Christmas parties and the like. I invariably leave my traditional birthday dinner decision too late, then end up having to accept fourth or fifth choice of dining establishment possibilities. Predictably though at this stage of the game, birthdays don't have quite the same frisson of excitement that they had when I was a youngster, so perhaps that accounts for a certain amount of laxness on my part. That and the fear of actually becoming another year closer to the unholy number of *sixty*.

Emiko has been ill for most of this week. She was laid low by what the doctor diagnosed as a stomach virus. A 'lot of it going about', apparently. She was in too much pain to go to work on Tuesday though she had little option on Wednesday because of two freelance contracts that she's duty bound to deal with. I did what I could to help, driving and carrying things. Thursday she was feeling a little better but still suffering from stomach pain intermittently and feeling weak. It was a busy day for both of us though, for several reasons. Thursday the 7th of December marked the 30th anniversary of my father's death. I drove over to Wakefield to pick my mother up from her home and together we drove out to the crematorium at Kettlethorpe to take some flowers. There's a tiny chapel of sorts in the crematorium gardens, a little red brick building houses a large, semi-ornate Book Of Rememberance. It is opened at the appropriate date of each day of each month, where the names of people who passed away on that date are recorded by hand in red and black gothic script with the year of their death next to their name. The wind was blowing hard, cold and wet as my mother and I entered the little building and looked down into the glass display case that contained the book. Two thirds of the way down the left hand page, my father's name, in the afore-mentioned immaculate gothic script, appeared: 'Walter Nelson, 7th December 1976.' We stood side by side, looking at the page in silence for a few seconds, almost as if the 30 year old ink might magically conjure my father's presence into the room. Then we talked fondly and wryly about him, noted the name of the only other person in the book who had died on the 7th of December 1976 and eventually, reluctantly, made our way outside to the rear of the building where a small, lean-to greenhouse-like annexe stood. It held rows of wall mounted zinc vases where flowers could be left as a memorial to loved ones. We took the wrapping paper from two bunches of white and yellow flowers we'd bought from Morrison's supermarket, just down the road from my mother's house, and placed them into two empty vases, halfway up the inside wall, opposite the outer, glassed wall. The second bunch was in remembrance of my grandmother, Ethel Griffiths, who had passed away a few years before my father. My mother opened her handbag and produced two messages that she had written on two nondescript pieces of lined notepaper. The messages were from herself and me, written in her neat and tidy old-school handwriting, a handwriting that puts mine to shame. One message was for my father and one for my grandmother. She sighed and noted that this was the very first time that the messages had not included the name of my brother Ian next to my mother's signature and mine.

We attached the pieces of paper to the zinc vases with a few elastic bands that my mother had also thoughtfully brought with her and adjusted the blooms so that they looked as attractive as we could possibly manage without Emi being there to add her professional flair. Then we wrapped up the stem ends that we'd trimmed from the greenery and stood back to see the finished effect, simultaneously scanning the surrounding vases, all with their own notes attached, messages from loving wives, husbands, sons and daughters. Each vase contained a life story of one kind or another, a life lost but not forgotten, expressed in faded flowers and a few inky words on damp paper.

On a bottom row, next to one particular vase, was a small, soft-toy teddy bear which had fallen on its side. My mother bent down to straighten it up and glanced at the card that was attached to it. From where I was standing, I could just make out the words, '... to my Daddy'. The rain beat down hard on the glass roof of the little greenhouse, driven by the cold wind that whistled in the eaves and under the door. We went outside and walked across to the main entrance path and to the spot where the local council authorities had cast my father's ashes, 30 years previous. My mother told me that she had once made enquiries, of the crematorium staff, about where this act had taken place and one official had looked it up in the book of records and then paced out the location for my mother. She led me over to it, an area just by the side of the stone-flagged path at the crematorium end. We stood now, in the rain, looking at this ambiguous patch of grass, vainly trying to materialise my father from the long dissolved powder of his remains.

I wanted to talk to him, to tell him about my life, to tell him about Emiko, to ask him hundreds of questions that I was too young and self-engrossed to ask when he was alive. Then, my mother and I sought the shelter of my car before driving away from the crematorium, passing the Kettlethorpe council estate and, just a few yards down from the crematorium, on the right-hand side of the road, the Kettlethorpe Youth Club building, the latter hardly changed since the 1960s. As we drove, my mother recalled a time, in my early teens, when I was out playing somewhere in Wakefield, with an amateur band I was involved in. Apparently, whilst I was out, a phone call came in to my parents', asking if the band could do another gig, later that same night, over at Kettlethorpe Youth Club. My father, who sometimes acted as manager for these early bands of mine, hopped in his car and drove to the gig in Wakefield to tell us about the request. The Wakefield gig must have been an early evening thing as my mother tells me that, afterwards, we packed up our gear and then went on to the Kettlethorpe Youth Club to play the second gig. I only vaguely recall this twin-booking windfall but I *do* remember one thing from the Kettlethorpe Youth Club gig and it is this: there was an open plan style staircase in the central entrance of the youth club, a very 1960s styled thing, quite modern then but maybe archaically so now. On these stairs I encountered and chatted with a very pretty girl. I can half see her face as I type these words. Can't recall her name though but she had a softness about her, a calmness. She possessed none of the common, vulgar presence that so many girls seemed to exude back then but had something deeper, gentler, quite lovely, refined even. I was very much taken by her and it seemed, from her warm smile and the inviting twinkle in her eye, that she felt the same about me. But I was relatively shy, lacked confidence and didn't make enough of an attempt to fan this tiny spark of mutual recognition into something bigger. We chatted, flirted and vanished into our respective futures. But I've never forgotten that encounter, one of those instances that actually happen far more frequently than we surmise. A situation where paths cross, where someone, out of the blue, connects with us in a profound way. Maybe you could call it a soul encounter, a precious, fleeting moment lost in time but forever remembered and cherished. Damn! What *was* her name?

Back to Thursday. From Kettlethorpe, my mother and I

then drove to Wakefield Cemetery where we cleaned out one of the glass vases on my Ian's grave and filled it with our third bunch of flowers. The wind was almost as cold as the terrible day when we watched his casket being lowered into the ground in April of this year. I miss him profoundly, much, much more than he would ever have expected. My mother, unsurprisingly, is still devastated, permanently wounded despite her outer attempts at stoicism. Ian's memorial headstone is not quite ready yet, so his grave is marked only by the metal framework that outlines the word 'DAD,' a remnant of a floral tribute from his three children that Emi prepared for Ian's funeral. No flowers on it now, of course, just the weather-beaten frame but, until the headstone is erected, it is the only object, other than three glass vases and some rain washed cards, that identifies his resting place. Mum and I agreed that it is time the headstone was in place. And it will be soon, I hope. We stood there in the cold rain, gazing down at the earth where Ian rests, thinking about how much we loved and miss him and how we wished we could have saved him from such a premature fate.

It suddenly struck me that, as a very young boy, I used to accompany my mother to Wakefield Cemetery in the 1950s to put flowers on the graves of my great-grandmother and great-grandfather. I would play amongst the gravestones with a toy balsa wood glider, (bought by my mother from a model shop then located at the bottom of Kirkgate) whilst my mother attended to the cleaning of vases and the changing of flowers. All those long years ago. And now, here are the two of us, mother in her late 70s, me rapidly approaching 60, placing flowers on my own brother's grave in that very same cemetery. Neither of us expected, back in those early, carefree 1950s, that this would be our future sorrow. No wonder it was raining.

I drove my mother to her home where her husband George was waiting, then set off for York. Emi had gone to work at the flower shop that morning, her stomach bug better than it had been but still not vanquished. She'd already booked the afternoon off as we'd had an invitation to attend a special event at Castle Howard, just north of York (for those of my diary readers unfamiliar with the place, it was used as one of the chief locations in the television series *Brideshead Revisited*). Earlier in the year, we'd signed up for an annual pass to Castle Howard. We visit there at regular intervals anyway and both of us adore the house and its glorious surroundings. One of the benefits of being a pass-card holder is that we get invited to special events, many of them not available to the general public. Today we were to be allowed into the house itself to view the Howard family's Christmas decorations followed by a brass band recital, mince pies, mulled wine and a torch-lit parade. Normally, the house is closed to the public in winter as the public wing of it is reclaimed by the Howard family for their Christmas entertaining.

It was a new experience for Emi and I to walk through the grounds of the house in winter. Normally, we're there during the spring or summer months when the atmosphere is quite different. But, to my delight, it is equally beguiling with a grey windy sky and naked trees. The interior of the house, when we entered and made our way through its corridors to the great hall, looked absolutely otherworldly. It was, by now, completely dark outside and the house was lit by hundreds of thick candles set on silver reflective trays, their glow flickering across the ancient carved marble bodies and heads of Greek and Roman gods and goddesses, some of them amusingly (and sometimes daringly) hung with festive tinsel and glass baubles. In the great hall, a log fire was blazing and opposite it stood a truly enormous Christmas tree, festooned by the Howards with their personal family decorations. And there were impressive Christmas trees throughout the entire house, each one beautifully trimmed and gleaming. Not Disney-like, not twee but transcendent. It was as if the entire building had been alchemically transformed into a fairytale palace, achingly gorgeous, filled with rare treasures. Choral music filled the air as if angels were hidden in the high corners of each magnificent room. I have to say that, despite being generally cynical about these things, I was transported, utterly enchanted. We slowly made our way through the huge house, eventually ending up in the Howard family's private chapel, a tiny jewel of Pre-Raphaelite splendour.

For many years, I've dreamed of creating a site-specific piece of music for this chapel. Now, on a candle-lit evening in early winter, I was seized by a stronger conviction than ever that this is something I must try to achieve before it becomes too late. I resolved to write to Simon Howard in person, to see what the possibilities for such a thing might be. It would involve a live instrumental performance from myself but with the possibility of some kind of vocal dimension being incorporated. (My good friend Harold Budd has suggested to me that a vocal work of a non-pop/rock nature might be worth my consideration. And he's right, of course.) I would also like to incorporate a small string section as part of the composition, though this may require more funding than may be available to me. It's nothing but pure idea now though, so much to be resolved before it would have a chance of being realised as an actual performance.

But something to work towards, next year. Let me see if I can outline my ideas in a letter to Mr. Howard. He may find the proposal of no interest. Then again ...

After leaving the chapel, we gathered around yet another gaily lit Christmas tree, this time outside on the north face of the house, where a brass band played carols and the invited guests were treated to mince pies and mulled wine. The Howards walked around, checking that everyone was enjoying the evening. Far away behind and slightly below us, one of Castle Howard's lakes gleamed in the December darkness while two white swans, faintly visible in the gloom, glided silently on its glassy surface. Then the torchlight parade from the house, through the grounds, to the stable courtyard where a Father Christmas Grotto had been set up for the children. All in all, a lovely, relaxing, memorable evening.

Then Emi and I drove to Leeds. This was to pick up some items that Emi needed from the flower market which was opening unusually late that evening. Once the car was loaded with these items, we then set off to the village of Ledsham for a cosy dinner for two in the ancient Chequers Inn, one of our favourite haunts. Two glasses of wine and a plate of mussels later, I sat back in the passenger seat as Emi drove us home to spend the rest of the evening snuggled up together on the sofa in front of the television. A hectic day but one that made us realise how blessed we were.

By direct contrast, I came across some really sad bickering amongst a tiny handful of fans on my website forum, fuelled by some deliberately vindictive postings elsewhere. I'm regularly amazed by how steamed up over absolutely nothing some people get. Certain troubled souls seem use either me or my work as a pitiful excuse to vent their own inner demons on the world at large. Terribly flattering, in a way, but completely self-defeating in the long run. It's doomed to failure and serves no positive purpose. If nothing else, it confirms my thoughts about the whole silly business of being fantasied over as a 'rock star' or whatever role I fulfil in some people's lives these days. That a few isolated fans feel the need to so intensely focus their energy on the minutiae of my existence is not so much a mystery as a tragedy. But ever since I've had a career in music, I've been forced to deal with some rather odd people, a tiny minority of them seriously troubled. But then again, I'm not alone in this. Virtually every other musician of my acquaintance has suffered the same experience at some point or other, and my management have often warned me about allowing certain people get too close. Maybe this kind of problem goes with the job, although I wish it didn't. I'm far too gullible, and I suppose I find it hard to say 'No' to people. The number of times my instincts have warned me to stay clear of someone or other, yet I've gone ahead and trusted them, only to be betrayed later. You'd think I'd have learned my lesson by now. My own fault, no doubt. On the other hand, I'm definitely blessed with a great number of loyal, genuine, sensible, calm and respectful fans of whom I'm proud. They reflect the care and thought that goes into the music and are wonderful ambassadors for my work. They are a joy to meet and are respectful of my privacy when I need it.

It's just that there have always been a few, let's just say, 'over-enthusiastic' ones, teetering, some people have suggested, on the edge of being psychopathically unbalanced. It seems that they just don't know where the boundary lies and end up regarding their heroes as personal property, always a recipe for disaster, in my experience. The crazy thing is, the more I try to disillusion them, to lift the scales from their eyes, the more they obsess and cling to their manias. I become a kind of life-raft for them, vehemently attacked because they've mistakenly come to depend upon me and my work for the propping up of their own sense of self. Ego, resentment, jealousy, there's evidence that all these things enter into the equation. As someone with a long-time interest in what makes people tick, I find this sort of phenomena immensely interesting. A social psychiatrist, I suspect, would have an absolute field day.

It's sad but a certain amount of personal provocation does get aimed in my direction, and in the direction of sincere, well-balanced fans, too. Maybe it stems from a latent masochistic streak or something. Perhaps these people are desperate to get me to hurl insults at them. Whatever the psychology, it seems I fulfil a very powerful role in their lives. Which, as you might expect, freaks me out no end. It's not something I set out to achieve, quite the opposite. But, ultimately, who cares? It's only pop music. And it's only in pop music that this sort of rubbish happens. In that respect, it's quite common and utterly banal.

Anyway, Christmas shopping in Harrogate on Saturday. The annual Charles Rennie Mackintosh Society festive gathering on Sunday (films, tea and sandwiches.) My music parked until next week when I need to knuckle down to some serious work before Christmas takes over my attentions completely.

I must complete the adaptation of *Dreamland Illuminated*, (the Memory Codex soundtrack,) that I intend to make the centrepiece of a new album. I'm adding some extra instrumentation to parts of the almost 40 minute piece, to make it work as a 'stand-alone' composition. This album will gather together various odds and ends that haven't found a home on recent albums. In some ways it will work in the manner of the Nelsonica convention specials. The album will have the title *Gleaming Without Light*. I also have a new project to work on: I've been invited to remake/remodel a track of my choosing from Mitchell Froom's first solo album, an invitation which I consider to be both an honour and a challenge.

Then there's the Be Bop Decca Sessions album to mix and assemble. It's called *Tomorrow The World*. I intend to add radio interviews and some 'official' bootleg live recordings to the package too. Then there's the EMI box set to consider with Mark Powell who is putting it all together. Plus update work on Paul Sutton-Reeves *Music In Dreamland* book. Somewhere amongst all that, I have to fit in Christmas and family duties. Not quite the usual holiday time then. Or is it? Nothing at all to complain about, though. I love every ticking minute!

·

FRIDAY 29TH DECEMBER 2006

2006 almost gone and Christmas gone in the blink of an eye. I spent the week before Christmas in a stressed-out panic, trying to make sure that everything and everyone was taken care of, presents bought, cards sent, plenty of food in the larder, enough wine to host a Bacchanalian revel, the usual Yuletide madness that, no matter how carefully I try to plan ahead, always ends up being a last-minute scramble. And for what? Christmas melts away faster than the fabled snow that never arrives. Eat, drink, fall asleep on the sofa and it's gone.

I did manage to get my son and daughter their main requested gifts: a Korg AX 3000 G guitar effects processor for Elliot and a Line 6 DL4 Delay modeller for Elle. A few fun stocking fillers were purchased to round things out for them. I also bought gifts for my eldest daughter Julia and my grandson Luke but their plan to travel from their home in London to spend Christmas or New Year in Yorkshire has been changed at the last minute. I'll hold on to everything until they manage to get up here.

For Emi, I bought mostly clothes and lingerie. Many men would not naturally relish the choosing of (and shopping for) clothes for their wives but for me it's an absolutely delightful and creative task. I'm pretty much dependable when it comes to finding items for Emi. Nothing to do with fashion (which, the more confident one becomes, the more one should ignore). It's more about elegance and style rather than High Street trends. (Or, at least that's the plan.) I'm quite prepared to spend as much time as necessary to track down something that little bit special and I know instinctively when I've found the right thing. Emi, flatteringly, trusts my taste, even though her own is sophisticated and finely honed. Luckily, from past experience, it's very rare that I get it wrong. This Christmas, she loved everything I bought and all of it fits her perfectly. Of course, I do get the added benefit of a private fashion show as she tries each garment on!

Emi bought me a new watch for my collection, a hand knitted fisherman's hat from Whitby, a hand-knitted scarf in lemon, grey and black from the same town, a book dealing with the history of British comics, a facsimile edition of a 1939 *Dandy* annual, a bottle of 'Aqua Di Parma' cologne (one of my favourite fragrances,) and several other bits and pieces.

We've been together for 13 years now (and known each other longer) yet I still can't believe my good fortune. How an unsophisticated kid from a council estate in Yorkshire ended up living with such a lovely treasure is not only a mystery to me but a continuing miracle. Wakefield and Tokyo, for much of our lives we were half a world apart but, somehow, fate brought us together. I could never have predicted such an exotic future when I was a young man

On Christmas Eve we both went to the art house cinema in the centre of town and watched a special screening of Frank Capra's *It's A Wonderful Life*. This involved a pre-film buffet with mulled wine which we were allowed take into the cinema with us. It was a full house and Emi and I had to sit apart from each other as only single seating arrangements were left. The mulled wine I'd happily consumed caused a few drowsy moments during the film but I responded to the story's sentimental ending with the customary tear-damp eyes. A pleasant way to spend Christmas Eve, nevertheless.

On Christmas Day we were both invited to join our friends, Steve and Julia, for the traditional feast at their house just down the lane from ours. They've been kind enough to let us share their festive family gathering for several years now and the Christmas meal is always a delight. Julia has a genuine talent for cooking and entertaining and all our taste buds were given a tremendous treat. A terrific meal and excellent company. During the woozy, boozy afternoon, Julia's mother, Julia's husband Steve and myself initiated a joyful, spontaneous jam session in the music room. Steve on drums, Julia's mum on piano and myself on guitar. Great fun. I'd never actually played *Begin The Beguine* before but I managed to figure it out as we went along, my D' Angelico New Yorker plugged into one of Steve and Julia's children's amplifiers. It almost sounded as if we'd rehearsed it. Julia's mother is a fine pianist and Steve used to play drums in a band before his business began to occupy so much of his time. I think he'd like to play more often if circumstances allowed. After much wine was consumed and gifts exchanged, Emi and I rolled home to spend the rest of the evening crashed out on the sofa, watching a DVD of Ken Russel's evocative television dramatisation of British composer Edward Elgar's life. Christmas lights twinkled merrily in the corners of the room, rows of greetings cards lined the low wooden ceiling beams, candles flickered in etched crystal jars as the Elgar dramatisation unfolded, enhancing my mood of fireside melancholy. Strains of *Nimrod* conjuring a lost England of dreams. A kind of wrapped-in-cotton-wool-cloudy blissfulness enveloped the two of us. Wonderful.

Christmas suits this place. Our home looks even more warm and colourful than usual with all the seasonal decorations. Took me quite a while to get everything organised but the end result was worth it. Reminds me of the childhood Christmases I shared with my brother Ian when we once-upon-a-time believed in Santa Claus, back in the 1950s when we lived at 28 Conistone Crescent, Eastmoor Estate, on the edge of Wakefield. Our parents always went to great trouble to ensure that it was a magical time for us. Even though we were a working-class family living in a council flat, Christmas morning always brought wonders. The front room was miraculously transformed into an indoor toy shop window, overflowing with endless delights: Meccano sets, Dinky Toys, Hornby train sets, Scalextric sets, *Eagle*, *Beano*, *Beezer* and *Topper* annuals, gaily decorated paint boxes, coloured 'Lakeland' pencils in wooden boxes, magician's outfits, cowboy hats and cap-guns in holsters, Airfix, Revell and Monogram model kits — all displayed with great visual skill on the living room carpet beneath the half-bay art-deco framed window. My brother Ian and I, awake early and eager, would kneel in front of this shining bounty, still in our red 'Ladybird' brand dressing gowns. We would carefully look at each gift in turn as our parents observed our mounting excitement. And all around us, the garlands, balloons, lights and other Christmas decorations, whilst not nearly as high-tech or elaborate as today's fare, shone with the most evocative colour schemes and shapes, so very much of their time.

Those long distant years are vividly etched in memory. Sometimes it feels as if I only need to move a few inches to my left and I'll be back there again, as if I'd stepped through a thin veil of time, a doorway to way back when. There's a lyric in an old Simon and Garfunkel song, (called, I think, *Photograph*). The lyric says: 'preserve your memories, they're all that's left you ...' Sentimental nonsense? Well, yes and no.

Here in the present, the future rushes towards us at such an unforgiving pace that it's no surprise that we sometimes regard the past as offering us a nebulous, peaceful haven, a moment's respite from the harsh pressures of the now. Yet this tendency to wallow in nostalgia is as much a curse as a blessing. I'm certainly not immune to its seductive charms and not nearly as brave and present in the here and now as I ought to be. For all my criticism of those who perpetually yearn for the return of their golden years, I still, when cold winds blow, furtively seek sanctuary in the warm candle-lit corridors of memory. If I stand back and attempt some kind of objectivity, I see that this might indicate a somewhat contradictory creature, and, if truth were told, a confused, headlight dazzled one too. On the surface, it doesn't quite add up.

How can someone who savours the likes of Coltrane, Partch, Faure, Milhaud, Feldman (and so on) find simple pleasure in the light, inconsequential music that was once broadcast by 'Uncle Mac' on the 'Children's Favourites' BBC radio programmes of the 1950s? I mean, come on — *The Big Rock Candy Mountain? The Runaway Train? Inchworm? Teddy Bear's Picnic? Sparky And His Magic Piano?* For goodness sake! Why should that be? Where lurks the critical faculty when I allow myself such indulgences?

How can a bookworm who delights in the literary pleasures of Kerouac, Ginsberg and Burroughs, who has pondered the mystical writings of Jacob Bohme, the occult speculations of A.O. Spare, the Zen musings of Suzuki, the sexo-political theories of Reich, etc, etc, how can *this* man still have an appetite for the adventures of Dan Dare, Jack Flash, Jimmy And His Magic Patch, General Jumbo, Marvelman, and all the other fanciful denizens of the British children's comics of the post-war years? How too, can I become absorbed in and inspired by the films of Jean Cocteau, Orson Wells, Maya Deren, Fritz Lang, Kenneth Anger, Harry Smith, Jack Smith and dozens of others of their luminous ilk and yet *still* shed a pathetic tear at the conclusion of *It's A Wonderful Life?* Or watch a compilation video of the Morecambe and Wise Christmas shows? Makes no sense. Then again, maybe to a perceptive psychologist, it does. Perhaps it's not so complicated, maybe I simply want it *all*, to reach out and grasp as much as possible, to embrace everything, to pull it all together and put it all into some sort of context.

What context would that be? Why, that of my own mysterious, unfathomable existence of course! I'm simply looking for myself amongst all the glittering rubble, the gilded ruins of my life. I'm made up of all this conflicting material, these myriad, random assemblies of *stuff* and yet, like everyone else, I'm ultimately, essentially, separate from these things. I simply curate them, contain them like a museum. A museum that I sometimes haunt like a ghost.

I often worry unduly about this paradoxical mess of seminal potage. At other times I simply ignore it and go with the flow. Cultural barriers can too easily be imposed from without far too many people taking their cues from the media, cherry picking their art passions for effect, a desperate attempt to impress those whom they perceive as their peers. (If not that, then at least to convince themselves of their own 'good' taste.)

Such barriers are also imposed from within, erected out of a kind of fear of the unknown, a fear of appearing 'different', a fear of being an outsider trapped within a uniform society. But surely this should be seen as an outmoded attitude nowadays? Haven't we gone beyond such limitations? Or are we returning to a more rigid, dogmatic, conservative ethos? The attitude of many who seek some kind of artistic perspective, is that there is no such thing as 'low' culture or 'high' culture. It's all one continuous ribbon: just *culture*. Class structures, privilege and wealth are redundant, irrelevant. Anything and everything can be considered as cultural grist-to-the-mill. Everything is up for grabs, inspirational, intrinsically valuable. The modern creative soul knows no bounds and little shame. Such a wide-open attitude goes way beyond post-modernism, beyond irony, beyond 'art' even. It's an ongoing, evolutional revelation, the timeless ticking of the human dream machine. Even the most mundane of moments is seen to contain a wealth of meaning and personal resonance. Perhaps the entire universe is available for transformation. Everything we are capable of comprehending is potentially transcendent. But how many people realise this and grasp that potential? For many of us, it's impossible to ignore the constant cynicism that permeates our society. The cynicism that screams at us from the pages of newspapers, from the media in general, from the streets. It's so ingrained nowadays that we often take it as the norm, a given condition of contemporary life. Nor is it breaking news that a deep undercurrent of despair runs beneath all the rabid consumerism, the jostling for status and position, the cults of celebrity, the empty aspirations of middle-class society, the transparent manipulations of our political puppet masters. Pointless to point the finger, we're all implicated and involved, both as individuals and as a collective society, whether we realise it or not.

At the risk of adding even more cynicism to the equation, I'll say this: Christmas definitely shines a harsh light on our vain attempts to chase after an illusory, fragmentary happiness. It's right there in front of our eyes. Just take a moment to look around. There was little of what might once have been called Christmas cheer in the streets those last few days before the shops finally closed their doors. Instead there were stern, even angry faces, people pushing their way through the crowds in wild-eyed desperation, gangs of youths in ugly shell suits, screaming abuse at each other, drunken gaggles of tinsel-wreathed girls spilling beer into their ample Wonderbra cleavages. Scenes of cheap, tacky debauchery that reminded me of the apocalyptic visions of Hogarth and Bosch. The annual siege mentality. A feverish desperation expressed in overflowing shopping bags and whispered curses. And this in a city that prides itself as one of England's finest. Lovely.

Actually, I have to admit that it fascinates me in an appalling way. I stand back and look at it as if I'm visiting from another world and yet I'm as inextricably woven into its chaotic fabric as anyone else. The act of observation and the reporting of it here only adds to the vulgar, nauseous effect. Nevertheless, you can't deny folks their jollies, especially at this time of year.

Maybe I'm just a decadent old snob but I do prefer my odd moments of debauchery to include some sort of redeeming aesthetic, a sensual dandyism, if you will: a finely turned ankle in an elegant, subtly fetishist shoe, a sweet bosom nestled in intricate black French lace, a moment of delicate, aching beauty prolonged to the point of religious ecstasy. Is there some kind of musky, velvety, suburban elitism at play here? Well, yes, quite possibly. Or at least there would be, given half the chance. But then, I also see myself as an old romantic who enjoys a tender kiss, a hint of perfume and the gleam of starlight to accompany his behind-the-gasworks fumbling. (No surprise this as I was a young romantic too, once upon a time. Check out those early Be Bop Deluxe songs for the damning evidence.) However, whether it's a sign of a failing libido or just plain old repulsion, lardy women exhibiting their spotty backsides whilst stooping to recover their clip-on reindeer's antlers outside Yates' Wine Lodge don't do a damned thing for me, I'm sorry to admit. Merry Christmas, girls. And make the most of it.

No matter how hard we try to surround ourselves with seasonal symbols, how much we spend in the High Street, how much we eat or drink, there's something terminally unfulfilling and empty at the end of it all. Our neighbour, Archbishop John Sentamu (yes, he's a local lad for the moment, at least until Cantebury calls) would probably say the same thing, but he would also, inevitably, add the Christian message of salvation as the solution. Archbishop Sentamu is, from all I've read about him, a good man and a fine example to us all (he even wonders through the village without ecclesiastical entourage, dressed in rather sharp fashionable clothes) but, God forgive me, Christianity, or at least the Church that claims its custody, seems somehow insufficient to the complexity of the modern malaise. Faith alone is never enough. 'Be ye as little children …' but beware strangers bearing toys. It's a wicked world and peace, love and understanding is under constant threat.

Perhaps the new thing, the best hope for our society, is an internal reprogramming, an adjustment of values, a total re-alignment of our expectations. Maybe it's time for our contemporary mean-spirited cynicism to be abandoned in favour of an open-hearted optimism, a warm and generous positivity. A sunnier disposition if you like. I could add, 'Yeah, and pigs will fly,' but then that would be my own lazy cynicism rearing its ugly head. Maybe it's not asking too much at all, perhaps such a fundamental, simple attitude shift would separate the winners from the losers, or transform the losers into winners. The new optimists, the yea-sayers, the 'inclusionists', the positivists, the all-embracers, perhaps this is what we must become if the future is to be saved from the ravages of the present. Knowledge, of self, first and foremost, then the glorious by-product: universal understanding and compassion. Lost keys to a bright tomorrow?

But I'm drifting way off course here. As I usually do. I'll

return to my reporting of the seasonal day to day: on Boxing Day my mother, her husband George, his daughter Jennifer (who is visiting from Australia where she lives), Elle and Elliot, all came to our house for a tasty buffet Emi had prepared. George has given me, as a Christmas gift, an old accordion of his. It's a beautiful object in its own right, before I even begin to play it. Which I can't at the moment, but I'll keep trying. (My old friend Roger Eno would coax a grand shanty out of it, as would the lovely Kate St. John, accordioneers both).

Elliot gave me a boxed set of DVDs archiving the old American television *Superman* series from the 1950s (the live action ones, not the Fleischer cartoons). For my birthday, a week earlier, he'd bought me another DVD set containing the entire series of *Supercar*, an early Gerry Anderson produced creation. Elliot is acquainted with my inner child and knows how to indulge it. Elle bought me some cosmetic things (as girls do) plus a beautifully scented candle and a set of Jean Cocteau fridge magnets which she bought in Paris. It seems that Cocteau has become a modern day product, just like his pal Picasso. 'Art, Empire, Industry' as I once sang, 30 years ago now.

On Wednesday, we went to visit my sister-in-law Diane in Wakefield. It is her first Christmas without my brother Ian and I can only imagine how she must feel. Ian's passing has over-shadowed all our enjoyments this Christmas. It's been impossible to deal with the seasonal demands without feeling a deep sadness at his absence. We all miss him so much. Ian's headstone was finally erected, just before the Christmas weekend, eight or nine months after his passing. Emi and I drove to Wakefield Cemetery on the day before Christmas Eve to view the memorial stone in situ. It was dark, cold and wet when we got there but we were able to drive Emi's car into the cemetery and park it with its headlights illuminating the grave. I have to admit that, whilst the headstone has been much anticipated, the sight of it provoked a dark anguish. It somehow underlined the awful finality of the situation. Emi and I placed fresh flowers in the vases that have been built into the headstone. Ian's name stood out in silver letters, carved as much into the cold night as the grey marble.

Every time I visit the cemetery, I struggle to grasp the enormity of the loss. It's still hard to believe that I won't be able to share a joke with him again, or recall together a memory of our happy childhood. Then, for an awful moment, the truth hits and hits brutally hard. It is always going to be tough, painful and sad, no matter how many years pass. There's absolutely no way around that. This thing will never completely settle. I just hope that our love for him counts for something, if only for love itself.

Today, Emi had to go to work at the flower shop (as she did yesterday). And my car won't start. A completely flat battery. I've caught a cold and haven't had the energy to sort the problem out. Feeling lethargic and unenthusiastic. A slump, a low, a kind of despair. Perhaps it's nothing more than post-Christmas depression. I'm not sure even if I care.

The two prototype Nelsonic Transitone guitars were returned to the Cambell American company a few weeks back. A recent conversation with Dean Campbell informed me that I should be receiving my proper, finished production model soon. The official limited edition production orders should start rolling in two or three weeks time, all being well. Now the slow ramp to the new year, the gradual shifting of gears, the dread of things to come. Optimism needed now, more than ever. Such is life. Roll on spring, yellow flowers and pink blossoms. At this very moment though, wind and hail cracks on the skylight night of my lamp lit studio.

.

POMONA BOOKS

Pomona is a wholly independent publisher dedicated to bringing before the public the work of prodigiously talented writers. Our books can be purchased on-line at:

www.pomonauk.com

Pomona backlist